INTRODUCING HTML 5

SECOND EDITION

New Riders

VOICES THAT MATTER™

BRUCE LAWSON
REMY SHARP

Introducing HTML5, Second Edition

Bruce Lawson and Remy Sharp

New Riders
1249 Eighth Street
Berkeley, CA 94710
510/524-2178
510/524-2221 (fax)

Find us on the Web at: www.newriders.com
To report errors, please send a note to errata@peachpit.com

New Riders is an imprint of Peachpit, a division of Pearson Education

Project Editor: Michael J. Nolan
Development Editor: Margaret S. Anderson/Stellarvisions
Technical Editors: Patrick H. Lauke (www.splintered.co.uk),
Robert Nyman (www.robertnyman.com)
Production Editor: Cory Borman
Copyeditor: Gretchen Dykstra
Proofreader: Jan Seymour
Indexer: Joy Dean Lee
Compositor: Danielle Foster
Cover Designer: Aren Howell Straiger
Cover photo: Patrick H. Lauke (splintered.co.uk)

ISBN 13: 978-0-321-78442-1
ISBN 10:   0-321-78442-1

9 8 7 6 5 4 3 2 1

Printed and bound in the United States of America

ACKNOWLEDGEMENTS

Huge thanks to coauthor-turned-friend Remy Sharp, and friend-turned-ruthless-tech-editor Patrick Lauke: *il miglior fabbro*. At New Riders, Michael Nolan, Margaret Anderson, Gretchen Dykstra, and Jan Seymour deserve medals for their hard work and their patience.

Thanks to the Opera Developer Relations Team, particularly the editor of dev.opera.com, Chris Mills, for allowing me to reuse some materials I wrote for him, Daniel Davis for his description of `<ruby>`, Shwetank Dixit for checking some drafts, and David Storey for being so knowledgeable about Web Standards and generously sharing that knowledge. Big shout to former team member Henny Swan for her support and lemon cake. Elsewhere in Opera, the specification team of James Graham, Lachlan Hunt, Philip Jägenstedt, Anne van Kesteren, and Simon Pieters checked chapters and answered 45,763 daft questions with good humour. Nothing in this book is the opinion of Opera Software ASA.

Ian Hickson has also answered many a question, and my fellow HTML5 doctors (**www.html5doctor.com**) have provided much insight and support.

Many thanks to Richard Ishida for explaining `<bdi>` to me and allowing me to reproduce his explanation. Also to Aharon Lanin. Smoochies to Robin Berjon and the Mozilla Developer Center who allowed me to quote them.

Thanks to Gez Lemon and mighty Steve Faulkner for advice on WAI-ARIA. Thanks to Denis Boudreau, Adrian Higginbotham, Pratik Patel, Gregory J. Rosmaita, and Léonie Watson for screen reader advice.

Thanks to Stuart Langridge for drinkage, immoral support, and suggesting the working title "HTML5 Utopia." Mr. Last Week's creative vituperation provided loadsalaffs. Thanks, whoever you are.

Thanks to John Allsopp, Tantek Çelik, Christian Heilmann, John Foliot, Jeremy Keith, Matt May, and Eric Meyer for conversations about the future of markup. Silvia Pfeiffer's blog posts on multimedia were invaluable to my understanding.

Stu Robson braved IE6 to take the screenshot in Chapter 1, Terence Eden took the BlackBerry screenshots in Chapter 3, Julia Gosling took the photo of Remy's magic HTML5 moustache in Chapter 4, and Jake Smith provided valuable feedback on early drafts of my chapters. Lastly, but most importantly, thanks to the thousands of students, conference attendees, and Twitter followers for their questions and feedback.

This book is in memory of my grandmothers, Marjorie White-head, 8 March 1917–28 April 2010, and Elsie Lawson 6 June 1920–20 August 2010.

This book is dedicated to Nongyaw, Marina, and James, without whom life would be monochrome.

—*Bruce Lawson*

Über thanks to Bruce who invited me to coauthor this book and without whom I would have spent the early part of 2010 complaining about the weather instead of writing this book. On that note, I'd also like to thank Chris Mills for even recommending me to Bruce.

To Robert Nyman, my technical editor: when I was in need of someone to challenge my JavaScript, I knew there would always be a Swede at hand. Thank you for making sure my code was as sound as it could be. Equally to Patrick Lauke, who also whipped some of my code, and certainly parts of my English, into shape.

Thanks to the local Brighton cafés, Coffee@33 and Café Délice, for letting me spend so many hours writing this book and drinking your coffee.

To my local Brighton digital community and new friends who have managed to keep me both sane and insane over the last few years of working alone. Thank you to Danny Hope, Josh Russell, and Anna Debenham for being my extended colleagues.

Thank you to Jeremy Keith for letting me rant and rail over HTML5 and bounce ideas, and for encouraging me to publish my thoughts. Equal thanks to Jessica for letting us talk tech over beers!

To the HTML5 Doctors and Rich Clark in particular for inviting me to contribute—and also to the team for publishing such great material.

To the whole #jquery-ot channel for their help when I needed to debug, or voice my frustration over a problem, and for being someplace I could go rather than having to turn to my cats for JavaScript support.

To the #whatwg channel for their help when I had misinterpreted the specification and needed to be put back on the right path. In particular to Anne Van Kesteren, who seemed to always have the answers I was looking for, perhaps hidden under some secret rock I'm yet to discover.

To all the conference organisers that invited me to speak, to the conference goers that came to hear me ramble, to my Twitter followers that have helped answer my questions and helped spur me on to completing this book with Bruce: thank you. I've tried my best with the book, and if there's anything incorrect or out of date: ~~blame Bruce~~ buy the next edition. ;-)

To my wife, Julie: thank you for supporting me for all these many years. You're more than I ever deserved and without you, I honestly would not be the man I am today.

Finally, this book is dedicated to Tia. My girl. I wrote the majority of my part of this book whilst you were on our way to us. I always imagined that you'd see this book and be proud and equally embarrassed. That won't happen now, and even though you're gone, you'll always be with us and never forgotten.

—*Remy Sharp*

CONTENTS

INTRODUCTION

Welcome to the second edition of the Remy & Bruce show. Since the first edition of this book came out in July 2010, much has changed: support for HTML5 is much more widespread; Internet Explorer 9 finally came out; Google Chrome announced it would drop support for H.264 video; Opera experimented with video streaming from the user's webcam via the browser, and HTML5 fever became HTML5 hysteria with any new technique or technology being called HTML5 by clients, bosses, and journalists.

All these changes, and more, are discussed in this shiny second edition. There is a brand new Chapter 12 dealing with the realities of implementing all the new technologies for old browsers. And we've corrected a few bugs, tweaked some typos, rewritten some particularly opaque prose, and added at least one joke.

We're two developers who have been playing with HTML5 since Christmas 2008—experimenting, participating in the mailing list, and generally trying to help shape the language as well as learn it.

Because we're developers, we're interested in building things. That's why this book concentrates on the problems that HTML5 can solve, rather than on an academic investigation of the language. It's worth noting, too, that although Bruce works for Opera Software, which began the proof of concept that eventually led to HTML5, he's not part of the specification team there; his interest is as an author using the language for an accessible, easy-to-author, interoperable Web.

Who's this book for?

No knowledge of HTML5 is assumed, but we do expect that you're an experienced (X)HTML author, familiar with the concepts of semantic markup. It doesn't matter whether you're more familiar with HTML or XHTML DOCTYPEs, but you should be happy coding any kind of strict markup.

While you don't need to be a JavaScript ninja, you should have an understanding of the increasingly important role it plays in modern web development, and terms like DOM and API won't make you drop this book in terror and run away.

Still here? Good.

What this book isn't

This is not a reference book. We don't go through each element or API in a linear fashion, discussing each fully and then moving on. The specification does that job in mind-numbing, tear-jerking, but absolutely essential detail.

What the specification doesn't try to do is teach you how to use each element or API or how they work with one another, which is where this book comes in. We'll build up examples, discussing new topics as we go, and return to them later when there are new things to note.

You'll also realise, from the title and the fact that you're comfortably holding this book without requiring a forklift, that this book is not comprehensive. Explaining a 700-page specification (by comparison, the first HTML spec was three pages long) in a medium-sized book would require Tardis-like technology (which would be cool) or microscopic fonts (which wouldn't).

What do we mean by HTML5?

This might sound like a silly question, but there is an increasing tendency amongst standards pundits to lump all exciting new web technologies into a box labeled HTML5. So, for example, we've seen SVG (Scalable Vector Graphics) referred to as "one of the HTML5 family of technologies," even though it's an independent W3C *graphics* spec that's ten years old.

Further confusion arises from the fact that the official W3C spec is something like an amoeba: Bits split off and become their own specifications, such as Web Sockets or Web Storage (albeit from the same Working Group, with the same editors).

So what we mean in this book is "HTML5 and related specifications that came from the WHATWG" (more about this exciting acronym soon). We're also bringing a "plus one" to the party—Geolocation—which has nothing to do with our definition of HTML5, but which we've included for the simple reason that it's really cool, we're excited about it, and it's part of NEWT: the *New Exciting Web Technologies*.

Who? What? When? Why?
A short history of HTML5

History sections in computer books usually annoy us. You don't need to know about ARPANET or the history of HTTP to understand how to write a new language.

Nevertheless, it's useful to understand how HTML5 came about, because it will help you understand why some aspects of HTML5 are as they are, and hopefully preempt (or at least soothe) some of those "WTF? Why did they design it like *that*?" moments.

How HTML5 nearly never was

In 1998, the W3C decided that they would not continue to evolve HTML. The future, they believed (and so did your authors) was XML. So they froze HTML at version 4.01 and released a specification called XHTML 1.0, which was an XML version of HTML that required XML syntax rules such as quoting attributes, closing some tags while self-closing others, and the like. Two flavours were developed (well, actually three, if you care about HTML Frames, but we hope you don't because they're gone from HTML5). XHTML Transitional was designed to help people move to the gold standard of XHTML Strict.

This was all tickety-boo—it encouraged a generation of developers (or at least the professional-standard developers) to think about valid, well-structured code. However, work then began on a specification called XHTML 2.0, which was a revolutionary change to the language, in the sense that it broke backwards-compatibility in the cause of becoming much more logical and better-designed.

A small group at Opera, however, was not convinced that XML was the future for all web authors. Those individuals began extracurricular work on a proof-of-concept specification that extended HTML forms without breaking backward-compatibility. That spec eventually became Web Forms 2.0, and was subsequently folded into the HTML5 spec. They were quickly joined by individuals from Mozilla and this group, led by Ian "Hixie" Hickson of Opera, continued working on the specification privately with Apple "cheering from the sidelines" in a small group that called itself the WHATWG (Web Hypertext Application Technology Working Group, **www.whatwg.org**). You can see this genesis still in the copyright notice on the WHATWG version of the spec "© Copyright 2004–2011 Apple Computer, Inc., Mozilla Foundation, and Opera Software ASA (note that you are licensed to use, reproduce, and create derivative works)."

Hickson moved to Google, where he continued to work full-time as editor of HTML5 (then called Web Applications 1.0).

In 2006 the W3C decided that they had perhaps been overly optimistic in expecting the world to move to XML (and, by extension, XHTML 2.0): "It is necessary to evolve HTML incrementally. The attempt to get the world to switch to XML, including quotes around attribute values and slashes in empty tags and namespaces, all at once didn't work," said Tim Berners-Lee.

The resurrected HTML Working Group voted to use the WHATWG's Web Applications spec as the basis for the new version of HTML, and thus began a curious process whereby the same spec was developed simultaneously by the W3C (co-chaired by Sam Ruby of IBM and Chris Wilson of Microsoft, and later by Ruby, Paul Cotton of Microsoft, and Maciej Stachowiak of Apple), and the WHATWG, under the continued editorship of Hickson.

In search of the spec

Because the HTML5 specification is being developed by both the W3C and WHATWG, there are different versions of it. Think of the WHATWG versions as being an incubator group.

The official W3C snapshot is **www.w3.org/TR/html5/**, while **http://dev.w3.org/html5/spec/** is the latest editor's draft and liable to change.

The WHATWG has dropped version numbers, so the "5" has gone; it's just "HTML,—the living standard." Find this at **http://whatwg.org/html** but beware there are hugely experimental ideas in there. Don't assume that because it's in this document it's implemented anywhere or even completely thought out yet. This spec does, however, have useful annotations about implementation status in different browsers.

There's a one-page version of the complete WHATWG specifications called "Web Applications 1.0" that incorporates everything from the WHATWG at **http://www.whatwg.org/specs/web-apps/current-work/ complete.html** but it might kill your browser as it's massive with many scripts.

A lot of the specification is algorithms really intended for those implementing HTML (browser manufacturers, for example). The spec that we have bookmarked is a useful version for the Web at **http://developers. whatwg.org**, which removes all the stuff written for implementers and presents it with attractive CSS, courtesy of Ben Schwarz. This contains the experimental stuff, too.

Confused? **http://wiki.whatwg.org/wiki/FAQ#What_are_the_various_versions_of_the_spec.3F** lists and describes these different versions.

Geolocation is not a WHATWG spec. You can go to **http://www.w3.org/TR/geolocation-API/** to find it.

The process has been highly unusual in several respects. The first is the extraordinary openness; anyone could join the WHATWG mailing list and contribute to the spec. Every email was read by Hickson or the core WHATWG team (which included such luminaries as the inventor of JavaScript and Mozilla CTO Brendan Eich, Safari and WebKit Architect David Hyatt, and inventor of CSS and Opera CTO Håkon Wium Lie).

Good ideas were implemented and bad ideas rejected, regardless of who the source was or who they represented, or even where those ideas were first mooted. Additional good ideas were adopted from Twitter, blogs, and IRC.

In 2009, the W3C stopped work on XHTML 2.0 and diverted resources to HTML5 and it was clear that HTML5 had won the battle of philosophies: purity of design, even if it breaks backwards-compatibility, versus pragmatism and "not breaking the Web." The fact that the HTML5 working groups consisted of representatives from all the browser vendors was also important. If vendors were unwilling to implement part of the spec (such as Microsoft's unwillingness to implement <dialog>, or Mozilla's opposition to <bb>) it was dropped. Hickson has said, "The reality is that the browser vendors have the ultimate veto on everything in the spec, since if they don't implement it, the spec is nothing but a work of fiction." Many participants found this highly distasteful: Browser vendors have hijacked "our Web," they complained with some justification.

It's fair to say that the working relationship between W3C and WHATWG has not been as smooth as it could be. The W3C operates under a consensus-based approach, whereas Hickson continued to operate as he had in the WHATWG—as benevolent dictator (and many will snort at our use of the word *benevolent* in this context). It's certainly the case that Hickson had very firm ideas of how the language should be developed.

The philosophies behind HTML5

Behind HTML5 is a series of stated design principles (**http://www.w3.org/TR/html-design-principles**). There are three main aims to HTML5:

- Specifying current browser behaviours that are interoperable

- Defining error handling for the first time

- Evolving the language for easier authoring of web applications

Not breaking existing web pages

Many of our current methods of developing sites and applications rely on undocumented (or at least unspecified) features incorporated into browsers over time. For example, XMLHttpRequest (XHR) powers untold numbers of Ajax-driven sites. It was invented by Microsoft, and subsequently reverse-engineered and incorporated into all other browsers, but had never been specified as a standard (Anne van Kesteren of Opera finally specified it as part of the WHATWG). Such a vital part of so many sites left entirely to reverse-engineering! So one of the first tasks of HTML5 was to document the undocumented, in order to increase interoperability by leaving less to guesswork for web authors and implementors of browsers.

It was also necessary to unambiguously define how browsers and other user agents should deal with invalid markup. This wasn't a problem in the XML world; XML specifies "draconian error handling" in which the browser is required to stop rendering if it finds an error. One of the major reasons for the rapid ubiquity and success of the Web (in our opinion) was that even bad code had a fighting chance of being rendered by some or all browsers. The barrier to entry to publishing on the Web was democratically low, but each browser was free to decide how to render bad code. Something as simple as

```
<b><i>Hello mum!</b></i>
```

(note the mismatched closing tags) produces different DOMs in different browsers. Different DOMs can cause the same CSS to have a completely different rendering, and they can make writing JavaScript that runs across browsers much harder than it needs to be. A consistent DOM is so important to the design of HTML5 that the language itself is defined in terms of the DOM.

In the interest of greater interoperability, it's vital that error handling be identical across browsers, thus generating the exact same DOM even when confronted with broken HTML. In order for that to happen, it was necessary for someone to specify it. As we said, the HTML5 specification is well over 700 pages long, but only 300 or so are relevant to web authors (that's you and us); the rest of it is for implementers of browsers, telling them *exactly* how to parse markup, even bad markup.

Web applications

An increasing number of sites on the Web are what we'll call web applications; that is, they mimic desktop apps rather than traditional static text-images-links documents that make up the majority of the Web. Examples are online word processors, photo-editing tools, mapping sites, and so on. Heavily powered by JavaScript, these have pushed HTML 4 to the edge of its capabilities. HTML5 specifies new DOM APIs for drag and drop, server-sent events, drawing, video, and the like. These new interfaces that HTML pages expose to JavaScript via objects in the DOM make it easier to write such applications using tightly specified standards rather than barely documented hacks.

Even more important is the need for an open standard (free to use and free to implement) that can compete with proprietary standards like Adobe Flash or Microsoft Silverlight. Regardless of your thoughts on those technologies or companies, we believe that the Web is too vital a platform for society, commerce, and communication to be in the hands of one vendor. How differently would the Renaissance have progressed if Caxton held a patent and a monopoly on the manufacture of printing presses?

Don't break the Web

There are exactly umpty-squillion web pages already out there, and it's imperative that they continue to render. So HTML5 is (mostly) a superset of HTML 4 that continues to define how browsers should deal with legacy markup such as <font>, <center>, and other such presentational tags, because millions of web pages use them. But authors should not use them, as they're obsolete. For web authors, semantic markup still rules the day, although each reader will form her own conclusion as to whether HTML5 includes enough semantics, or too many elements.

As a bonus, HTML5's unambiguous parsing rules should ensure that ancient pages will work interoperably, as the HTML5 parser will be used for all HTML documents once it's implemented in all browsers.

What about XML?

HTML5 is not an XML language (it's not even an SGML language, if that means anything important to you). It *must* be served as text/html. If, however, you need to use XML, there is an XML serialisation called XHTML5. This allows all the same features, but (unsurprisingly) requires a more rigid syntax (if you're used to coding XHTML, this is exactly the same as you already write). It *must* be well-formed XML and it *must* be served with an XML MIME type, even though IE8 and its antecedents can't process it (it offers it for downloading rather than rendering it). Because of this, we are using HTML rather than XHTML syntax in this book.

HTML5 support

HTML5 is moving very fast now. The W3C specification went to last call in May 2011, but browsers were implementing HTML5 support (particularly around the APIs) long before then. That support is going to continue growing as browsers start rolling out features, so instances where we say "this is only supported in browser X" will rapidly date—which is a good thing.

New browser features are very exciting and some people have made websites that claim to test browsers' HTML5 support. Most of them wildly pick and mix specs, checking for HTML5, related WHATWG-derived specifications such as Web Workers and then, drunk and giddy with buzzwords, throw in WebGL, SVG, the W3C File API, Media Queries, and some Apple proprietary whizbangs before hyperventilating and going to bed for a lie-down.

Don't pay much attention to these sites. Their point systems are arbitrary, their definition of HTML5 meaningless and misleading.

As Patrick Lauke, our technical editor, points out, "HTML5 is not a race. The idea is not that the first browser to implement all will win the Internet. The whole idea behind the spec work is that all browsers will support the same feature set consistently."

If you want to see the current state of support for *New Exciting Web Technologies*, we recommend **http://caniuse.com** by Alexis Deveria.

Let's get our hands dirty

So that's your history lesson, with a bit of philosophy thrown in. It's why HTML5 sometimes willfully disagrees with other specifications—for backwards-compatibility, it often defines what browsers actually do, rather than what an RFC document specifies they ought to do. It's why sometimes HTML5 seems like a kludge or a compromise—it is. And if that's the price we have to pay for an interoperable open Web, then your authors say, "*Viva* pragmatism!"

Got your seatbelt on?

Let's go.

CHAPTER 1

Main Structure

Bruce Lawson

ALTHOUGH MUCH OF the attention that HTML5 has received revolves around the new APIs, there is a great deal to interest markup monkeys as well as JavaScript junkies. There are 30 new elements with new semantics that can be used in traditional "static" pages. There is also a swathe of new form controls that can abolish JavaScript form validation altogether.

So, let's get our hands dirty. In this chapter, we'll transform the current markup structure of <div>s into a semantic system. New HTML5 structural elements like <nav>, <header>, <footer>, <aside>, and <article> designate specific types of content. We'll look at how these work, and how HTML5 documents have an unambiguous outline and are—arguably—more "semantic."

The <head>

First things first: the DOCTYPE:

```
<!DOCTYPE html>
```

That's it. No unwieldy string that even the most prolific web authors need to cut and paste. No URLs. No version number. That's all. It's not so much an instruction as an incantation: it's required by browsers that need the presence of a DOCTYPE to trigger standards mode, and this is the shortest string that does this reliably. We've written in uppercase so that it's both HTML and XML compliant, and suggest you do the same.

Then we need to define the document's character encoding. Not doing so can result in an obscure but real security risk (see **http://code.google.com/p/doctype/wiki/ArticleUtf7**). This should be in the first 512 bytes of the document. Unless you can think of a splendid reason not to use it, we recommend UTF-8 as the character encoding:

```
<!DOCTYPE html>
<meta charset=utf-8>
```

Take a look at that `<meta>` tag very carefully. Those who are accustomed to writing XHTML will notice three oddities. The first is that the `<meta>` tag is much shorter than the tag we are familiar with—`<meta http-equiv="Content-Type" content="text/html; charset=UTF-8">`. This is still possible, but the shorter way is better as it's easier to type and works everywhere already.

You'll also notice that I haven't quoted the attribute `charset="utf-8"`. Neither have I self-closed the tag `<meta charset=utf-8 />`.

HTML5 is not an XML language, so you don't need to do those things. But you can if you prefer. All of these are equally valid HTML5:

```
<META CHARSET=UTF-8>
<META CHARSET=UTF-8 />
<META CHARSET="UTF-8">
<META CHARSET="UTF-8" />
<meta charset=utf-8>
<meta charset=utf-8 />
<meTa CHARset="utf-8">
<meTa CHARset="utf-8" />
```

Pick a style and stick with it

Just because you can use any of the aforementioned syntaxes doesn't mean you should mix them all up, however. That would prove a maintenance nightmare, particularly in a large team.

Our advice is to pick a style that works for you and stick with it. It doesn't matter which you choose; Remy prefers XHTML syntax while Bruce prefers lowercase, attribute minimisation (so `controls` rather than `controls="controls"`) and only quoting attributes when it's necessary, as in adding two classes to an element—so `<div class=important>` but `<div class="important logged-in">`. You'll see both styles in this book, as we each work as we feel most comfortable and you need to be able to read both.

As a brave new HTML5 author, you're free to choose—but having chosen, keep to it.

Why such appallingly lax syntax? The answer is simple: browsers never cared about XHTML syntax if it was sent as text/html—only the XHTML validator did. Therefore, favouring one form over the other in HTML5 would be entirely arbitrary, and cause pages that didn't follow that format to be invalid, although they would work perfectly in any browser. So HTML5 is agnostic about which you use.

While we're on the subject of appallingly lax syntax rules (from an XHTML perspective), let's cheat and, after adding the document title, go straight to the content:

```
<!DOCTYPE html>
<meta charset=utf-8>
<title>Interesting blog</title>
<p>Today I drank coffee for breakfast. 14 hours later,
¬ I went to bed.</p>
```

If we validate this exhilarating blog, we find that it validates fine, yet it has no `<html>` tag, no `<head>`, and no `<body>` (**Figure 1.1**).

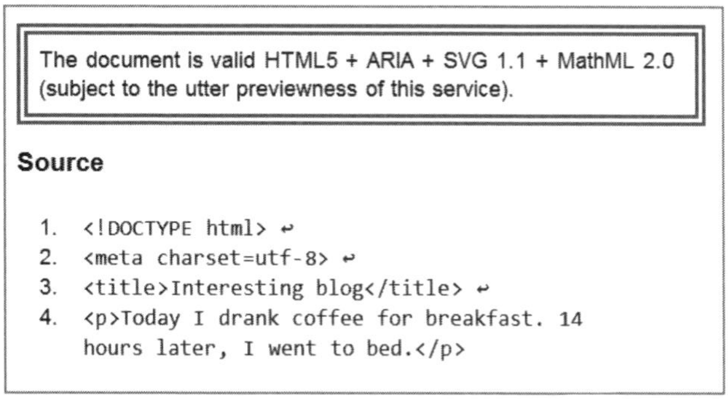

FIGURE 1.1 Shockingly, with no head, body, or HTML tag, the document validates.

The document is valid HTML5 + ARIA + SVG 1.1 + MathML 2.0 (subject to the utter previewness of this service).

Source

1. `<!DOCTYPE html>` ↵
2. `<meta charset=utf-8>` ↵
3. `<title>Interesting blog</title>` ↵
4. `<p>Today I drank coffee for breakfast. 14 hours later, I went to bed.</p>`

This is perhaps one of those *WTF?* moments I mentioned in the introduction. These three elements are (XHTML authors, are you sitting down?) entirely optional, because browsers assume them anyway. A quick glance under the browser hood with Opera Dragonfly confirms this (**Figure 1.2**).

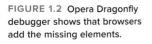

```
<!DOCTYPE html>
<html>
  <head>
    <meta charset="utf-8"/>
    <title>Interesting blog</title>
  </head>
  <body>
    <p>Today I drank coffee for breakfast. 14 hours later, I went to bed.</p>
  </body>
</html>
```

Figure 1.3 shows it using the Internet Explorer 6 developer tools.

```
1   <!DOCTYPE HTML PUBLIC "-//W3C//DTD HTML Strict//EN"><META http-equiv="Content-Ty
2
3   <HTML><BODY><P>
4
5   Today I drank coffee for breakfast. 14 hours later, I went to bed.
6
7   </P></BODY></HTML>
```

FIGURE 1.3 Internet Explorer 6, like all other browsers, adds missing elements in the DOM. (Old versions of IE seem to swap `<title>` and `<meta>`, however.)

Because browsers do this, HTML5 doesn't require these tags. Nevertheless, omitting these elements from your markup is likely to confuse your coworkers. Also, if you plan to use AppCache (see Chapter 7) you'll need the `<html>` element in your markup. It's also a good place to set the primary language of the document:

`<html lang=en>`

A visually-impaired user might come to your website with screenreading software that reads out the text on a page in a synthesized voice. When the screenreader meets the string "six" it will pronounce it very differently if the language of the page is English or French. Screenreaders can attempt to guess at what language your content is in, but it's much better to unambiguously specify it, as I have here.

IE8 and below require the <body> element before they will apply CSS to style new HTML5 elements, so it makes sense to use this element, too.

So, in the interest of maintainability, we'll add those optional elements to make what's probably the minimum maintainable HTML5 page:

```
<!DOCTYPE html>
<html lang=en>
<head>
<meta charset=utf-8>
<title>Interesting blog</title>
</head>
<body>
<p>Today I drank coffee for breakfast. 14 hours later,
¬I went to bed.</p>
</body>
</html>
```

Does validation matter anymore?

Given that we have such forgiving syntax, we can omit implied tags like `<html>`, `<head>`, and `<body>`, and—most importantly—because HTML5 defines a consistent DOM for any bad markup, you might be asking yourself if validation actually matters anymore. We've asked ourselves the same question.

Our opinion is that it's as important as it's ever been as a quality assurance tool. But it's only ever been a tool, a means to an end—not a goal in itself.

The goal is semantic markup: ensuring that the elements you choose define the meaning of your content as closely as possible, and don't describe presentation. It's possible to have a perfectly valid page made of nothing but display tables, divs, and spans, which is of no semantic use to anyone, Conversely, a single unencoded ampersand can make an excellently structured, semantically rich web page invalid, but it's still a semantic page.

When we lead development teams, we make passing validation a necessary step before any code review, let alone before making code live. It's a great way to ensure that your code really does what you want. After all, browsers may make a consistent DOM from bad markup but it might not be the DOM you want.

Also, HTML5 parsers aren't yet everywhere, so ensuring valid pages is absolutely what you should aim for to ensure predictable CSS and JavaScript behaviours.

We recommend using **http://validator.w3.org/** or **http://html5.validator.nu**. We expect that there will be further developments in validators, such as options to enforce coding choices—so you can choose to be warned for not using XHTML syntax, for example, even though that's not required by the spec. One such tool that looks pretty good is **http://lint.brihten.com**, although we can't verify whether the validation routines it uses are up-to-date.

Using new HTML5 structural elements

In 2004, Ian Hickson, the editor of the HTML5 spec, mined one billion web pages via the Google index, looking to see what the "real" Web is made of. One of the analyses he subsequently published (**http://code.google.com/webstats/2005-12/classes.html**) was a list of the most popular class names in those HTML documents.

More recently, in 2009, the Opera MAMA crawler looked again at class attributes in 2,148,723 randomly chosen URLs and also ids given to elements (which the Google dataset didn't include) in 1,806,424 URLs. See **Table 1.1** and **Table 1.2**.

TABLE 1.1 Class Names

POPULARITY	VALUE	FREQUENCY
1	footer	179,528
2	menu	146,673
3	style1	138,308
4	msonormal	123,374
5	text	122,911
6	content	113,951
7	title	91,957
8	style2	89,851
9	header	89,274
10	copyright	86,979
11	button	81,503
12	main	69,620
13	style3	69,349
14	small	68,995
15	nav	68,634
16	clear	68,571
17	search	59,802
18	style4	56,032
19	logo	48,831
20	body	48,052

TABLE 1.2 ID Names

POPULARITY	VALUE	FREQUENCY
1	footer	288,061
2	content	228,661
3	header	223,726
4	logo	121,352
5	container	119,877
6	main	106,327
7	table1	101,677
8	menu	96,161
9	layer1	93,920
10	autonumber1	77,350
11	search	74,887
12	nav	72,057
13	wrapper	66,730
14	top	66,615
15	table2	57,934
16	layer2	56,823
17	sidebar	52,416
18	image1	48,922
19	banner	44,592
20	navigation	43,664

As you can see, once we remove obviously presentational classes, we're left with a good idea of the structures that authors are trying to use on their pages.

Just as HTML 4 reflects the early Web of scientists and engineers (so there are elements like <kbd>, <samp>, and <var>), HTML5 reflects the Web as it was during its development: 30 elements are new, many of them inspired by the class and id names above, because that's what developers build.

So, while we're in a pragmatic rather than philosophical mood, let's actually use them. Here is a sample blog home page marked up as we do in HTML 4 using the semantically neutral <div> element:

```
<div id="header">
 <h1>My interesting life</h1>
</div>
<div id="sidebar">
 <h2>Menu</h2>
 <ul>
  <li><a href="last-week.html">Last week</a></li>
  <li><a href="archive.html">Archives</a></li>
 </ul>
</div>
<div class="post">
 <h2>Yesterday</h2>
 <p>Today I drank coffee for breakfast. 14 hours later,
 ¬I went to bed.</p>
</div>
<div class="post">
 <h2>Tuesday</h2>
 <p>Ran out of coffee, so had orange juice for breakfast.
 ¬It was from concentrate.</p>
</div>
<div id="footer">
 <p><small> This is copyright by Bruce Sharp. Contact me to
 ¬negotiate the movie rights.</small></p>
</div>
```

By applying some simple CSS to it, we'll style it:

```
#sidebar {float:left; width:20%;}
.post {float:right; width:79%;}
#footer {clear:both;}
```

Diagrammatically, the page looks like **Figure 1.4**.

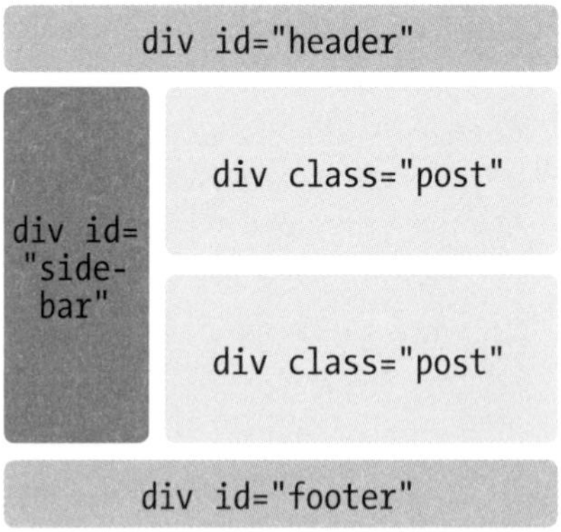

FIGURE 1.4 The HTML 4
structure of our blog.

While there is nothing at all wrong with this markup (and it'll continue working perfectly well in the new HTML5 world), most of the structure is entirely unknown to a browser, as the only real HTML element we can use for these important page landmarks is the semantically neutral <div> (defined in HTML 4 as "a generic mechanism for adding structure to documents").

So, if it displays fine, what's wrong with this? Why would we want to use more elements to add more semantics?

It's possible to imagine a clever browser having a shortcut key that would jump straight to the page's navigation. The question is: How would it know what to jump to? Some authors write <div class="menu">, others use class="nav" or class="navigation" or class="links" or any number of equivalents in languages other than English. The Opera MAMA tables above suggest that menu, nav, sidebar, and navigation could all be synonymous, but there's no guarantee; a restaurant website might use <div class="menu"> not as navigation but to list the food choices.

HTML5 gives us new elements that unambiguously denote landmarks in a page. So, we'll rewrite our page to use some of these elements:

```
<header>
 <h1>My interesting life</h1>
</header>
<nav>
 <h2>Menu</h2>
 <ul>
  <li><a href="last-week.html">Last week</a></li>
```

```
  <li><a href="archive.html">Archives</a></li>
  </ul>
 </nav>
 <article>
  <h2>Yesterday</h2>
  <p>Today I drank coffee for breakfast. 14 hours later,
  ¬ I went to bed.</p>
 </article>
 <article>
  <h2>Tuesday</h2>
  <p>Ran out of coffee, so had orange juice for breakfast.
  ¬ It was from concentrate.</p>
 </article>

 <footer>
  <p><small>This is copyright by Bruce Sharp. Contact me to
  ¬ negotiate the movie rights.</small></p>
 </footer>
```

Diagrammatically, the HTML5 version is shown in **Figure 1.5**.

FIGURE 1.5 The HTML5
structure of our blog.

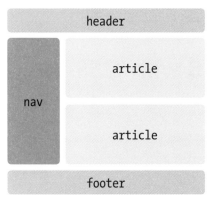

Before we look in detail at when to use these new elements and
what they mean, let's first style the basic structures of the page.

Why, oh why, is there no <content> element?

It's easy to see how our hypothetical "jump to nav" shortcut key would work, but a more common require-ment is to jump straight to the main content area. Some accessibility-minded designers add a "skip links" link at the very top of the page, to allow screen reader users to bypass navigation items. Wouldn't it be great if browsers provided a single keystroke that jumped straight to the main content?

Yet in HTML5 there is no `<content>` element to jump to, so how would the browser know where the main content of a page begins?

Actually, it's simple to determine where it is, using what I call the Scooby Doo algorithm. You always know that the person behind the ghost mask will be the sinister janitor of the disused theme park, simply because he's the only person in the episode who isn't Fred, Daphne, Velma, Shaggy, or Scooby. Similarly, the first piece of content that's not in a `<header>`, `<nav>`, `<aside>`, or `<footer>` is the beginning of the main content, regardless of whether it's contained in an `<article>`, or `<div>`, or whether it is a direct descendent of the `<body>` element.

This would be useful for screenreader users, and mobile device manufacturers could have the browser zoom straight in to the central content, for example.

If you're wishing there were a <content> element as a styling hook, you can use WAI-ARIA and add `role=main` to whatever element wraps your main content, which also provides a styling hook via CSS attribute selectors (not available in IE6), for example, `div[role=main] {float:right;}` (see Chapter 2 for more on WAI-ARIA).

Styling HTML5 with CSS

In all but one browser, styling these new elements is pretty sim-ple: You can apply CSS to any arbitrary element, because, as the spec says, CSS "is a style sheet language that allows authors and users to attach style . . . to structured documents (e.g., HTML documents and XML applications)" and XML applications can have any elements you want.

Therefore, using CSS we can float <nav>, put borders on <header> and <footer>, and give margins and padding to <article> almost as easily as we can with <div>s.

Although you can use the new HTML5 elements now, older browsers don't necessarily understand them. They don't do anything special with them and they treat them like unknown elements you make up.

What might surprise you is that, by default, CSS assumes that elements are display:inline, so if you just set heights and widths to the structural elements as we do <div>s, it won't work properly in ye olde browsers until we explicitly tell the browser that they are `display:block`. Browsers contain a rudimentary, built-in style sheet that overrides the default inline styling for those elements we think of as natively block-level (one such style sheet can be found at **http://www.w3.org/TR/CSS2/ sample.html**). Older browsers don't have rules that define new HTML elements such as <header>, <nav>, <footer>, <article> as `display:block`, so we need to specify this in our CSS. For modern browsers, our line will be redundant but harmless, acting as a useful helper for older browsers, which we all know can linger on well beyond their sell-by dates.

So, to style our HTML5 to match our HTML 4 design, we simply need the styles

```
header, nav, footer, article {display:block;}
nav {float:left; width:20%;}
article {float:right; width:79%;}
footer {clear:both;}
```

And a beautiful HTML5 page is born. Except in one browser.

Styling HTML5 in Internet Explorer 6,7,8

In old (but sadly, not dead) versions of Internet Explorer, CSS is properly applied to the HTML 4 elements that IE does support, but any new HTML5 elements that the browser doesn't know remain unstyled. This can look . . . unpleasant.

The way to cajole old IE into applying CSS to HTML5 is to poke it with a sharp JavaScript-shaped stick. Why? This is an inscrutable secret, and if we told you we'd have to kill you. (Actually, we don't know.) If you add the following JavaScript into the head of the page

```
<script>
 document.createElement('header');
 document.createElement('nav');
 document.createElement('article');
 document.createElement('footer');
</script>
```

IE will magically apply styles to those elements, provided that there is a <body> element in the markup. You need only create each element once, no matter how many times it appears on a page.

Remember, HTML5 itself doesn't require a body element, but this heady brew of Internet Explorer 8 (and earlier versions),

CSS, HTML5, and JavaScript does. IE9 works like the other browsers and doesn't need JavaScript.

> **NOTE** The `<script>` element no longer requires you to specify the type of script; JavaScript is assumed by default. This works on legacy browsers also so you can use it right away.

Although this JavaScript is unnecessary for other browsers, it won't cause them any harm. However, you might wish to give your page a speed optimisation and only download and execute this script in IE by surrounding it with conditional comments (see **http://dev.opera.com/articles/view/supporting-ie-with-conditional-comments/**).

Enabling Script

Alternatively, you can use Remy's tiny HTML5-enabling script **http://remysharp.com/2009/01/07/html5-enabling-script/** that will perform this for all new elements in one fell swoop, and which also includes Jon Neal's IE Print Protector (**http://www.iecss.com/print-protector**) that ensures that HTML5 elements also appear styled correctly when printing documents in IE.

A user with JavaScript turned off, whether by choice or corporate security policy, will be able to access your content but will see a partially styled or unstyled page. This may or may not be a deal-breaker for you. (A user with ancient IE and no JavaScript has such a miserable web experience, your website is unlikely to be the worst they encounter.) Simon Pieters has shown that, if you know what the DOM looks like, you can style some HTML5 without JavaScript but it's not particularly scalable or maintainable; see "Styling HTML5 markup in IE without script" at **http://blog.whatwg.org/styling-ie-noscript**.

Other legacy browser problems

There are other legacy browser problems when styling HTML5. Older versions of Firefox (prior to version 3) and Camino (before version 2) had a bug that **http://html5doctor.com/how-to-get-html5-working-in-ie-and-firefox-2/** has dealt with.

We don't propose to compose an exhaustive list of these behaviours; they are temporary problems that we expect to quickly disappear as new browser versions come out and users upgrade to them.

When to use the new HTML5 structural elements

We've used these elements to mark up our page, and styled them, and although the use of each might seem to be self-evident from the names, it's time to study them in a little more detail.

<header>

In our example above, as on most sites, the header will be the first element on a page. It contains the title of the site, logos, links back to the home page, and so on. The spec says:

"The header element represents a group of introductory or navigational aids . . . Note: A header element is intended to usually contain the section's heading (an h1–h6 element or an hgroup element), but this is not required. The header element can also be used to wrap a section's table of contents, a search form, or any relevant logos."

Let's dissect this. The first thing to note is that a `<header>` element is not required; in our example above, it's superfluous as it surrounds just the <h1>. Its value is that it groups "introductory or navigational" elements, so here's a more realistic example:

```
<header>
 <a href="/"><img src=logo.png alt="home"></a>
 <h1>My interesting blog</h1>
</header>
```

Many websites have a title and a tagline or subtitle. To mask the subtitle from the outlining algorithm (so making the main heading and subtitle into one logical unit; see Chapter 2 for more discussion), the main heading and subtitle can be grouped in the new <hgroup> element:

```
<header>
<a href="/"><img src=logo.png alt="home"></a>
<hgroup>
<h1>My interesting blog</h1>
<h2>Tedium, dullness and monotony</h2>
</hgroup>
</header>
```

The header can also contain navigation. This can be very useful for site-wide navigation, especially on template-driven sites where the whole of the <header> element could come from a template file. So, for example, the horizontal site-wide navigation on **www.thaicookery.co.uk** could be coded as shown. You can see the result in **Figure 1.6**.

```
<header>
 <hgroup>
  <h1>Thai Cookery School</h1>
  <h2>Learn authentic Thai cookery in your own home.</h2>
 </hgroup>
 <nav>
  <ul>
   <li>Home</li>
   <li><a href="courses.html">Cookery Courses</a></li>
   <li><a href="contact.html">Contact</a></li>
  </ul>
 </nav>
</header>
```

FIGURE 1.6 Header for www.thaicookery.co.uk.

Of course, it's not required that the <nav> be in the <header>. The Thai cookery example could just as easily be marked up with the main <nav> outside the <header>:

```
<header>
 <hgroup>
  <h1>Thai Cookery School></h1>
  <h2>Learn authentic Thai cookery in your own home.</h2>
 </hgroup>
</header>
<nav>
 <ul>
```

```
  <li>Home</li>
  <li><a href="courses.html">Cookery Courses</a></li>
  <li><a href="contact.html">Contact</a></li>
 </ul>
</nav>
```

It depends largely on whether you believe that site-wide navigation belongs in the site-wide header, and also on pragmatic considerations about ease of styling. Take, for example, my personal site, which has a very long site-wide navigation on the left of the content area, which can be much longer than a post. Putting this <nav> in the <header> would make it very hard to put the main content in the right place and have a footer, so in this case, the site-wide navigation is outside the <header>, and is a sibling child of the <body>, as in this example (**Figure 1.7**).

FIGURE 1.7 Typical page with site-wide navigation out of the main header area.

Note that currently we're creating only the main <header> for the page; there can be multiple <header>s—we'll come to that in Chapter 2.

<nav>

The <nav> element is designed to mark up navigation. Navigation is defined as links around a page (for example, a table of contents at the top of an article that links to anchor points on the same page) or within a site. But not every collection of links is <nav>; a list of sponsored links isn't <nav>, and neither is a page of search results, as that is the main content of the page.

To <nav> or not to <nav>?

I was previously guilty of navitis—the urge to surround any links to other parts of a site as <nav>.

I cured myself of it by considering who will benefit from use of the <nav> element. We've previously speculated about a shortcut that would allow an assistive technology user to jump to navigation menus. If there are dozens of <nav>s, it will make it hard for the user to find the most important ones. So I now advocate marking up only the most important nav blocks, such as those that are site-wide (or section-wide) or tables of contents for long pages.

A good rule of thumb is to use a <nav> element if you could imagine the links you're considering wrapping having a heading "Navigation" above them. If they are important enough to merit a heading (regardless of whether the content or design actually requires such a heading), they're important enough to be <nav>.

As the spec says, "Not all groups of links on a page need to be in a nav element—the element is primarily intended for sections that consist of major navigation blocks."

Conversely, the spec suggests that the "legal" links (copyright, contact, freedom of information, privacy policies, and so on). that are often tucked away in the footer should not be wrapped in a <nav>: "It is common for footers to have a short list of links to various pages of a site, such as the terms of service, the home page, and a copyright page. The footer element alone is sufficient for such cases; while a nav element can be used in such cases, it is usually unnecessary."

We advise you to ignore what the spec says—use <nav> for these. Many sites also include a link to accessibility information that explains how to request information in alternate formats, for example. Typically, people who require such information are those who would benefit the most from user agents that can take them directly to elements marked up as <nav>.

As with <header>s and <footer>s (and all of the new elements), you're not restricted to one <nav> per page. You might very well have site-wide <nav> in a header, a <nav> which is a table of contents for the current article, and a <nav> below that which links to other related articles on your site.

The contents of a <nav> element will probably be a list of links, marked up as an unordered list (which has become a tradition since Mark Newhouse's seminal "CSS Design: Taming Lists" (**http://www.alistapart.com/articles/taminglists/**) or, in the case of breadcrumb trails, an ordered list. Note that the <nav> element is a wrapper; it doesn't replace the <ol> or <ul> element but wraps around it. That way, legacy browsers that don't understand the element will just see the list element and list items and behave themselves just fine.

FIGURE 1.8 **My blog sidebar, (once upon a time) mixing navigation with colophon information and pictures of hunks.**

> **NOTE** Before you throw down this book in disgust at my changing my mind, it's important to emphasise that there is rarely One True Way™ to mark up content. HTML is a general language without a million elements to cover all eventualities (it just feels that way sometimes)!

While it makes sense to use a list (and it gives you more hooks for CSS), it's not mandatory. This is perfectly valid:

```
<nav>
 <p><a href="/">Home</a></p>
 <p><a href="/about">About</a></p>
</nav>
```

You can include headings for navigation, too:

```
<nav>
 <h2>Pages</h2>
 <ul>
  <li><a href="/about">About me</a></li>
  <li><a href="/news">News</a></li>
 </ul>

 <h2>Categories</h2>
 <ul>
  <li><a href="/happy">Happy Pirates</a></li>
  <li><a href="/angry">Angry Pirates</a></li>
 </ul>
</nav>
```

Grouping <nav> and other elements in a sidebar

Many sites have a sidebar that includes multiple blocks of navigation and other non-navigation content. Take, for example, my personal site **www.brucelawson.co.uk** (**Figure 1.8**).

The sidebar on the left of the main content has one nav area containing sublists for pages, categories, archives, and most recent comments. In the first edition of this book, I recommended that these be marked up as a series of consecutive <nav> elements; I've changed my mind and now surround the sublists with one overarching <nav>. (If you have two or more blocks of important navigation that are not consecutive, by all means use separate <nav> elements.)

All my main site navigation is contained in an <aside> element that "can be used for typographical effects like pull quotes or sidebars, for advertising, for groups of nav elements, and for other content that is considered separate from the main content of the page" (**http://dev.w3.org/html5/spec/semantics.html#the-aside-element**).

```
<aside>
 <nav>
  <h2>Pages</h2>
   <ul> .. </ul>
  <h2>Categories</h2>
   <ul> .. </ul>

  <h2>Recent comments</h2>
   <ul> ... </ul>
 </nav>

 <section>
  <h2>blah blah</h2>
  <a href="...">Web hosting by LovelyHost</a>
  <img src="...">
  <p>Powered by <a href="...">WordPress</a></p>
  <p><a href="...">Entries (RSS)</a> and <a href="...">
  ¬ Comments (RSS)</a></p>
 </section>
</aside>
```

Note that the "blah blah" section is not marked up as <nav>, as the link to my web host, a picture of me, and two RSS links don't seem to me to be a "section that consist[s] of major navigation blocks" as the spec defines <nav>. It's wrapped in a <section> so that the sidebar headings remain the same level in the outlining algorithm (see Chapter 2 for more information).

<footer>

The <footer> element is defined in the spec as representing "a footer for its nearest ancestor sectioning content or sectioning root element." ("Sectioning content" includes article, aside, nav, and section, and "sectioning root elements" are blockquote, body, details, fieldset, figure, and td.)

Note that, as with the header element, there can be more than one footer on a page; we'll revisit that in Chapter 2. For now, we have just one footer on the page that is a child of the body element. As the spec says, "When the nearest ancestor sectioning content or sectioning root element is the body element, then it applies to the whole page."

The spec continues, "A footer typically contains information about its section, such as who wrote it, links to related documents, copyright data, and the like."

Our footer holds copyright data, which we're wrapping in a `<small>` element, too. `<small>` has been redefined in HTML5; previously it was a presentational element, but in HTML5 it has semantics, representing side comments or small print that "typically features disclaimers, caveats, legal restrictions, or copyrights. Small print is also sometimes used for attribution, or for satisfying licensing requirements."

Your site's footer probably has more than a copyright notice. You might have links to privacy policies, accessibility information (why are you hiding that out of the way?), and other such links. I'd suggest wrapping these in <nav>, despite the spec's advice (see previous <nav> section).

The spec says "Some site designs have what is sometimes referred to as 'fat footers'—footers that contain a lot of material, including images, links to other articles, links to pages for sending feedback, special offers . . . in some ways, a whole 'front page' in the footer." It suggests a <nav> element, within the `<footer>`, to enclose the information.

When tempted to use a "fat footer," consider whether such links actually need <nav> at all—navitis can be hard to shake off. Also ask yourself whether such links are actually part of a `<footer>` at all: would it be better as an `<aside>` of the whole page, a sibling of `<footer>`?

<article>

The main content of this blog's home page contains a few blog posts. We wrap each one up in an `<article>` element. `<article>` is specified thus: "A self-contained composition in a document, page, application, or site and that is, in principle, independently distributable or reusable, e.g., in syndication. This could be a forum post, a magazine or newspaper article, a blog entry, a user-submitted comment, an interactive widget or gadget, or any other independent item of content."

A blog post, a tutorial, a news story, comic strip, or a video with its transcript all fit perfectly into this definition. Less intuitively, this definition also works for individual emails in a web-based email client, maps, and reusable web widgets. For `<article>` don't think newspaper article, think article of clothing—a discrete item. Note that, as with `<nav>`, the heading is part of the article itself, so it goes inside the element. Thus

```
<h1>My article</h1>
<article>
 <p>Blah blah</p>
</article>
```

is incorrect; it should be

```
<article>
 <h1>My article</h1>
 <p>Blah blah</p>
</article>
```

There are many more interesting facets to `<article>` which (you've guessed it) we'll look at in the next chapter.

What's the point?

A very wise friend of mine, Robin Berjon, wrote, "Pretty much everyone in the Web community agrees that 'semantics are yummy, and will get you cookies,' and that's probably true. But once you start digging a little bit further, it becomes clear that very few people can actually articulate a reason why.

"The general answer is 'to repurpose content.' That's fine on the surface, but you quickly reach a point where you have to ask, 'Repurpose to what?' For instance, if you want to render pages to a small screen (a form of repurposing) then <nav> or <footer> tell you that those bits aren't content, and can be folded away; but if you're looking into legal issues digging inside <footer> with some heuristics won't help much . . .

"I think HTML should add only elements that either expose functionality that would be pretty much meaningless otherwise (e.g., <canvas>) or that provide semantics that help repurpose for Web browsing uses." **www.alistapart.com/comments/ semanticsinhtml5?page=2#12**

As Robin suggests, small screen devices might fold away non-content areas (or zoom in to the main content areas). A certain touch or swipe could zoom to nav, or to footer or header. A search engine could weight links in a footer less highly than links in a nav bar. There are many future uses that we can't guess at—but they all depend on unambiguously assigning meaning to content, which is the definition of semantic markup.

Summary

In this chapter, we've taken our first look at HTML5 and its DOCTYPE. We've structured the main landmarks of a web page using `<header>`, `<footer>`, `<nav>`, `<aside>`, and `<article>`, providing user agents with more semantics than the meaningless generic `<div>` element that was our only option in HTML 4, and styled the new elements with the magic of CSS.

We've seen its forgiving syntax rules such as optional uppercase/lowercase, quoting and attribute minimisation, omitting implied elements like head/body, omitting standard stuff like `type="text/javascript"` and `type="text/css"` on the `<script>`, and `<style>` tags and we've even shown you how to tame the beast of old IE versions. Not bad for one chapter, eh?

CHAPTER 2

Text

Bruce Lawson

NOW THAT YOU'VE marked up the main page landmarks with HTML5 and seen how a document's outline can be structured, this lesson looks deeper to show how you can further structure your main content.

To do this, you'll mark up a typical blog with HTML5. We've chosen a blog because over 70 percent of web professionals have a blog (**www.aneventapart.com/ alasurvey2008**), and everyone has seen one. It's also a good archetype of modern websites with headers, footers, sidebars, multiple navigation areas, and a form, whether it's a blog, a news site, or a brochure site (with products instead of news pieces). We'll then move on to a case study with a real website to see where you would use the new structures, followed by a look at new elements and global attributes.

Structuring main content areas

Take a look at the main content area of a blog (**Figure 2.1**). There may be multiple articles, each containing metadata and the actual textual content of that article.

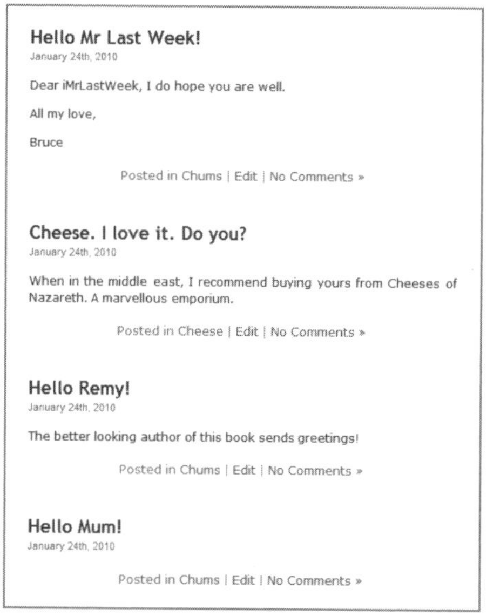

FIGURE 2.1 **A series of articles on a typical blog.**

Here's some typical markup (simplified from the default WordPress theme):

```
<div class="post">
<h2>Memoirs of a Parisian lion-tamer</h2>
<small>January 24th, 2010</small>
  <div class="entry">
    <p>Claude Bottom's poignant autobiography is this
    ¬ summer's must-read.</p>
  </div>
  <p class="postmetadata">Posted in <a href="/?cat=3">
  ¬ Books category</a> | <a     href="/?p=34#respond">
  ¬ No Comments</a></p>
</div>
```

There is nothing majorly wrong with this markup (although we would query use in HTML 4 of the presentational `<small>` element for the date). It will work fine in all browsers, but apart from the heading for the blog post, there is no real structure—just meaningless `<div>`s and paragraphs.

HTML 4 gives us generic structures to mark up content. <div>, for example, is just a generic box that tells the browser, "Here's some stuff, it all belongs together," but it doesn't mean anything; there's no semantic value beyond "these belong together." Where possible, we'll replace generic boxes with new HTML5 elements, while still using <div> where there isn't an appropriate element, just as we did in HTML 4.

Let's concentrate on an individual article first. As you saw in Chapter 1, you can replace the outer <div class="post"> with <article>, but you can go further still. The HTML5 <header> and <footer> elements can be used multiple times on a page, each time referring to the section it's in.

> **NOTE** All quotes describing the elements, unless otherwise noted, are from the HTML5 specification as it read at the time of writing.

The heading and the time of posting are introductory matter and thus the job for <header>, right? Similarly, the metadata about the post that is currently in a paragraph with class="postmetadata" is better marked up in HTML5 as a <footer>, which the spec says "typically contains information about its section, such as who wrote it, links to related documents, copyright data, and the like."

Diagrammatically, the revised structure is shown in **Figure 2.2**.

FIGURE 2.2 A single blog article using new HTML5 structures.

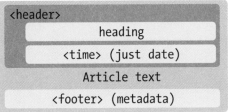

```
<article>
  <header>
    <h2>Memoirs of a Parisian lion-tamer</h2>
    <time datetime=2010-01-24>January 24th,
    ¬ 2010</time>
  </header>
  <p>Claude Bottom's poignant autobiography is this
  ¬ summer's must-read.</p>
  <footer>
    Posted in <a href="/?cat=3" >Books category</a>.
    ¬ <a href="/?p=34#respond">No Comments</a>
  </footer>
</article>
```

Let's look at this in more detail.

The <time> element

The new element `<time>` is used for unambiguously encoding dates and times for machines, while still displaying them in a human-readable way. The uses of this in web pages aren't hard to imagine: a browser could offer to add future events to a user's calendar; content aggregators could produce visual timelines of events; a Thai-localised browser could offer to transform dates into Thai Buddhist era dates, which are numerically 543 years greater than their corresponding Western-style years.

The spec says, "The time element represents either a time on a 24-hour clock, or a precise date in the proleptic Gregorian calendar, optionally with a time and a time-zone offset."

The machine-readable part of the `<time>` element is usually encapsulated in the element's datetime attribute. The content inside the element is what gets presented to end users.

```
<time datetime=2009-11-13>13 November 2009</time>
<time datetime=2009-11-13>13<sup>th</sup> November last
¬ year</time>
<time datetime=2010-11-13>Bruce's 21st birthday</time>
<time datetime=2010-11-13T02O:00Z>8PM on my birthday</time>
<time datetime=20:00>8 PM</time>
```

If you're happy to have the machine-readable format visible to the end user as well, you don't need to use a separate datetime attribute. User agents should then simply pick the content of the element and interpret it:

```
<time>20:00</time>
```

Machine-readable dates and times

To be machine-readable, dates must be in the format YYYY-MM-DD and may also include a time, prefixed with "T" to separate the date and time, in the format HH:MM. Optionally you can append seconds (separated from the minutes with a colon). Fractions of a second are allowed after a full stop mark.

As you've seen above, you can give a time on the 24-hour clock with no date information.

If you're giving time and date together, you need to show the time zone: that's either "Z" for Coordinated Universal Time (UTC), or an offset from UTC in hours and minutes, prefixed with a plus or minus.

Putting that all together: "1979-10-14T12:00:00.001-04:00" represents one millisecond after noon on October 14, 1979, in Eastern Standard Time during daylight saving time (UTC-4 hours).

Reddit.com combines a relative time ("8 hours ago") as the text content of the element, with a title attribute showing the human-readable full time on hover:

```
<p>Submitted <time title="Sun Jul 3 02:15:49 2011 GMT"
¬ datetime="2011-07-03T02:15:49.881631+00:00">8 hours</time>
¬ ago</p>
```

The only trouble with `<time>` is that it must contain a positive date on the proleptic Gregorian calendar—meaning you can't encode a date before the Christian era. Neither can you encode imprecise dates such as "July 1904." This seriously limits its use for sites such as museums, history/encyclopedia pages, or family trees, where precise dates may not be known.

A consortium of search engines, Bing, Google, and Yahoo!, has launched an initiative called schema.org to create and support a series of common markup patterns. This growing set of schemas use HTML5 Microdata (see later in this chapter):

" . . . in ways recognized by major search providers. Search engines including Bing, Google and Yahoo! rely on this markup to improve the display of search results, making it easier for people to find the right web pages (**www.schema.org**)."

NOTE As this second edition goes to press, the Working Group is discussing removing `<time>` from HTML and, to replace it, magicking up a more generic—and therefore less useful—`<data>` element. We hope that this won't happen but before you use it, please see www.introducinghtml5.com to find any errata to this book. Or look at the spec!

Note that schema.org uses the <time> element to express dates, but uses the full ISO 8601 date format rather than HTML5's cut-down date format, so "2011-09" is a legitimate date, expressing an unspecified day in September 2011. Similarly, durations can be specified via a "P" prefix (for period):

```
<time itemprop="cookTime" datetime="PT1H30M">1.5 hours</time>
```

As we've seen, neither of these schema.org examples have datetime attributes that will validate as HTML5. This puts responsible developers in a quandary—should you aim for the personal karma of valid code, or the tangible business benefits of helping search engines understand your content?

It's silly to force developers to choose, so hopefully the Working Group will see sense and loosen the restrictions on the `<time>` element.

The pubdate attribute

The Boolean attribute pubdate indicates that this particular `<time>` is the publication date of an `<article>` or the whole `<body>` content.

You might be wondering why the pubdate attribute is needed at all. Why not just assume that any `<time>` element in an `<article>`'s `<header>` is its publication date?

Consider this example:

```
<article>
  <header>
    <h1>Come to my party on <time datetime=2010-12-01>1
    ¬ December</time></h1>
      <p>Published on <time datetime=2010-06-20 pubdate>20
      ¬ June 2010</time></p>
  </header>
  <p>I'm throwing a party at Dr Einstein's Cabaret
  ¬ Roller-disco Bierkeller Pizza-parlour-a-gogo. Do come
  ¬ and dance to Rusty Trombone's Swingin' Brass Band.
  ¬ (Formal dress and lewd hat required.)</p>
</article>
```

You'll see that there are two dates within the `<header>`: the date of the actual party and the publication date of the article. The pubdate attribute is required to remove any ambiguity. And yes, you are invited—just don't get drunk this time.

More fun with headers and footers

The main surprise with our article makeover is that each article can have its own `<header>` and `<footer>`. This means that, in addition to the "main" header and footer on a page, each article can have its own headers and footers as well. They can be separately styled with CSS: for instance, body>header and body>footer target the main headers and footers (assuming that they're direct descendants of `<body>`), whereas article>header and article>footer target the inner structures.

To include old versions of Internet Explorer, you can take advantage of specificity. Define generic header and footer styles, and then redefine/override them for article header and article footer:

```
header {display:block; color:red; text-align:right;}
¬ /*page header */
article header {color:blue; text-align:center;}
¬ /*article header */
```

Note that so far you've introduced no ids or classes as hooks for CSS.

Using multiple <footer>s on the same element

The spec says, "Footers don't necessarily have to appear at the end of a section, though they usually do," and it allows an element to have two or more footers. A simplified version of the example in the spec is

```
<body>
 <footer><a href="/">Back to index...</a></footer>
 <h1>Lorem ipsum</h1>
 <p>Lorem ipsum</p>
 <footer><a href="/">Back to index...</a></footer>
</body>
```

The reason for this is that the elements are supposed to be non-presentational. If "back to index" is the footer below the article, and you choose to have another "back to index" above the article, too, you should use the same element for the same content, regardless of where it appears.

Using <blockquote> <footer>s

Very groovily, `<blockquote>` can have a footer, which is a very useful way of citing the source in a way that's unambiguously associated with the quotation but also nicely presented to your users (HTML4 has the cite attribute on <blockquote> which in theory serves this purpose by allowing authors to provide a link to the original source, but no browsers do anything with it so the source isn't displayed anywhere to the user:

```
<blockquote>
  Thou look'st like antichrist, in that lewd hat.
  <footer>Ananias <cite>Scene 4.3, <a  href="http://
  ¬ www.gutenberg.org/files/4081/4081-h/4081-h.htm">The
  ¬ Alchemist</a></cite> (Ben Jonson)</footer>
</blockquote>
```

Since the first edition of this book, it's been suggested that using <footer> inside <blockquote> for attributing the source of the quotation is wrong, because according to the spec, "Content inside a blockquote must be quoted from another source," and attribution isn't a quote. However, this seems incorrect; often you "tidy" quotes by adding ellipses, silently correcting spelling and such, which isn't strictly quoting. Also, many web publications include the attribution inside the quotation, which isn't allowed by the spec at the moment (see fellow HTML5 Doctor Oli Studholme's research at **http://oli.jp/2011/blockquote/**). Therefore, we consider that disallowing the use above is a spec bug.

Adding blog posts and comments

So, you have a page with a header, footer, navigation, and content areas containing several articles (blog posts), each with its own header and footer. But wait...what is a blog without comments?

The specification mentions this case, and recommends the use of nested <article>s: "When article elements are nested, the inner article elements represent articles that are in principle related to the contents of the outer article. For instance, a blog entry on a site that accepts user-submitted comments could represent the comments as article elements nested within the article element for the blog entry."

So let's do that. Note as well that blog comments are typically shown in chronological order and have information such as author's name and URL—in short, header information. Diagrammatically it looks like **Figure 2.3**.

FIGURE 2.3 The structure of a blog post, with comments as nested articles.

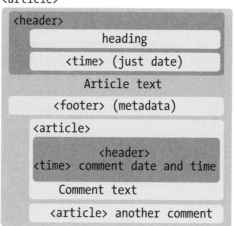

The code is as you'd expect, with comments highlighted:

```
<article>
  <header>
    <h1>Come to my party on <time datetime=
    ¬ 2010-12-01>1 December</time></h1>
      <p>Published on <time datetime=2010-06-20 pubdate>
      ¬ 20 June 2010</time></p>
  </header>
```

```
  <p>I'm throwing a party at Dr Einstein's Cabaret
  ¬Roller-disco Bierkeller Pizza-parlour-a-gogo. Do come
  ¬and dance to Rusty Trombone's Swingin' Brass Band.
  ¬(Formal dress and lewd hat required.)</p>
<footer>Published in the Parrtay!! category by Bruce
¬</footer>

  <article> <!-- comment -->
   <header>
    Comment from <a href="http://remysharp.com">Remy
    ¬Sharp</a> at <time datetime="2010-05-01T08:45Z">
    ¬8.45 on 1 May 2010</time>
   </header>
   <p>I'll be there. I very much enjoy a bit of Rusty
   ¬Trombone.</p>
  </article> <!-- end comment -->

  <article> <!-- comment -->
   <header>
    Comment from <a href="http://splintered.co.uk">Patrick
    ¬Lauke</a> at <time datetime="2010-05-02T10:45Z">10.45
    ¬on 2 May 2010</time>
   </header>
   <p>Sorry mate. Am off to Bath to see TubaGirl.</p>
  </article> <!-- end comment -->

 </article> <!-- end blogpost -->
```

Working with HTML5 outlines

Some word processing applications have a function to show you the outline of a document. For example, **Figure 2.4** shows this chapter in Microsoft Word 2007's outline view.

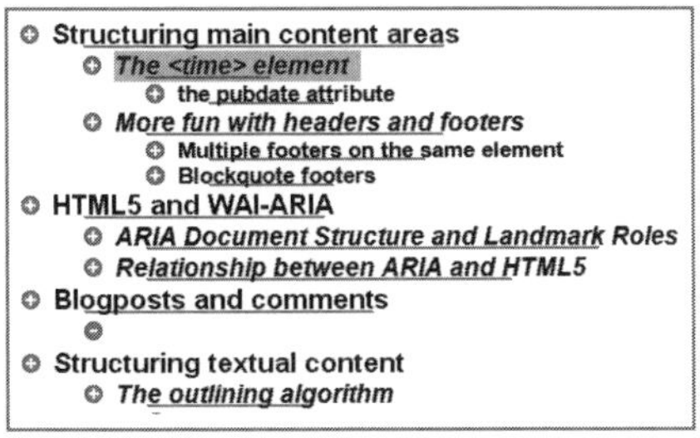

FIGURE 2.4 Microsoft Word 2007's outline view.

HTML5 has a tightly defined outlining algorithm that allows user agents to produce a similar outline from a web page. Just as with a word-processing package, this could be used to give the user a quick overview of the web page (and, of course, there's no reason why the web page shouldn't actually be a word-processing application). The other main use for the outlining algorithm is for syndication: grabbing content and inserting it somewhere else and ensuring that the destination web page still has a logical structure.

A word of warning: This section of the chapter is pretty dense, and it hasn't been implemented by any browsers yet (although there is a JavaScript implementation at **http://code.google.com/p/h5o/**, which has been wrapped as a Chrome extension from the same URL, and as an Opera extension at **https://addons.opera.com/addons/extensions/details/html5-outliner/**). You need to understand the concept of the document outline to know when to use <section>, <aside>, or <div>.

One major departure from HTML 4, and an important concept to grasp before you proceed, is that certain HTML5 elements—<article>, <section>, <nav>, and <aside>—are *sectioning content*, which begin new sections in the outline. To explain this concept, let's take this simple code:

```
<h1>Hello</h1>
<div>
 <h1>World</h1>
</div>
```

To illustrate how this algorithm works, I'm using a web-based utility at **http://gsnedders.html5.org/outliner/**, as no browser currently has this logic embedded. The outline this code generates is as you would expect (**Figure 2.5**).

FIGURE 2.5 **A simple outline.**

Figure 2.6 shows what happens if you change the meaningless <div> to an <article>, which is sectioning content:

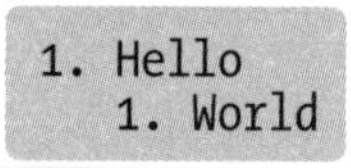

```
<h1>Hello</h1>
<article>
 <h1>World</h1>
</article>
```

FIGURE 2.6 **A document outline after <div> is replaced by <article>.**

The presence of sectioning content has shifted its content to be hierarchically "below" the content that preceded it. Or, to put it more simply: the <h1> inside the article is a logical <h2> because

<article> has started a new section. Using <section>, <nav>, or <aside> instead of <article> does the same thing, as they are all sectioning content.

In fact, it doesn't matter what level of heading you use here; the outlining algorithm cares about nesting and relative levels, so this code

```
<h3>Hello</h3>
<article>
 <h6>World</h6>
</article>
```

produces exactly the same result as Figure 2.6.

You might be saying, "So what. What's the use for that?" Well, firstly, it means you're not restricted to six levels of headings, as you are in HTML 4. A heading element nested inside seven levels of <section>, <article>, <nav>, or <aside> (or any combination of them) becomes a logical <h7> element (however, unless you're marking up legal documents or some other horrors, you should reconsider your content if you need so many levels).

Another advantage is with syndication. Suppose Remy posts an article:

```
<article>
 <h1>What I did on my holiday</h1>
 <p>I went to Narnia. I was bitten by a trilobite. Then I
 ¬ came home.</p>
</article>
```

From TBL '91 to XHTML 2 to HTML5

All very newfangled, isn't it? Well, no; the idea that logical headings should depend on their nesting in <section>s was first floated in 1991 by Sir Tim Berners-Lee himself:

"I would in fact prefer, instead of <H1>, <H2> etc for headings . . . to have a nestable <SECTION>..</SECTION> element, and a generic <H>..</H> which at any level within the sections would produce the required level of heading."

For some reason this didn't make it into HTML. It was revived for XHTML2 and re-revived by HTML5, but without an <h> element— for backwards-compatibility reasons, <h1> to <h6> are used instead.

Let's say you run a large online newspaper and naturally wish to syndicate this story. When the magic syndication machines slot it into your template, the resulting code is

```
<h1>The Monotonous Times</h1>
<section>
 <h2>Breaking news</h2>
  <article>
   <h1>What I did on my holiday</h1>
   <p>I went to Narnia. I was bitten by a trilobite.
   ¬ Then I came home.</p>
  </article>
 ..
</section>
```

It's obvious that "breaking news" is higher in the hierarchy of headings than the title of Remy's blog post, but due to a mismatch between Remy's template and your template, there's an <h2> that is more important than the <h1>.

Checking the outline, however, shows us that everything is as it should be (**Figure 2.7**). You clever thing, you.

FIGURE 2.7 The outlining algorithm produces the correct outline in syndication, too.

```
1. The Monotonous Times
   1. Breaking news
      1. What I did on my holiday
```

<nav>, <aside>, and untitled sections

A quick word about the outlining tools, as you'll probably get into the habit of checking your document outlines as part of your development process, much as you regularly validate your code and check it in different browsers.

Generally, if a tool finds sectioning content that has no heading, it will report it. So this snippet

```
<article>
 <p>I have no heading</p>
</article>
```

gives the outline "Untitled Section." For <section>s and <article>s, this is a useful warning, as these elements nearly always begin with a heading.

However, inside `<nav>` and `<aside>` it's perfectly legitimate not to have a heading. You may want to do it for some <nav> blocks, such as "Most popular posts" or "Recent comments," but you probably don't want a heading on your main site <nav> that just says "Navigation."

Therefore, if you see "Untitled Section," don't automatically assume that you should put a heading there. Treat it as a warning, not an error.

<hgroup>

Sometimes you have a heading and a subheading, or tagline. Slashdot uses "News for nerds, stuff that matters"; dev.opera has "Follow the Standards. Break the Rules"; Metafilter is a "community weblog." How do you mark up those taglines? In HTML 4, you could use

```
<h1>Metafilter</h1>
<p>community weblog</p>
```

> **NOTE** We haven't used a <header> element in this <article>. <header> is a grouping element that collects together introductory content; as you only have headings already grouped in <hgroup>, there's no need for a further layer of grouping. It wouldn't be an error to use it, but it's superfluous in this example.

but that doesn't feel right, as the subtitle feels like it should be a heading. An alternate method of marking this up could be

```
<h1>Metafilter</h1>
<h2>community weblog</h2>
```

but then every header on the site would need to be <h3> to <h6> as they're subordinate to the tagline. In HTML5, the subtitle can be marked up as a heading element but removed from the document outline, like so:

```
<hgroup>
  <h1>Metafilter</h1>
  <h2>community weblog</h2>
</hgroup>
```

This gives the outline shown in **Figure 2.8**.

```
1. Metafilter
```

FIGURE 2.8 **The outline shows only "Metafilter" as part of the outline.**

The spec for <hgroup> says, "For the purposes of document summaries, outlines, and the like, the text of hgroup elements is defined to be the text of the highest-ranked h1–h6 element descendant of the hgroup element."

So:

```
<hgroup>
  <h2>Get the beers in! Here comes</h2>
  <h1>Remy Sharp!</h1>
</hgroup>
```

shows the text "Remy Sharp" in the outline, as that's the highest-ranking heading element in the group.

Sectioning roots

Note that certain elements—<blockquote>, <body>, <details>, <fieldset>, <figure>, <td>—are said to be *sectioning roots*, and can have their own outlines, but the sections and headings inside these elements do not contribute to the outlines of their ancestors. This is because, for example, you could quote several sections of an article in a <blockquote>, but those quoted sections don't form part of the overall document outline.

In the following example:

```
<h1>Unicorns and butterflies</h1>
<nav>
 <h2>Main nav</h2>
...
</nav>
<article>
 <h2>Fairies love rainbows!</h2>
 <p>According to Mr Snuggles the fluffy kitten, fairies
¬ like:</p>
 <blockquote>
  <h3>Pretty dainty things</h3>
  <p>Fairies love rainbows, ribbons, and ballet shoes</p>
  <h3>Weaponry</h3>
  <p>Fairies favour Kalashnikovs, flick knives, and
  ¬ depleted uranium missiles</p>
 </blockquote>
</article>
```

the outline does not include the contents of blockquote: (**Figure 2.9**).

FIGURE 2.9 **The outline does not include content in a sectioning root.**

```
1. Unicorns and butterflies
   1. Main nav
   2. Fairies love rainbows!
```

Styling headings in HTML5

All this clever stuff presents a challenge to authors of CSS. Given that

```
<article><section><h1>...</h1></section></article>
<article><article><h1>...</h1></article></article>
<section><section><h1>...</h1></section></section>
<section><aside><h1>...</h1></aside></section>
<h3>...</h3>
```

can potentially be the same logical levels, you might wish to apply the same styling to them. This can lead to gigantic blocks of rules in your style sheets. There has been some talk of a new CSS pseudo-class or pseudo-element like :heading(n) (as internally the browser will "know" what level a heading is from the outlining algorithm) which would simplify styling:

```
*:heading(1) {font-size: 2.5em;}   /* a logical <h1> */
*:heading(2) {font-size: 2em;}     /* a logical <h2> */
```

However, at the time of this writing, this is but a wonderful dream. As a stopgap, Mozilla is experimenting with a new selector grouping mechanism in Firefox nightlies called :-moz-any() that allows a form of CSS shorthand—go to **http://hacks.mozilla. org/2010/05/moz-any-selector-grouping/** to learn more.

Perhaps, for this reason, you would be tempted to use only <h1> elements to simplify styling, and let the outlining algorithm do the rest. After all, the spec says, "Sections may contain headings of any rank, but authors are strongly encouraged to either use only h1 elements, or to use elements of the appropriate rank for the section's nesting level." But you shouldn't (yet) as it harms accessibility.

The outlining algorithm and accessibility

A recent survey by WebAIM showed that 57 percent of screen reader users use a site's headings structure as their first method to find information on a lengthy site. (See the full survey for more vital information at **www.webaim.org/projects/screenreadersurvey3**). These people use the hierarchy of headings both to give themselves a mental overview (an outline!) of the document they're in and also to navigate through that content. Most screen readers

> **NOTE** Watch the excellent video entitled "Importance of HTML Headings for Accessibility" (**www.youtube.com/watch?v=AmUPhEVWu_E**). The video shows how a blind accessibility consultant navigates a page with JAWS. In an ideal world, it would be compulsory to watch and understand this video before you're allowed to call yourself a professional designer or developer. Sadly, it's not an ideal world.

have keyboard shortcuts that allow users to jump from heading to heading. For example, the JAWS screen reader (by far the most used package, according to the survey) uses the H key to jump from heading to heading, the 1 key to jump to the next <h1>, the 2 key to go to the next <h2>, and so on.

Currently, no browser builds an internal model of the page structure based on all the complex rules previously mentioned and therefore can't expose this model to any screen reader or assistive technology. So, using only <h1> wrecks the navigability and therefore hinders the accessibility of your page.

Our advice is again, follow the spec: "Use elements of the appropriate rank for the section's nesting level." That is, ensure that, in your pages, the hierarchy of headings is correct even without factoring in new HTML5 elements. It will also make writing CSS much easier.

In cases when articles are syndicated from one site to the other and the levels might be out of logical order, a completely unscientific Twitter poll of screen reader users suggested that badly nested section headers are better than all headings being at the same level (which is still better than no headings at all).

And, having done your best, wait for the browsers and the screen readers that sit on top of them to implement the outlining algorithm. As I said, it's not an ideal world.

What's the difference between <article> and <section>?

This is a question that is regularly asked of us at **html5doctor.com**.

An article is an independent, stand-alone piece of discrete content. Think of a blog post, or a news item in a document-based site. In a web application, an `<article>` could be individual emails within an email application or stories in a web-based feed reader, as each email or story is a component of the application and can be independently reused. Think of `<article>` not as a newspaper or magazine article, but as a discrete entity like an article of clothing.

\<article>

Consider this real-world blog/news article:

```
<article>
<h1>Bruce Lawson Is World's Sexiest Man</h1>
<p>Legions of lovely ladies voted luscious lothario Lawson
¬ as the World's Sexiest Man today.</p>
<h2>Second-sexiest man concedes defeat</h2>
<p>Remington Sharp, JavaScript glamourpuss and Brighton
¬ roister-doister, was gracious in defeat. "It's cool
¬ being the second sexiest man when number one is Awesome
¬ Lawson" he said from his swimming pool-sized jacuzzi full
¬ of supermodels.</p>
</article>
```

It could be syndicated, either by RSS or other means, and makes sense without further contextualisation. Just as you can syndicate partial feeds, a "teaser" article is still an article:

```
<article>
<a href=full-story.html>
  <h1>Bruce Lawson is World's Sexiest Man</h1>
  <p><img src=bruce.png alt="bruce lawson">Legions of lovely
  ¬ ladies voted luscious lothario Lawson as the World's
  ¬ Sexiest Man today.</p>
  <p>Read more</p>
</a>
</article>
```

"Block-level" links

Note from this example that you can wrap links around "block-level" elements. In the HTML 4 spec, this is not allowed, so you would probably have links around the heading, the teaser paragraph, and the phrase "read more" all pointing to the same destination.

However, it turns out that all browsers quite happily (and consistently) allowed links to be placed around various block-level elements (with a bit of coaxing—see **www.mattwilcox.net/sandbox/html5-block-anchor/test.html**), and it was only the old HTML spec that didn't allow it, so in HTML5 one link can surround the whole \<article>. As the browsers already handle wrapping links around block-level elements, and there is an obvious use-case, there was no reason to artificially keep the structure as invalid.

It's always been a good idea (for accessibility and usability alike) to "front-load" important information at the start of links. Now, with the possibility of having even larger chunks of content wrapped up as a link, this is even more important (hat tip, Steve Faulkner—**http://www.paciellogroup.com/blog/2011/06/html5-accessibility-chops-block-links**).

As you've seen, comments on blog posts are ⟨article⟩s inside a parent ⟨article⟩. There are other uses for this nesting besides comments—for example, a transcript to a video:

```
<article>
<h1>Stars celebrate Bruce Lawson</h1>
<video>...</video>

<article class=transcript>
<h1>Transcript</h1>
  <p>Supermodel #1: "He's so hunky!"</p>
  <p>Supermodel #2: "He's a snogtabulous bundle of gorgeous
  ¬manhood! And I saw him first, so hands off!"</p>
</article>

</article>
```

The transcript is complete in itself, even though it's related to the video in the outer ⟨article⟩. Remember: The spec says, "When article elements are nested, the inner article elements represent articles that are in principle related to the contents of the outer article."

⟨section⟩

NOTE A ⟨section⟩ generally begins with a heading that introduces it. An exception to this might be a ⟨section⟩ that will have a heading injected using JavaScript. If you wouldn't use a heading, or you want some wrapping element purely for styling purposes you probably should be using a ⟨div⟩.

Compared to ⟨article⟩, ⟨section⟩ is *not* "a self-contained composition in a document, page, application, or site and that is intended to be independently distributable or reusable." It's either a way of sectioning a page into different subject areas, or sectioning an article into, well, sections.

Consider this HTML 4 markup—the rules from Remy's previous job in an off-Broadway production of *The Wizard of Oz:*

```
<h1>Rules for Munchkins</h1>
<h2>Yellow Brick Road</h2>
  <p>It is vital that Dorothy follows it—so no selling
  ¬bricks as "souvenirs"</p>
<h2>Fan Club uniforms</h2>
  <p>All Munchkins are obliged to wear their "I'm a friend
  ¬of Dorothy!" t-shirt when representing the club</p>
  <p><strong>Vital caveat about the information above:
  ¬does not apply on the first Thursday of the month.
  ¬</strong></p>
```

Does the "Vital caveat about the information above" refer to the whole article, that is, everything under the introductory <h1>, or does it refer only to the information under the preceding <h2> ("Fan Club uniforms")? In HTML 4, that paragraph would fall under the <h2>, and there's no easy way to semantically change this. In HTML5, the <section> element makes its meaning unambiguous (which is what we really mean as web developers when we use the word "semantic"):

```
<article>
<h1>Rules for Munchkins</h1>

 <section>
  <h2>Yellow Brick Road</h2>
  <p>It is vital that Dorothy follows it—so no selling
  ¬bricks as "souvenirs"</p>
 </section>

 <section>
  <h2>Fan Club uniforms</h2>
  <p>All Munchkins are obliged to wear their "I'm a friend
  ¬of Dorothy!" t-shirt when representing the club</p>
 </section>

 <p><strong>Vital caveat about the information above:
 ¬does not apply on the first Thursday of the month.
 ¬</strong></p>
</article>
```

Figure 2.10 illustrates this diagrammatically.

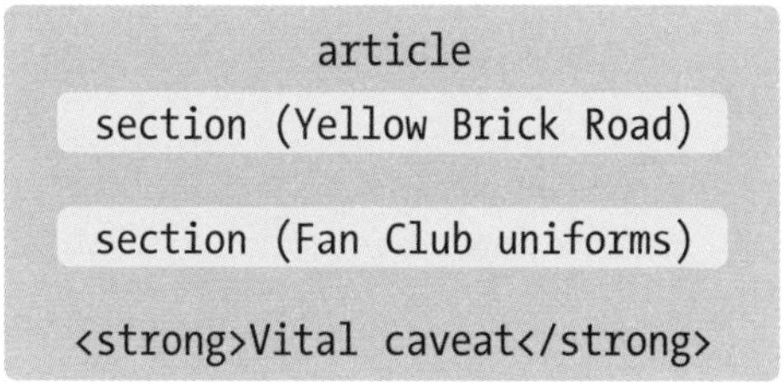

FIGURE 2.10 **Now you can see that the vital caveat refers to the whole** <article>.

```
              article
     section (Yellow Brick Road)

     section (Fan Club uniforms)

     <strong>Vital caveat</strong>
```

If it had been inside the final section element

```
<article>
...
<section>
  <h2>Fan Club uniforms</h2>
  <p>All Munchkins are obliged to wear their "I'm a friend
  ¬of Dorothy!" t-shirt when representing the club</p>
  <p><strong>Vital caveat about the information above:
  ¬does not apply on the first Thursday of the month
  ¬</strong></p>
 </section>
</article>
```

it would unambiguously refer to that section alone, as illustrated in **Figure 2.11**.

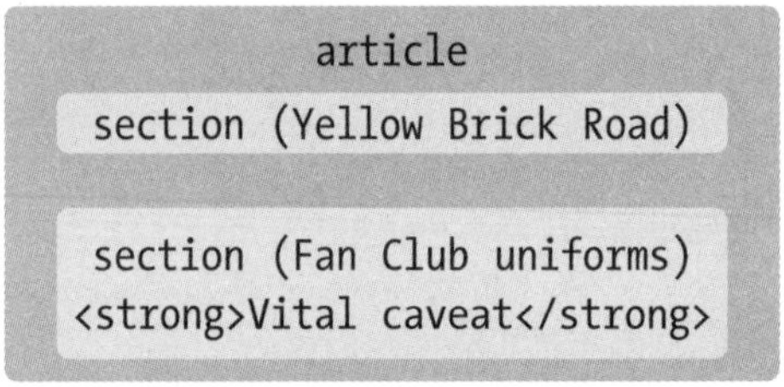

FIGURE 2.11 The `<section>` element removes any ambiguity.

It would *not* have been correct to divide up this article with nested article elements, as they are not independent discrete entities.

OK. So you've seen that you can have `<article>` inside `<article>` and `<section>` inside `<article>`. But you can also have `<article>` inside `<section>`. What's that all about then?

`<article>` inside `<section>`

Imagine that your content area is divided into two units: one for articles about llamas, the other for articles about root vegetables. That's my kind of content.

You're not obliged to mark up your llama articles separately from your root vegetable articles, but you want to demonstrate that the two groups are thematically distinct. Perhaps, because they're thematically distinct, you want them in separate columns, or you'll use CSS and JavaScript to make a tabbed interface.

In HTML 4, you'd use our good but meaningless friend `<div>`. In HTML5, you use `<section>`, which, like `<article>`, invokes the HTML5 outlining algorithm (whereas <div> doesn't, because it has no special structural meaning).

```
<section>
<h1>Articles about llamas</h1>

<article>
<h2>The daily llama: Buddhism and South American camelids
¬</h2>
<p>blah blah</p>
</article>

<article>
<h2>Shh! Do not alarm a llama</h2>
<p>blah blah</p>
</article>

</section>

<section>
<h1>Articles about root vegetables</h1>

<article>
<h2>Carrots: the orange miracle</h2>
<p>blah blah</p>
</article>

<article>
<h2>Eat more Swedes (the vegetables, not the people)</h2>
<p>blah blah</p>
</article>

</section>
```

Why didn't you mark the two <section>s up as <article>s instead? Because, in this example, each <section> is a collection of independent entities, each of which could be syndicated—but you wouldn't ordinarily syndicate the collection as an individual entity.

Note that a <section> doesn't need to contain lots of <article>s; it could be a collection of paragraphs explaining your creative commons licensing, an author bio, or a copyright notice. In our example, each article could contain sub-articles or sections, as explained earlier—or both.

> NOTE All of your which-structural-element-should-I-choose conundrums are easily solved with "The Amazing HTML5 Doctor Easily Confused HTML5 Element Flowchart of Enlightenment!" at www.html5doctor.com/flowchart.

Estelle Weyl has a good analogy at **www.standardista.com/html5-section-v-article**: "Think of a newspaper. The paper comes in sections. You have the sports section, real estate section, maybe home & garden section, etc. Each of those sections, in turn, has articles in it. And, some of those articles are divided into sections themselves.

In other words, you can have parent <section>s with nested <article>s that in turn have one or many <section>s. Not all pages' documents need these, but it is perfectly acceptable and correct to nest this way."

Case study: www.guardian.co.uk

Let's continue with the newspaper theme and look at a real site and work out where you would use the new structures. **Figure 2.12** shows a screenshot from my favourite newspaper, the *Guardian* (**www.guardian.co.uk**). Let's see how this could be represented in HTML5.

FIGURE 2.12 The *Guardian* homepage.

The following is how I would mark up this page; you might choose different structures, and that's OK. There's not necessarily "one true way" of doing this; it depends in part on how you intend to use the content—will you syndicate it, or pull it out of a database for display in several different page templates with a variety of heading hierarchies?

It's pretty easy to see the branding and introductory matter that forms the <header>, which also includes two <nav> structures for site-wide navigation (**Figure 2.13**).

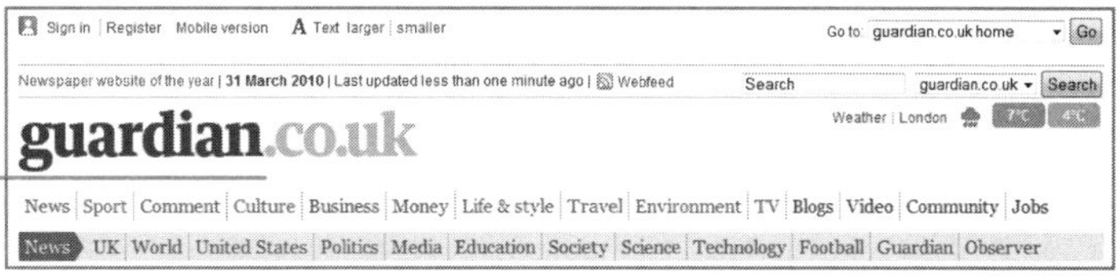

FIGURE 2.13 The *Guardian* homepage's branding and introductory matter.

THE GUARDIAN'S <header>

I've used two separate <nav>s because the top band ("News, Sport, Comment.") is site-wide, whereas the second band ("News, UK, World.") is section-wide. An alternative structural approach would be to have a single <nav> in the header, with the section-wide navigation as a sublist of the site-wide navigation:

```
<nav>
<ul>
<li><a href=...>News<a>
  <ul>
  <li><a href=...>News</a></li>
  <li><a href=...>UK</a></li>
  <li><a href=...>World</a></li>
  ...
  </ul>
</li>
...
</ul>
</nav>
```

FIGURE 2.14 The "breaking news" area of the *Guardian* homepage.

Immediately below the header is an area with the title "breaking news" and a "ticker" of text. Each summary is a link to an expanded story (**Figure 2.14**).

BREAKING NEWS

Breaking news: LATEST: Four schoolchildren seriously injured in coach crash in South Lanarkshire, Strathclyde police said. More details soon ...

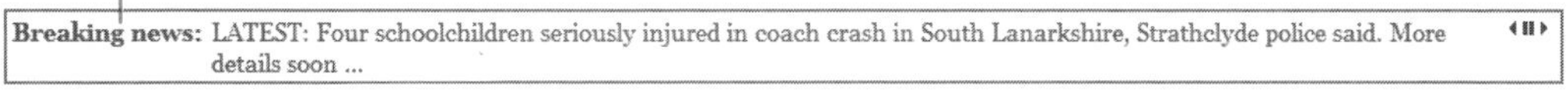

Aside from the JavaScript-controlled ticker effect, this "breaking news" is simply a list of links to other pages. Therefore, it matches the <nav> element. Don't be fooled by the fact that it's horizontal, with the heading on the same line; CSS will sort that out:

```
<nav>
<h2>Breaking news</h2>
<ul>
 <li><a href=...>Four schoolchildren injured...</a></li>
 <li><a href=...>Terrible thing happens to someone</a></li>
 ...
</ul>
</nav>
```

Although visually this area appears closely tied with the header, it's not introductory matter or site-wide navigation. The difference is subtle, but in my opinion, links to comments, TV, and sports pages are part of site-wide navigation, while navigating news stories on a news site is "shortcut navigation" to deeper content. Therefore, this is a <nav> after, rather than inside, the <header> element.

There's more navigation on the right of the main content area (**Figure 2.15**).

As you saw in Chapter 1, sidebars are often composed of navigation plus other non-nav stuff. We're using the <aside> element to group it all together.

```
<aside>
 <nav>
 <h2>guardianjobs</h2>
 <form role=search ... > ... </form>
 <ul>
  <li><a href=...>Upload your CV</a></li>
   ...
  </ul>
 <h2>Online Dating</h2>
 <ul>
   ...
 </ul>
  ...
 </nav>
<section>
<h2>Sponsored Features</h2>
<section>
</aside>
```

FIGURE 2.15
A sidebar of
navigation
on the right
side of the
Guardian
homepage.

Our navigation is a single <nav> element containing multiple unordered lists—each with its own heading (Jobs, Dating, CD box sets, Today's paper, and so on), styled with a blue-grey background and a thick red border-top.

> **NOTE** I've included a search form inside the <nav> (but outside the <ul>s); it seems appropriate to me to regard a search form as a navigational aid. I've also given it the ARIA role appropriate to its function.

However, contrary to my advice in the first edition of this book, I haven't wrapped each list in its own <nav> element, because my purpose is to help assistive technology users to find navigation. Lots of individual <nav>s next to each other would probably make it harder rather than easier for those users. This is speculation, however, and once assistive technologies support <nav>, this would need to be user-tested.

"Sponsored Features" isn't inside <nav> as it's not primary navigation; presumably, its main purpose is to advertise. There's nothing to stop us styling its heading the same as the headings inside the <nav> though, and that's what the design requires.

Now let's look at the main content area (**Figure 2.16**).

FIGURE 2.16 **The main content area of the** *Guardian* **homepage.**

MAIN CONTENT AREA ——

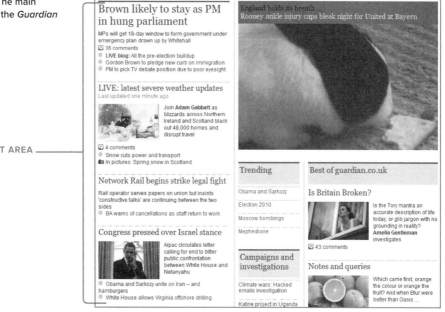

Unsurprisingly for a newspaper site, the main content area of the *Guardian* homepage is given over to news articles. It's important to notice that there is no overriding heading grouping the main articles (such as "top stories"); otherwise you could wrap the whole thing up in a <section>. Therefore, you just have a list of ‹article›s. Because ‹section› isn't appropriate here, if there is a need to wrap all the articles with an element for styling purposes, you'd use the semantically empty ‹div› element.

There is one featured article that consists mostly of an image, presumably because it's the most striking image available (**Figure 2.17**).

FIGURE 2.17 **The featured picture.**

This remains simply an ‹article›, although you might need a class or id to allow special styling.

Below the featured article, you have some sections that aren't the top stories; there is less information on the homepage, and they're primarily, but not solely, links to other pages. Each has its own heading ("Best of guardian.co.uk," "Latest multimedia," "What you're saying"), and then a group of articles. The natural elements are therefore ‹article›s within ‹section›s:

```
<section>
<h2>Best of guardian.co.uk</h2>
<article>
<h3>Is Britain broken?</h3>
...
</article>

<article>
<h3>Notes and queries</h3>
...
</article>

<article>
<h3>Tech Weekly live: Personal privacy</h3>
...
</article>
...
```

```
</section>

<section>
<h2>Latest multimedia</h2>
...
</section>
```

On the website (but not in the screenshot), there are also a couple more <nav> blocks ("Trending," "Campaigns and investigations") and a "fat footer" that, as we saw in Chapter 1, should be a couple of page-wide <nav> blocks outside the "real" <footer> that contains the usual privacy, terms and conditions, and accessibility information.

And there it is, ladies and gentlemen: an HTML5 version of **www.guardian.co.uk**. Like any other exercise in markup above the level of the trivial, there are legitimate differences of opinion. That's OK. HTML is a general language, so there aren't elements for every specific occasion. Choose the most appropriate element for the job and be consistent when marking up similar content throughout the site.

Understanding WAI-ARIA

The W3C Web Accessibility Initiative's Accessible Rich Internet Applications suite (WAI-ARIA) is an independent spec that "plugs the holes" in HTML 4 (or any other markup language) to help make web applications and web pages more accessible.

> **NOTE** If you start using these new ARIA attributes, you may notice that your HTML 4 pages won't validate anymore. As long as the rest of your markup is OK, that doesn't matter—accessibility trumps validity. The ARIA attributes won't cause any kind of DOM weirdness or cause any malfunction in browsers—like with CSS rules, they're just ignored if they're not understood.

Imagine that you have scripted a slider control. In HTML 4 there is no native slider, so you just have some HTML elements (an <input>, some images) with some JavaScript attached to act and look like a slider. There is no way to tell the operating system that the role of this widget is a slider and what its current state and value are. If the operating system doesn't know that vital information, assistive technology such as a screen reader can't convey it to the user either.

ARIA aims to bridge this situation by introducing a whole series of new attributes that browsers and assistive technologies can hook into.

So, using horrible old-school HTML you could—in theory—add ARIA to

```
<font size="+5" color="red">I should be a heading</font>
```

to make

```
<font size="+5" color="red" role="heading" aria-level="2">
¬I should be a heading</font>
```

This tells the user agent that this text is a heading, level 2. But of course, this would be nonsense, as HTML already has a perfectly valid and semantic way of defining this sort of structure with

```
<h2>I AM a heading</h2>
```

A developer might forget to bolt on the necessary ARIA attributes, whereas using the correct <h2> element has built-in "heading-ness" and built-in level so it's a lot more robust. ARIA is not a panacea or "get out of jail free" card for developers to start abusing markup and make everything out of <div>s and <span>s. Whenever possible, use the correct markup and use ARIA only in situations where the correct semantics can't be otherwise expressed (a slider in HTML 4 example, for instance).

The ARIA spec says, "It is expected that, over time, host languages will evolve to provide semantics for objects that previously could only be declared with WAI-ARIA. When native semantics for a given feature become available, it is appropriate for authors to use the native feature and stop using WAI-ARIA for that feature."

So something like HTML5 <nav> shouldn't need ARIA role=navigation added to it, because it should (in an ideal world) have that built-in. However, HTML5 is very new, whereas ARIA already has some support in assistive technology. So it shouldn't hurt to use the built-in element *plus* the ARIA information, and it can only help users who rely on assistive technology. The HTML5 validator therefore validates ARIA as well as HTML5 (whereas HTML 4 validators report ARIA information as an error because HTML 4 predates ARIA).

ARIA document structure and landmark roles

WAI-ARIA defines several roles that tell assistive technology about landmarks and the structure of a document. Some of these are:

- application
- article
- banner
- complementary
- contentinfo
- document
- form
- heading
- main
- navigation
- search

Looking at a simple page from an ARIA perspective, you might see what is shown in **Figure 2.18**.

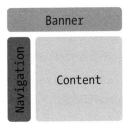

Some of these obviously match HTML5 elements, such as `<article>`, `<form>`, `<header>`, and `<nav>`.

Others lack an obvious one-to-one correspondence. For example, `role=banner` "typically includes things such as the logo or identity of the site sponsor, and site-specific search tool. A banner usually appears at the top of the page and typically spans the full width." That initially seems to match HTML5 `<header>`, but as you've seen, there can be multiple `<header>`s on a page. So the "page header" is the only one allowed to have `role=banner`.

Similarly, contentinfo is defined as "a large perceivable region that contains information about the parent document. Examples of information included in this region of the page are copyrights and links to privacy statements." This sounds like <footer>, but it's only the "page footer" and not each footer in a page with multiple footers.

role=main defines the "main content area" of a page. We discussed in Chapter 1 how that can be algorithmically deduced, but as assistive technologies can make use of ARIA *now*, it makes sense to add this role to the element you're using to group your main content. You can even use it as a hook for CSS in browsers that understand attribute selectors:

```
div[role=main] {color:red; background-color:yellow;
¬ font-family: "Comic Sans MS", cursive; ... }
```

There you have it: accessibility and gorgeous typography in perfect harmony.

Combining ARIA and HTML5

We recommend that you consider using ARIA where appropriate in addition to HTML5 as a transitional measure to improve accessibility that won't harm validation (but see the following note on screen readers). However, we don't do that in this book (as we're teaching you HTML5, not ARIA). A small polyfill at **http://github.com/yatil/accessifyhtml5.js** adds roles to the most common, generic HTML5 cases, but note that (sadly) it won't magically accessify heavy-duty AJAXed web apps.

ARIA resources

There is a useful cross-reference in the spec of HTML5 and ARIA at **http://dev.w3.org/html5/spec/embedded-content-0. html#annotations-for-assistive-technology-products-aria**. Steve Faulkner of The Paciello Group has a list of ARIA information that HTML5 doesn't have built-in at **www.paciellogroup.com/ blog/?p=585**.

For more information on ARIA in general, see Gez Lemon's "Introduction to WAI-ARIA" at **http://dev.opera.com/articles/ view/introduction-to-wai-aria/** and follow The Paciello Group's blog (**www.paciellogroup.com/blog/**). Two recommended books are *Universal Design for Web Applications* by Wendy Chisholm and Matt May (O'Reilly) and *Designing with Progressive*

Enhancement: Building the Web that Works for Everyone by Todd Parker, et al. (New Riders) for useful information on practical uses of ARIA.

The ARIA spec itself is at **www.w3.org/WAI/PF/aria/**.

A note on screen readers

Houston, we have a problem.

In 2007, I was concerned that no screen reader vendors were participating in the HTML5 specification process, so I wrote to the W3C to ask it to invite vendors to join. In 2009, I asked HTML editor Ian Hickson if any vendors had responded. He replied, "A couple did, but only to say they had little time for the standards process, which was quite disappointing. Since then, though, Apple has ramped up their efforts on their built-in Mac OS X screen reader software, and we do get a lot of feedback from Apple. So at least one screen reader vendor is actively involved."

A recent test (**http://www.accessibleculture.org/research/html5-aria-2011/**) shows that older versions of two widely used commercial screen readers cannot properly process content that is marked up with *both* HTML5 and ARIA (oh, the irony) or in `<nav>` elements inside a `<header>`. Not all screen readers misbehave, however; Apple VoiceOver does not omit content, JAWS 12 fixed bugs in versions 10 and 11, and the open-source NVDA screen reader (**www.nvda-project.org/**) speaks all content *and* allows navigation by ARIA landmarks.

Personally, I feel that if you are using the specification the right way, it's not your problem if a browser or screen reader cannot adequately deal with that content. However, that's my personal opinion; you might feel differently, or the legal situation where you are might require you to dumb down your code to accommodate those screen readers. Of course, they might fix the bugs by the time you read this book. In the meantime, **it's your responsibility to know your users and the law in your area.**

Even more new structures!

You ain't seen nothing yet. Actually, that's untrue: you've seen loads already. So while we're in the zone, let's look at other new elements of HTML5, and some of the changes from HTML 4. We'll look at global attributes allowed on any element, as well as wave "hi" to a few HTML5 features that we won't cover in this book.

Microdata

Microdata is a way to give extra semantics to your content without using more HTML elements. It's similar to RDFa and microformats, but is (arguably) simpler.

HTML5 element categories and content models

HTML 4 divided elements into "block-level" and "inline." These names are gone from HTML5, as they're inherently presentational; they simply reflect the way browsers display them with their default style sheets. There is nothing inherent to any HTML element that is "block" or "inline."

By default, CSS defines every element as `display:inline` until it's overridden by the browser's default style sheet or the gorgeous design that the sublimely talented designer that you are applies to the markup. (Don't blush, you know you are; everybody says so.)

In HTML5, we find lots of new content models, including *phrasing* (broadly equivalent to inline) and *flow* (broadly equivalent to block-level). Some elements (`<a>`, `<ins>`, `<del>`) can be both. You'll also recognize *heading* content like `<h1>..<h6>` and *sectioning* elements like `<article>`, `<section>`, `<nav>`, and `<aside>`.

There's also *embedded* (content that imports another resource into the document, or content from another vocabulary that's inserted into the document, such as `<audio>`, `<canvas>`, `<embed>`, `<iframe>`, `<img>`, `<math>`, `<object>`, `<svg>`, and `<video>`), *interactive* (`<a>`, `<audio>` [if the `controls` attribute is present], `<button>`, `<details>`, `<embed>`, `<iframe>`, and `<img>` [if the `usemap` attribute is present], `<input>` [if the `type` attribute is not in the `hidden` state], `<keygen>`, `<label>`, and `<menu>` [if the `type` attribute is in the `toolbar` state], `<object>` [if the `usemap` attribute is present], `<select>`, `<textarea>`, and `<video>` [if the `controls` attribute is present]), *metadata*, and others.

Don't get hung up on these. They're pretty intuitive: Apart from the fact that `<a>` now behaves like `<ins>` and `<del>` and can be "inline" or "block" (to use the old HTML 4 parlance), you won't notice anything different from before in terms of styling—particularly if you're using the HTML5 shiv (**http://code.google. com/p/html5shiv/**) to help old browsers along with the new HTML5 elements until their default presentation is added to the browsers' style sheets.

Microdata is composed of five attributes that can go on any HTML element. The most important are `itemscope`, `itemtype`, and `itemprop`.

`itemscope` defines the scope of one particular item; it says "this container is all about one single item."

Here is a <div> about this very book:

```
<div itemscope>
I love that Introducing HTML5 by Bruce Lawson and Remy Sharp
¬ (ISBN 0321784421)
</div>
```

`itemtype` allows me to specify a vocabulary so a parser or crawler will know what kind of information I'm marking up (this must be an absolute URL):

```
<div itemscope itemtype="http://schema.org/Book">
I love that Introducing HTML5 by Bruce Lawson and Remy Sharp
¬(ISBN 0321784421)
</div>
```

Using **itemprop** I can assign properties to the content:

```
<div itemscope itemtype="http://schema.org/Book">
I love that <span itemprop="name">Introducing HTML5</span>
 by <span itemprop="author"> Bruce Lawson</span> and
 <span itemprop="author">Remy Sharp</span>
 (ISBN <span itemprop="isbn">0321784421</span>)
</div>
```

Notice I've used the properties name for the book title, isbn for the ISBN, and author twice, for Bruce and that other guy.

The actual value that gets assigned to itemprop depends on the element it's on. It's generally the text content of the element, except:

- If the element also has an itemscope attribute, the value is the item created by the element.

- If the element is a <meta> element, the value is the value of the element's content attribute.

- If the element is an <audio>, <embed>, <iframe>, <img>, <source>, <track>, or <video> element, the value is the element's src attribute, resolved to an absolute URL.

- If the element is an <a>, <area>, or <link> element, the value is the element's src attribute, resolved to an absolute URL.

- If the element is an <object> element, the value is the element's data attribute, resolved to an absolute URL.

- If the element is a <time> element with a datetime attribute, the value is the value of the element's datetime attribute.

Microdata items can be nested, so I could give details for the authors using vCard. On the span containing the author name, we give it an itemprop of author, as that's its relationship to the book vocabulary, and we define the span as being a container "about" an individual, so give it an itemscope and an itemtype pointing at the hCard vocabulary:

> **NOTE** This is a silly micro-data example as it gives no further information about our authors than their names; the purpose is to demonstrate the nesting. Much fuller examples can be found in the spec at **www.whatwg.org/specs/web-apps/current-work/multipage/microdata.html#mdvocabs**.

```
<div itemscope itemtype="http://schema.org/Book">
I love that <span itemprop="name">Introducing HTML5</span>
 By
<span itemprop="author" itemscope itemtype=
¬"http://microformats.org/profile/hcard">
 <span itemprop="fn">Bruce Lawson</span>
</span>
and
 <span itemprop="author" itemscope itemtype=
¬"http://microformats.org/profile/hcard">
 <span itemprop="fn">Remy Sharp</span>
</span>
 (ISBN <span itemprop="isbn">0321784421</span>)
</div>
```

Microdata is as simple as that for the majority of use-cases. There are, however, two more attributes that we'll mention for completeness.

itemref

Sometimes, you might want to list additional elements for a user agent to crawl in order to find the name-value pairs of the item, because those elements aren't descendents of the element with the `itemscope` attribute. On the element with itemscope, you can list unique, space-separated tokens that are case-sensitive and correspond to IDs of elements in the same page.

itemid

If you want to, you can use an **itemid** attribute. This is a globally unique identifier—not just on your website, but on the whole Web. It could, for example, be an ISBN or a URL or anything that you can guarantee to be unique, really. Doing this sprinkles magical Semantic Web pixie dust all over your website, and crawlers and content aggregators will "know" that your content is talking about the same things as my content because they share the same itemid. (At time of writing, though, the Microdata vocabularies published by Bing, Google, and Yahoo! on schema.org don't use itemid at all.)

If you want to use itemid, you must use a vocabulary that supports global identifiers:

"The itemid attribute must not be specified on elements that do not have both an itemscope attribute and an itemtype attribute specified, and must not be specified on elements with an item-scope attribute whose itemtype attribute specifies a vocabulary that does not support global identifiers for items, as defined by that vocabulary's specification."

For more information about Microdata, we recommend

"Extending HTML5—Microdata" by Oli Studholme
http://html5doctor.com/microdata/

"Microdata Tutorial" by Tab Atkins, Jr.
www.xanthir.com/blog/b4570

"Using Multiple Vocabularies in Microdata" by Jeni Tennison
www.jenitennison.com/blog/node/161

The Microdata DOM API

Microdata also has an associated DOM API to manipulate items and properties which gives the `document.getItems()` method to grab a nodelist containing Microdata items on a page. Without an argument, the method gets all the items on a page, or passing an itemtype URL returns only items with that itemtype.

At time of writing, only pre-release versions of Opera 12 support the DOM API.

<aside>

In Chapter 1 you saw `<aside>` used to mark up sidebars. It represents "a section of a page that consists of content that is tangentially related to the content around the aside element, and which could be considered separate from that content. Such sections are often represented as sidebars in printed typography. The element can be used for typographical effects like pull quotes or sidebars, for advertising, for groups of nav elements, and for other content that is considered separate from the main content of the page."

Using an `<aside>` inside an `<article>`, for example, is the right place for tangentially related information or pull quotes about that article, but not, we hasten to add, page-wide navigation.

`<aside>` has an implied ARIA role of note, but can be given `role="complementary"` or (if it surrounds a search form) `role="search"`.

<bdi>

The spec says that `<bdi>` "represents a span of text that is to be isolated from its surroundings for the purposes of bidirectional text formatting." *Huh?* I asked Richard Ishida (@r12a on Twitter—follow him!), the W3C's internationalization lead, to explain this to me, and he was kind enough to write a blog post in response (**http://rishida.net/blog/?p=564**), which I have condensed here with his permission.

The HTML5 specification contains a bunch of new features to support bidirectional text in web pages. Languages written with right-to-left scripts—such as Arabic, Hebrew, Persian, Thaana, Urdu, and so on—commonly mix in words or phrases in English or some other language that uses a left-to-right script. The result is called bidirectional or bidi text.

HTML 4.01, coupled with the Unicode Bidirectional algorithm, already does a pretty good job of managing bidirectional text, but there are still some problems when dealing with embedded text from user input or from stored data.

Here's an example where the names of restaurants are added to a page from a database. This is the code, with the Hebrew shown using ASCII:

```
<p>Aroma - 3 reviews</p>
<p>PURPLE PIZZA - 5 reviews</p>
```

Figures 2.19 and **2.20** show what you'd expect to see, and what you'd actually see, respectively.

The problem arises because the browser thinks that the "-5" is part of the Hebrew text. This is what the Unicode Bidi Algorithm tells it to do, and usually it is correct. Not here though.

So the question is how to fix it? The trick is to use the `<bdi>` element around the text to isolate it from its surrounding content. (bdi stands for "bidi-isolate.")

```
<p><bdi>Aroma</bdi> - 3 reviews</p>
<p><bdi>PURPLE PIZZA</bdi> - 5 reviews</p>
```

The bidi algorithm now treats the Hebrew and "- 5" as separate chunks of content, and orders those chunks according to the direction of the overall context (in this instance, from left to right).

TOP RATED RESTAURANTS

Aroma - 3 reviews
★★★★☆
פיצה סגולה - 5 reviews
★★★★☆

FIGURE 2.19 How we'd like our web page to look.

TOP RATED RESTAURANTS

Aroma - 3 reviews
★★★★☆
5 - פיצה סגולה reviews
★★★★★

FIGURE 2.20 How our bidi page actually looks. Note the numeral "5" has been separated from the word "reviews." The content is now unintelligible.

You'll notice that the example above has `bdi` around the name Aroma too. Of course, you don't actually need that, but it won't do any harm. On the other hand, it means you can write a script in something like PHP that says:

```
foreach $restaurant echo "<bdi>".$restaurant['name']."
¬</bdi> - %1 reviews";
```

This way you can handle any name that comes out of the database, whatever language it is in.

Using the dir attribute with bdi

The `dir` attribute can be used on the `<bdi>` element to set the base direction. With simple strings of text like PURPLE PIZZA you don't really need it, however if your `<bdi>` contains text that is itself bidirectional you'll want to indicate the base direction.

Before HTML5, you could only set the `dir` attribute to `ltr` or `rtl`. The problem is that in a situation like the one described above, where you are pulling strings from a database or user, you may not know which of these to use.

That's why HTML5 has provided a new auto value for the `dir` attribute, and `bdi` comes with that set by default. The auto value tells the browser to look at the first strongly typed character in the element and work out from that what the base direction of the element should be. If it's a Hebrew (or Arabic, and so on) character, the element will get a direction of `rtl`. If it's, say, a Latin character, the direction will be `ltr`.

In rare instances this may not give the desired outcome, but in the vast majority of cases it should produce the expected result.

Note that this isn't implemented anywhere yet, but as information about it is so scarce, we've included it here.

<details>

I'm very fond of the `<details>` element. It's cool because it introduces native support for a common behaviour—an expanding/collapsing area—thereby removing the need for custom JavaScript (or, something I've seen on far too many sites to be funny, pulling in the full jQuery library).

```
<details>
 <summary>Photograph details</summary>
 <p>Photograph taken on <time datetime=2009-12-25>Xmas
¬ Day 09</time> with a Canon IXUSi.</p>
 <p><small>Copyright Bruce Lawson,
¬ <address>bruce@brucelawson.co.uk</address></small>.</p>
¬ </details>
```

The contents of the descendant `<summary>` element are focus-able and act as a control that, when activated by mouse or key-board, expand or collapse the remainder of the element. If no `<summary>` element is found, the browser supplies its own default control text, such as "details" or a localised version. Browsers will probably add some kind of icon, such as a down arrow, to show that the text is "expandable."

`<details>` can optionally take the open attribute to ensure that the element is already open when the page is loaded:

```
<details open>
```

At time of writing, `<details>` is only supported by Google Chrome 12. Use with care though, and test it well, as it has accessibility problems: it can't be controlled with a keyboard so requires a mouse. Hopefully this will be fixed in a future version of Chrome.

NOTE The `<details>` element isn't restricted to purely textual markup—it could be a login form, an explanatory video, a table of source data for a graph, or a description of the structure of a table for those who use assistive technology, have learning disabilities, or who (like me) simply don't "get" numbers.

`<figure>`

I've always felt a bit semantically grubby when adding a caption to explain a picture or to give attribution to the photographer, because the only way to do it has been with text that runs into surrounding content, with no way to explicitly associate it with the image. There simply haven't been any markup constructs for this before. Perhaps I'm just weird, but that's why I'm very glad to see the **`<figure>`** element that wraps an image (or a video, or a block of code, or a supporting quotation) and its caption, which goes in the `<figcaption>` element:

```
<figure>
<img src=welcome.jpg
>
<figcaption>
Bruce and Remy welcome questions
<small>Photo &copy; Bruce's mum</small>
</figcaption>
</figure>
```

Styling this markup can produce some nice effects (**Figure 2.21**).

FIGURE 2.21 `<figure>` and `<figcaption>` elements with some **CSS3** designer bling.

Bruce and Remy welcome questions
Photo © Bruce's mum

Notice that there is no `alt` attribute on the image. In the first edition, I had added a blank `alt=""`, but this was incorrect.

In figures where the figcaption text tells you all you need to know ("Pippa Middleton and Remy Sharp pose on the red carpet at the premier of the Jane Austen movie *Pride and ECMAScript*"), don't duplicate this in alt text because duplicated content can quickly become very annoying. Duplicated content can quickly become very annoying.

In the first edition, I tried to avoid duplicated content (which can quickly become very annoying) by also including `alt=""` on the `<img>` element. But if an image has empty alt text it is regarded as having an implied ARIA `role=presentation` (only there to enhance presentation). This removes the element from the page's accessibility tree (no user agent does this, yet, but that's the general plan).

As the image is not purely presentational (if it were, you wouldn't mark it up as a figure or give it a caption), you shouldn't have empty `alt`, you should use no alternate text at all, for example.

Steve Faulkner has written a very useful document "HTML5: Techniques for providing useful text alternatives" (that is a First Public Working Draft, therefore very, very susceptible to change) in which he writes:

"Circumstances in which it is not appropriate to use an empty or null alt attribute: An image is contained within a figure element and has an associated caption provided using the figcaption element." (**http://dev.w3.org/html5/alt-techniques/**)

On the other hand, you may think that the example above needs alt text `<img src=welcome.jpg alt="Bruce and Remy glower menacingly into the camera">` because otherwise the joke isn't communicated to a screen reader user.

As an accessibility bonus it's useful (but not mandatory) to add ARIA attributes to associate the image with the caption until browsers "understand" the figure element and do this automatically.

When there is no alt text, use `aria-labelledby` to associate the id of the `figcaption` to the `img`:

```
<figure>
<img src=welcome.jpg aria-labelledby=figcap219>
<figcaption id=figcap219>
Pippa Middleton and Remy Sharp pose on the red carpet at
¬ the premier of the Jane Austen movie <cite>Pride and
¬ ECMAScript</cite>
</figcaption></figure>
```

If there is alt text, use `aria-describedby`:

```
<figure>
<img src=welcome.jpg
alt="Bruce and Remy glower menacingly into the camera"
aria-describedby=figcap219>
<figcaption id=figcap219>
Bruce and Remy welcome questions
<small>Photo © Bruce's mum</small>
</figcaption></figure>
```

HTML5 and alt text on images

There has been much weeping and lamentation in the streets about the fact that, in certain circumstances, the validator won't punch you for omitting the `alt` attribute on `<img>` (although I will punch anyone referring to it as "the alt tag"):

- The presence of `<meta name=generator>` makes missing `alt` conforming.
- The presence of `title` makes missing `alt` conforming.
- The presence of `figcaption` makes missing `alt` conforming.

I recommend that 99.99 percent of the time, you should continue to use `alt` with an image, with purely decorative images getting empty `alt=""`. An occasional exception will be as we've discussed with images in `<figure>`. If the function of the image is *exactly* expressed in the `<figcaption>`, use no `alt` at all. The other 0.01% is when you're writing a template for automatically generated web pages that import images where it's impossible to get `alt`, for example, automatically including stills from a live webcam, in which case use `<meta name=generator>` in the head.

<mark>

The `<mark>` element allows you to do the markup equivalent of using a highlighter pen to bring out some words on a printed page. It's not the same as emphasis—for that you use `<em>`. But if you had some existing text and wanted to bring something to the fore that isn't emphasised in the text, you could use `<mark>` and style it to be italics, or with a yellow highlighter-pen background colour. In print, you'll often see the phrases "my italics" or "emphasis added."

The spec also says, "When used in the main prose of a document, it indicates a part of the document that has been highlighted due to its likely relevance to the user's current activity."

As an illustration, on my own site, I use an adapted version of Stuart Langridge's *searchhi* script (**www.kryogenix.org/code/browser/searchhi/**), which checks to see if the referrer to a page was a search engine and the search terms are in the query string. If they are, the script walks the DOM and surrounds each instance of a search term with a `<mark>` element, which is then styled a pretty pink. It would have been wrong to wrap these search terms in `<strong>` or `<em>` as they're not emphatic—and this would have changed the meaning of the content of our page—but are relevant to the user's current activity: arriving at a page on our site looking for information about a certain search term.

<ruby>, <rt>, <rp>

The `<ruby>` element is a useful addition for those writing content in some Asian languages. Daniel Davis has a very useful article, "The HTML5 `<ruby>` element in words of one syllable or less" (**http://my.opera.com/tagawa/blog/the-html5-ruby-element-in-words-of-one-syllable-or-less**), in which he explains how it works, along with the related `<rt>` and `<rp>` tags, in the context of Japanese (used with kind permission):

Any piece of Japanese text (banner ad, article, legal doc, and so on) uses a combination of kanji, hiragana, and katakana writing systems. It is sometimes the case that people reading the text can't read the kanji, especially because kanji characters can have more than one pronunciation. People and place names are one example of kanji having numerous or irregular pronunciations.

日 can be pronounced "nichi," "hi," or "ka"

本 can be pronounced "hon" or "moto"

日本 can be pronounced "nihon" or "nippon"

To help the reader, sometimes the pronunciation is written above the kanji using the hiragana alphabet. This is called *furigana* in Japanese and *ruby* in English (from the name of the small 5.5 pt type size used for similar sorts of annotations in British print tradition). It is often used in newspapers and books but not so much on websites, due to the difficulty of squeezing miniature text above larger text on a single line. The `<ruby>` element aims to solve this.

According to the current HTML5 spec, the `<ruby>` element is an inline element and is placed around the word or character you'd like to clarify, like so:

`<ruby>日本</ruby>`

By itself this does nothing, so you add the pronunciation either for each character or, as in this case and our personal preference, for the word as a whole. For this, you use the **`<rt>`** tag, meaning ruby text.

`<ruby>日本<rt>にほん</rt></ruby>`

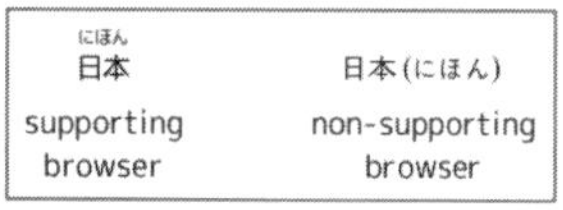

にほん
日本   日本(にほん)

supporting   non-supporting
browser   browser

FIGURE 2.22 In supporting browsers, ruby text is shown above main text. In nonsupporting browsers, ruby text is shown next to main text but in parentheses.

You could leave it like that and supporting browsers would show the hiragana pronunciation above the kanji text, but nonsupporting browsers would ignore the tags and show both the text and its pronunciation side by side. To solve this, you have another tag, **`<rp>`**, meaning ruby parentheses, which cleverly hides characters (namely parentheses) in supporting browsers. This means you can write the pronunciation in parentheses, which nonsupporting browsers will show, and supporting browsers will continue to show the pronunciation without parentheses above the main text (**Figure 2.22**).

`<ruby>日本<rp>(</rp><rt>にほん</rt><rp>)</rp></ruby>`

<wbr>

In Netscape 4 and now standardized by HTML5 to great rejoicing, the `<wbr>` element tells a browser it may (but is not required to) insert a line break here if it needs somewhere to break a line.

Redefined elements

HTML5 redefines the semantics of some existing elements as well as adding new ones. Here are a few old friends: some have radically changed, others have simply finessed their hairstyles.

<address>

As in HTML4, `<address>` is for contact details of the author, not as a generic element for postal addresses.

What's new is that you can have multiple addresses in a document, one inside each `<article>`. Author information associated with an `<article>` element does not apply to nested `<article>` elements, so a blog post in an `<article>` can have an `<address>` for its author, and each blog comment (which you remember is a nested `<article>`) can have the `<address>` of its commenter.

Bruce Lawson, Remy Sharp

FIGURE 2.23 An `<address>` containing a QR code as contact details.

Now we're all riders of the Information Superhighway, and we probably use electronic methods to contact authors, so contact details can be email address, postal address, or any others. These can be marked up as a microformat, RDFa, or Microdata if you wish (**Figure 2.23**).

```
<address>
<a href="http://introducinghtml5.com">
<img src=qr.png alt="">
Bruce Lawson, Remy Sharp</a>
</address>
```

Tangentially, formatting addresses (along with adding line breaks to poetry, lyrics, and code samples) is one of the few reasons remaining to use the `<br>` element:

```
<address>
Dunhackin<br>
123 Standards Boulevard<br>
Semantichester<br>
UK<br>
</address>
```

<cite>

In HTML 4, the `<cite>` element could be used to mark up the name of a speaker:

```
As <cite>Harry S. Truman</cite> said,<Q lang="en-us">
¬ The buck stops here.</Q>
```

HTML5 disallows this: "A person's name is not the title of a work—even if people call that person a piece of work—and the element must therefore not be used to mark up people's names."

This is bonkers. It makes existing content that conforms to the rules of HTML 4 nonconforming to the rules of HTML5, although it will never be flagged as invalid by a validator, as a machine has no way of knowing that "Harry S. Truman" is a name rather than the title of a biography called "Harry S. Truman."

In his article, "Incite a Riot," <cite>Jeremy Keith</cite> wrote, "Join me in a campaign of civil disobedience against the unnecessarily restrictive, backwards-incompatible change to the `<cite>` element (**http://24ways.org/2009/incite-a-riot**)."

I agree. Use `<cite>` for names if you want to.

<dl>

In HTML 4, `<dl>` was a definition list containing a term and one or more definitions for that term. This was nice and straightforward, but then the spec got itself all muddy and confused, as it also mentioned the potential use of `<dl>` to mark up dialogues, complete with code examples to that effect. It was regularly misused to mark up any name and value pairs regardless of whether one *defined* the other.

HTML5 widens the element to be "an association list consisting of zero or more name-value groups . . . Name-value groups may be terms and definitions, metadata topics and values, or any other groups of name-value data." Here's an example listing the books in Remy's collection, using `<dt>` and `<dd>` to group title and author(s).

```
<dl>
 <dt>History of French plastic sandals</dt>
 <dd>Phillipe Philloppe</dd>
 <dt>J-Lo's plastic surgery: a profile</dt>
 <dd>Hugh Jarce</dd>
 <dt>The Orpheus and Eurydice myth</dt>
```

```
  <dd>Helen Bach</dd>
  <dt>The Proctologist and the Dentist</dt>
  <dd>Ben Dover</dd>
  <dd>Phil McCavity</dd>
</dl>
```

<em>, <i>

Use `<em>` to mark up emphasis of the kind that subtly changes the meaning of a sentence; if the question is "Did you say you live in Paris?" the answer might be marked up as

```
<p>No, my <em>name</em> is Paris. I live in <em>Troy</em>.
¬Cloth-ears.</p>
```

If you have relative levels of importance, you can nest `<em>` elements to make the contents extra emphatic.

The spec tell us that the `<i>` element "represents a span of text in an alternate voice or mood, or otherwise offset from the normal prose, such as a taxonomic designation, a technical term, an idiomatic phrase from another language, a thought, a ship name, or some other prose whose typical typographic presentation is italicized."

Here are some examples of `<i>` where `<em>` would *not* be appropriate:

```
<p>The <i>Titanic</i> sails at dawn.</p>
<p>The design needs a bit more <i lang=fr>ooh la la</i>.</p>
<p>You, sir, deserve a jolly good kick up the <i>gluteus
maximus</i>!</p>
```

<hr>

The `<hr>` element is now media-independent and indicates "a paragraph-level thematic break." A commenter on HTML5doctor.com put it nicely: "It's the markup equivalent of the '* * *' that is often used in stories and essays." We were about to write it off as a historical curiosity when fellow HTML5 Doctor Oli Studholme wrote, "<hr> is used as a section separator quite frequently in Japanese design. They're generally hidden via CSS but visible when viewed on cHTML cell phone browsers, which only support very basic CSS and don't get the visual design (and with it the visual separation of sections)."

Unless your audience has significant numbers of users of these phones, we recommend you use sectioning content and headings instead, with CSS for pretty dividers and forget about <hr>. That way you have less markup, and besides, it's hard to style <hr> consistently across browsers.

<ol>

Our old friend the unordered list hasn't been redefined, but it does have two new attributes.

In HTML 4, the start attribute on `<ol>` was deprecated, as it was deemed presentational. Luckily, HTML5 reverts this wrong decision. If you want an ordered list to start at line five rather than line one, use:

```
<ol start=5>
```

Something nice that isn't yet implemented in any browser is the reversed attribute. Consider the following example:

```
<h3>Top five dreamy mega-hunks</h3>
<ol reversed>
 <li>Brad Pitt</li>
 <li>George Clooney</li>
 <li>Orlando Bloom</li>
 <li>Remy Sharp</li>
 <li>Bruce Lawson</li>
</ol>
```

This creates a list that counts down from five (Mr. Pitt) to one (me). Sorry, Brad, George, and Orlando—but what do you guys know about HTML5?

<s>

In HTML 4.01, we had the `<strike>` and `<s>` elements to present some text with a line through it. HTML5 retains `<s>` to represent content that is no longer accurate or no longer relevant and that therefore has been "struck" from the document. You'd use it to show a pre-special offer price:

```
<p>Photograph of Remy Sharp in mankini. <s>&pound;100</s>
¬ Now: 12 pence.</p>
```

<small>

The `<small>` element has been completely redefined, from a generic presentational element to make text appear smaller to actually representing "small print," which "typically features disclaimers, caveats, legal restrictions, or copyrights. Small print is also sometimes used for attribution, or for satisfying licensing requirements."

You might not notice this redefinition, as your browser will probably render the content in smaller type, just as before. But the new semantic means that `<small>` also corresponds to the really quickly spoken part at the end of radio advertisements, so a screen reader might mimic that for its default aural rendering.

If the whole page is a "legalese" page, don't use `<small>`. In that case, the legal text *is* the main content, so there is no need to use an element to differentiate the legalese. It's only for short runs of text. `<small>` has no bearing on `<strong>` or `<em>` elements.

<strong>, <b>

The `<strong>` element represents strong importance for its contents but, unlike `<em>`, it does not change the meaning of the sentence. For example,

`<p><strong>Warning! This banana is dangerous.</strong></p>`

You can nest `strong` elements to make them extra-important.

The `<b>` element "represents a span of text to which attention is being drawn for utilitarian purposes without conveying any extra importance and with no implication of an alternate voice or mood, such as key words in a document abstract, product names in a review, actionable words in interactive text-driven software, or an article lede."

For example:

```
<p>Remy never forgot his fifth birthday—feasting on
¬ <b>powdered toast</b> and the joy of opening his gift:
¬ a <b>Log from Blammo!</b>.</p>
```

<u>

The `<u>` element is another one that used to be presentational but has now been given a New! Improved! semantic meaning, in what feels more like a mopping-up exercise than a useful definition.

The spec says it "represents a span of text with an unarticulated, though explicitly rendered, non-textual annotation, such as labeling the text as being a proper name in Chinese text (a Chinese proper name mark), or labeling the text as being misspelt."

Removed elements

Some elements you may know from HTML 4 have been made completely obsolete in HTML5, such as <applet> (use <embed> instead), <big>, <blink>, <center>, <font>, and <marquee>. They will not validate and must not be used by authors. Frames are gone (but <iframe> remains). Good riddance.

HTML5 browsers must still render these dear departed elements, of course, as there are plenty of them still out there in the wild. But you must avoid them as if they were tarantulas, zombies, man-eating tigers, plutonium sandwiches, or Celine Dion songs.

Global attributes

There are several new global attributes, which can be added to any element. They are covered in this section.

accesskey

The accesskey attribute allows a developer to specify a keyboard shortcut that activates or focuses the element. It was added to HTML 4 to promote accessibility. Because of discoverability problems, but primarily because most possible combinations conflict with keystrokes in assistive technologies, it was rarely used.

Because HTML5 is for web applications, and power users like to use keyboard shortcuts, accesskey isn't removed from HTML5 and is now allowed on any element.

To prevent clashes with other applications or the browser's own keyboard shortcuts, you can now specify a number of alternatives in the accesskey attribute. The spec gives this example:

```
<input type="search" name="q" accesskey="s 0">
```

explaining that "the search field is given two possible access keys, 's' and '0' (in that order). A user agent on a device with a full keyboard might pick Ctrl+Alt+S as the shortcut key, while a user agent on a small device with just a numeric keypad might pick just the plain unadorned key 0."

contenteditable

Invented by Microsoft, and reverse-engineered and implemented by all other browsers, `contenteditable` is now officially part of HTML5.

This adoption of `contenteditable` means two things for browsers: first, users can edit the contents of elements with this attribute, so the element must be selectable and the browser must provide a caret to mark the current editing position; second, you can make the text bold, change the font, add lists, headings, and so on. `contenteditable` is a Boolean attribute, so it can be set to true or false. Although markup capitalisation is irrelevant, the `DOM` attribute (if you were to set it programmatically through JavaScript) requires `contentEditable` (note the capital *E*). The DOM also has `isContentEditable` to assess whether an element is editable—since the `contentEditable` flag could have been inherited from a parent element.

You can also set `document.designMode = 'on'` (notice, not `'true'`) to enable the entire document to be editable. This can only be done using JavaScript—there is no equivalent attribute that can be written in your HTML.

Finally, any content that is selected (highlighted) by the user can have a number of commands run against it, such as `document.execCommand('bold')`. Typical keyboard commands to make text bold or italic (such as CTRL+B and CTRL+I respectively on Windows/Linux) affect the DOM in the editable element, adding `<b>` and `<i>` around them.

If you want to use `contenteditable` for some form of CMS, you will want to save the changes to your server at some point. There's no particular API method for doing this, but since your user's changes have modified the DOM, you need to send the `innerHTML` of the editable element (or entire document if using `designMode`) back to the server for saving in your CMS.

data-* (custom data attributes)

HTML5 allows custom attributes on any element. These can be used to pass information to local scripts.

Previously, to store custom data in their markup, authors would do something annoying like use classes: `<input class="spaceship shields-5 lives-3 energy-75">`. Then your script would need to waste time grabbing these class names, such as `shields-5`, splitting them at a delimiter (a hyphen in this example) to extract the value—all very hacky and arguably an abuse of the class attribute, which is intended (according to HTML 4.01) as a hook for styling or for "general purpose processing by user agents."

In his 2007 book, *ppk on JavaScript,* Peter-Paul Koch explains how to do this and why he elected to use custom attributes in some HTML 4 pages, making the JavaScript leaner and easier to write but also making the page technically invalid. As it's much easier to use `data-shields=5` for passing name/value pairs to scripts, HTML5 legitimises and standardises this useful, real-world practice and gives us a simple, standardised API to easily access and manipulate these custom attributes.

When the `data-*` attributes are fully supported in a browser, JavaScript can access the properties using `element.dataset.foo` (where the `data-foo` attribute contains the value).

This is currently supported in all browsers except Internet Explorer, but the polyfill at **http://gist.github.com/362081** can help with that.

Otherwise scripts can access the values via the traditional `get`/`setAttribute` methods. The advantage of the `dataset` property over `setAttribute` is that it can be enumerated a lot more easily. Say, for instance, you needed to get all the values stored in the `data-*` attributes; using the native functionality the code is straightforward and as you'd expect (without any optimisation):

```
var values = [];
for (var key in element.dataset) {
  values.push(element.dataset[key]);
}
```

However, to do this today, although the code has the same result, it's not so accessible to newer developers or folk that are less savvy with JavaScript and the DOM:

> **NOTE** Custom data attributes are only meant for passing information to the site's own scripts, for which there are no more appropriate attributes or elements. The spec says "These attributes are not intended for use by software that is independent of the site that uses the attributes" and are therefore not intended to pass information to crawlers or third-party parsers. That's a job for microformats, Microdata, or RDFa.

```
var attributes = el.attributes,
    values = [];
for (var i = 0; i < attributes.length; i++) {
  if (attributes[i].name.indexOf('data-') === 0) {
    values.push(test.attributes[i].nodeValue);
  }
}
```

When fully implemented in browsers, setting a dataset attribute automatically sets the content attribute on the element giving you a shorthand syntax for setting custom data. So instead of having to do

```
element.setAttribute('data-author', 'Remy and Bruce');
```

You can simple execute

```
elemenent.dataset.author = 'Remy and Bruce';
```

This syntax will automatically set the attribute on the DOM node as well as change the `dataset.name` property.

draggable

`draggable` indicates that the element can be dragged using the drag-and-drop API (see Chapter 8).

hidden

This `hidden` attribute is analogous to `aria-hidden`, which tells the browser that the content of this element shouldn't be rendered in any way. It hides the content, but keeps it "in the wings," so that, for instance, you could use JavaScript later on to remove the attribute and cause the element to "pop" into being.

Quoting the specification (rather than attempting to paraphrase it any further): "The `hidden` attribute must not be used to hide content that could legitimately be shown in another presentation. For example, it is incorrect to use `hidden` to hide panels in a tabbed dialog, because the tabbed interface is merely a kind of overflow presentation—one could equally well just show all the form controls in one big page with a scrollbar. It is similarly incorrect to use this attribute to hide content just from one presentation—if something is marked hidden, it is hidden from all presentations, including, for instance, screen readers."

Even if you know that you'll be "unhiding" stuff later with some scripting, you should treat hidden stuff as if it literally wasn't there. So don't add links pointing to content that's hidden and don't tie other elements to it with `aria-describedby` or `aria-labelledby`.

id

You don't need us to explain what our old chum `id` is. But now you can begin the value of id with a digit, just like you always have been able to do with `class`. Yay to the max, that's phat, as people a quarter of my age probably say.

itemscope, itemprop, itemtype, itemref, itemid

These attributes are associated with the Microdata specification.

role, aria-*

As you've already seen, HTML5 treats WAI-ARIA as legal additions to the language—meaning they'll quite happily validate.

spellcheck

This Boolean attribute tells the browser to check the element's spelling and grammar—generally, an `<input>` or `<textarea>`, but it could be anything because anything can be set to be `contenteditable`. If it's missing, "the default state indicates that the element is to act according to a default behavior, possibly based on the parent element's own `spellcheck` state."

tabindex (=-1)

`tabindex` is a largely archaic concept that allows you to specify the order in which elements are focused when the user navigates a page with the keyboard (traditionally using the Tab key, though some browsers—most notably Opera—may use different key combinations for this).

This was quite popular when sites were built using deeply nested layout tables in which the document order of focusable elements would often be markedly different from its visual rendering order and logical tab order. Because no one above the level of WYSIWYG-wielding wannabe has used tables for layout since Mozart went stegosaurus hunting, nowadays this is not usually necessary. The default tab order is determined by the order in which elements appear in your markup, so a properly ordered and structured document should never require additional tabbing hints.

However, tabindex does have a useful side effect. Normally, only links, form elements, and image map areas can be focused via the keyboard. Adding a tabindex can make other elements also focusable, so executing a focus() command from JavaScript would move the browser's focus to them. However, this would also make these elements keyboard-focusable, which may not be desirable.

Using a negative integer (by convention, tabindex=-1) allows the element to be focused programmatically, "but should not allow the element to be reached using sequential focus navigation."

It's very useful in overcoming a bug in IE whereby, under some circumstances, elements such as headings that were targets of in-page links were never focused for screen reader users, leaving the information inaccessible. (See **www.juicystudio.com/ article/ie-keyboard-navigation.php** for more information.) In HTML 4, "-1" was an invalid value for the attribute, and the attribute itself was invalid on any element other than form fields and links. However, as it works in browsers now and it solves a real problem, HTML5 legalises it everywhere. Yay!

Removed attributes

<table border=...>

Of course, there's no question that someone like you wouldn't use tables to lay out a page, but just in case you are maintaining or tweaking these old-school monsters, there are only two allowed values for the border attribute: the empty string and "1". These simply give a hint to user agents that the table is for layout. A better way to do this, however, is with the newfangled ARIA role=presentation, which is interesting as its children don't inherit it—so a table can be marked as presentational, but its contents (a form inside one of the table cells, for instance) does not also get marked as presentational in the eyes of screen-readers and other ARIA-consuming user agents.

Of course, if you need groovy borders for your data tables, use CSS. This is really here just for backwards compatibility.

<table summary=...>

Previous versions of HTML had a summary attribute on `<table>`, which was not to be rendered visually but was purely "for user agents rendering to non-visual media such as speech and Braille." This is now nonconforming. One reason for this is that data that can't be seen can fall out of step with the visual data that it describes. This might happen when a harassed developer updates the data in the table and, because the hidden summary is invisible to a quick visual check, fails to update the summary as well to correspond with the visible data. An incorrect summary of the table data is worse than no summary at all.

It's been argued that it would be better to require user agents to render table summaries visually, but unfortunately WCAG 1, the original web accessibility guidelines, *required* a table summary, so there are many layout tables with the helpful summary "This is a layout table" and it's unlikely that the Web would be improved by revealing each of those.

It seems to me that if a website has a structure complex enough that it needs summarising to visually impaired users, non-screen reader users might also benefit from that information. Therefore, the spec gives numerous suggestions for presenting this information visually: surrounding the table, in the table's caption, in a `<details>` element, next to the table in the same `<figure>`, next to the table in a `<figcaption>`, or simply in prose.

<img longdesc=...>

The attribute `longdesc` was a very rarely used attribute on images that pointed to a separate page which described the image in detail. It's been removed from HTML5, largely because few authors ever used it, and few of those who did authored it correctly. Nevertheless, it is much beloved by screen reader users, 60 percent of whom say it's "somewhat" or "very" useful (**http://webaim.org/projects/screenreadersurvey3/#longdesc**) and no comparable method exists to provide the same form of extended description, so you'll need to use other mechanisms (such as the `<details>` element) to describe an image.

Features not covered in this book

For completeness, here are some of the most interesting features of HTML5 that, for reasons of page count or lack of implementation, aren't discussed further.

<embed>

Of course `<embed>` is well-known and has been used for years, but was always an outlaw element that never validated. But like that other outlaw, Robin Hood, it was widely supported because it performed a useful function: It's the only way to get plugins such as Flash to work reliably in all browsers, which explains its overwhelmingly common usage (see 2008 stats at **http:// dev.opera.com/articles/view/mama-plug-ins/**). Because of this, there's no reason to keep it from validating. HTML5 paves that particular cowpath and finally includes it into the formal language specification.

But hang on. Isn't HTML5 supposed to replace all these plugin-based technologies? Contrary to the sensationalist headlines of some journalists, HTML5 won't magically replace plugins overnight, and now we can embed them into HTML5 without incurring the wrath of the validator.

<keygen>

This element, which is already well supported in all browsers other than the big IE elephant in the room, is used in situations where your form needs to send a public key. Take a look at **http://en.wikipedia.org/wiki/Public_key** to learn more about public-key cryptography.

And if you're still lost, you don't actually need this element!

<menu>, <command>

These are exciting elements that allow you to define toolbars or context menus for your application, with icons and associated commands that execute scripts when activated. They're cooler than a bucket full of Lou Reeds. However, no browser yet supports them, so we don't discuss them further.

\<style scoped\>

The `scoped` attribute on a style element tells the browser to apply the styles to the element that the `<style scoped>` element is in, and its children. Thus, it is found inside elements in the document's `<body>` rather than only in the `<head>` where style elements have hitherto been confined. This allows for highly localised styling right inside your HTML; for instance, an `<article>` that contains a scoped style block can be syndicated and retain its special styles.

However, no browser supports it yet.

Summary

Phew, that was quite a ride, wasn't it? You've seen a lot of new structures, new elements, and quite a few changes to existing elements. If you've studied our markup examples carefully, you also know the favoured weaponry of fairies, so beware if you're a goblin or an orc.

HTML5 allows us to mark up common website structures with dedicated elements, rather than empty `<div>` or `<span>` elements. However, these elements are still completely necessary parts of the language. Just as with HTML 4, you should use these generic containers when there are no more appropriate elements—but now you have a larger arsenal of semantically more meaningful elements to choose from. You've also seen that some of these new elements have conceptually built-in roles to help assistive technologies. However, while we're in this transitional period and browser (and, more importantly, screen reader/assistive technology) support for these built-in roles may still be lacking, you can (validly and legally) add extra ARIA information.

It probably seems pretty complex, but take my word for it: as you use these new constructs, they soon become much easier to understand ... so get stuck in!

CHAPTER 3

Forms

Bruce Lawson

ONE OF THE problems with HTML 4 forms is that they're just dumb fields. Validation is required on the server, of course, but you have to duplicate it in the user's browser with JavaScript to give them the seamless experience they deserve. Given that almost every web page has some kind of form—search, comments, sign-up, and so on—wouldn't it be great if browsers had built-in validation for some of the most common data types that we collect?

You guessed it: HTML5 forms provide exactly that.

We ♥ HTML, and now it ♥s us back

HTML5 makes developing forms quicker. There are some nice goodies like the addition of two HTTP types of form action (update and delete) to go with the current get and post. But the coolest features for developers—which will be transparent to bosses and consumers, but they'll make our lives much easier—are new form input types which can give us special UIs and built-in error reporting.

> **NOTE** These form enhancements aren't implemented across the board yet. Opera has the most extensive support, followed by the WebKit browsers and Firefox. At the time of this writing, Internet Explorer 10 Platform Preview 2 has some support. Exciting times!

Eventually, you won't need JavaScript validation at all for these fundamental data types, although you can't mothball your scripts yet—the new input types degrade gracefully but will need your JavaScript until the golden future when everyone has an HTML5 browser (or your boss tells you that users of ancient browsers will just have to put up with server-side-only form checking). In Chapter 12, we show you a methodology called *polyfilling* to ensure that old browsers (and only old browsers) are given a JavaScript helping hand, while you just code to the standard.

New input types

The new form fields were the genesis of the spec that became HTML5, and this is where we see the principle of specifying backwards-compatible extensions to the language in action. The extensions are largely new values of the type attribute of the input element. HTML4 specifies that browsers should assume <input type=text> if you don't specify a type attribute, or you use an unknown type. Therefore, legacy browsers that don't understand the new extensions will fall back to the default and allow the user to enter data in a plain text field. This fallback can be detected in script and polyfilled if required so old browsers can mimic the new behaviours.

The specification makes no requirements on how browsers should present the new input types to the user or report errors, and so on. Different browsers and different devices will present different user interfaces; compare, for example, the different ways that a select box is shown in Safari on a desktop and an iPhone (**Figure 3.1**).

FIGURE 3.1 The same select
box rendered in Safari/Windows
(left) and Safari/iPhone (right).

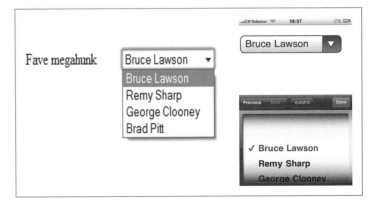

FIGURE 3.1 The same select
box rendered in Safari/Windows
(left) and Safari/iPhone (right).

The manner in which the browser reports errors is similarly unde-fined. **Figure 3.2** shows errors generated when a required field isn't completed before submission in Opera, Firefox, and Google Chrome. Below, you can see the same error in the Japanese-localised Opera. Because the messages are part of the browser, they are automatically localised, meaning much less work for a developer and a more usable experience for the consumer.

FIGURE 3.2 Automatically
generated error messages in
Opera, Firefox, Chrome, and
Japanese Opera (below).

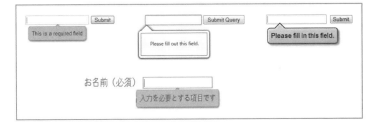

The email input type

The markup `<input type=email>` tells the browser that it should not allow the form to be submitted if the user has not entered what looks like a valid email address—that is, it doesn't check whether the email address exists or not, only whether it's in a valid format. As with all input types, the user may submit the form with this field empty unless the `required` attribute is present.

The `multiple` attribute indicates that the value of the field can be a list of comma-separated, valid email addresses. This does not require that the user enter a comma-separated list manually; a browser may choose to pop up a list of the user's contacts from his mail client or phone contacts list, with checkboxes and then construct the comma-separated list behind the scenes.

Currently browsers aren't this helpful, but because this type is now unambiguous and machine readable/understandable, the browser knows what the intention of the author is and can conceivably offer more contextually-relevant UI. For example, the experimental Firefox Contacts add-on **http://mozillalabs.com/blog/2010/03/contacts-in-the-browser** collects contacts from various sources, which it uses to offer addresses when a user comes across an `<input type=email>`. Through the W3C draft Contacts API (**http://dev.w3.org/2009/dap/contacts/**), it also exposes this contact information to website scripts.

The URL input type

`<input type=url>` causes the browser to ensure that the value entered in the field is a correct URL. A browser may offer assistance to the user—for example, Opera automatically prepends "http://" to URLs that don't have a protocol (that is, the user didn't type in http:// or ftp:// or whatever). A URL need not be a web URL; the page could, for example, be a web-based HTML editor in which the user may wish to use the `tel:` pseudo-protocol.

The date input type

The option `<input type=date>` is one of my favourites. We've all seen web pages that require the user to enter a date for a flight, concert ticket, and the like. Because dates are tricky to enter (is the format DD-MM-YYYY or MM-DD-YYYY or YYYY-MM-DD?), developers code JavaScript date picker widgets that vary wildly in appearance, usability, and accessibility between sites.

Using `<input type=date>` solves this problem by providing a native datepicker widget that's rendered directly by the browser. Opera, for example, pops up a calendar widget (**Figure 3.3**).

On the BlackBerry browser in BlackBerry Device Software version 5.0, the date input control used to implement the date input field is the same Java component used within the native BlackBerry calendar app (although it isn't integrated with the calendar app). See **Figure 3.4**.

FIGURE 3.3 Opera renders a
calendar widget.

FIGURE 3.4 <input type=date>
on the BlackBerry browser.

Of course, these are still early days. In the future, though,
it's conceivable that, beyond simply showing a shiny new
datepicker, the browser could do something far cleverer, and
call up the native calendar app so you could browse dates to
see your prior appointments. The point is that the browser can
now understand what you mean. Previously, date pickers were—
from the perspective of the browser—nothing more than <div>s,
<span>s, and links with lots of JavaScript behaviour attached.
Now the browser knows that you're in fact entering an actual
time and date and can offer richer controls and integration with
other time/date information.

The time input type

<input type=time> allows input of a time in 24-hour format and
validates it. Once again, the actual user interface is left to the
browser; it could be as simple as entering numbers and throwing an error if the user enters an hour greater than 24 or one
minute greater than 59, or it could be far more elaborate: a
clock face, for example, with draggable hands. The user interface could also allow for entry of a time zone offset.

The datetime input type

Date and time that we've just seen can be combined using
<input type=datetime> to validate a precise date and time.
Local date and time works as datetime except that the browser
doesn't allow the user to add (or change) a time zone offset.

The month input type

Using `<input type=month>` allows entry and validation of a month. Although the month value is stored internally as a number between 1 and 12, the browser may offer a selection method that uses the names of the months instead. You could do this with a select box with 12 options, January to December, but this doesn't localise. Using an HTML5 month input type, a French-localisation of a browser could offer a drop-down with Janvier instead of January, for example. That's more work for the browser *and less work for web developers,* and that's the way it should be.

The week input type

`<input type=week>` allows entry and validation of a week number. While this could be a simple input field allowing a user to input a number, it's more complex in practice: some years have 53 weeks. Therefore, the format is 2010-W07 for the seventh week in the year 2010.

Opera offers a date picker UI, which populates the input field with the week number of any selected date rather than the dates YYYY-MM-DD format (**Figure 3.5**).

FIGURE 3.5 Opera's rendering of `<input type=week>`.

The number input type

Not surprisingly, `<input type=number>` validates numeric entry. It is not meant for telephone numbers, as these are often typed with spaces, brackets, plus signs, hyphens etc; use `<input type=tel>` for those.

It works perfectly with the `min`, `max`, and `step` attributes (see below). In Opera and Chrome, it is rendered as a spinner control that will not go beyond the upper and lower limits (if specified) and which progresses by the increment specified in `step`, although a user can also type the value (**Figure 3.6**). The spin controls are outside the input area in Opera, and inside the input area in Chrome. The spec is rightly unprescriptive on the UI of these new controls.

FIGURE 3.6 Opera (left) and Chrome (right) rendering `<input type=number>`.

There's a nasty gotcha on desktop browsers that don't offer a special, numeric-only UI. Currently, typing alphabetic characters into type=number fields doesn't throw a validation error in Opera or Chrome. This seems to me to be highly counter-intuitive behavior. It's because the browser doesn't get as far as validating the input, as it never even replaces the current value of the field with the non-numeric characters that you typed. Unfortunately, the UI suggests that you've entered alphabetics and they've been accepted.

The range input type

Using `<input type=range>` renders as a slider. **Figure 3.7** shows it in Chrome.

FIGURE 3.7 Chrome's rendering of `<input type=range>`.

Previously, sliders needed to be faked by hijacking an input and using JavaScript and images for the pointers. Because these were not native in the browser, great care had to be taken—and extra code written—to ensure keyboard accessibility. Now that sliders are native to HTML, the responsibility is removed from the developer, leading to leaner code and greater accessibility for keyboard users.

See the example in the "Putting all this together" section of this chapter for more information. It works perfectly with the `min`, `max`, and `step` attributes (see below).

The search input type

This input type, `<input type=search>`, expects a search term. In Safari there is also an unspecified proprietary attribute that adds a history of recent results, using the `results=n` attribute. The difference between search and text type is only stylistic, and in Safari on the Mac, it takes the operating system's default rounded-corners style for search—which can nonetheless be overwritten with some proprietary CSS (hat-tip to Wilfred Nas for this):

```
input[type="search"] {-webkit-appearance: textfield;}
```

The tel input type

`<input type=tel>` expects a telephone number. There is no special validation; it doesn't even enforce numeric-only input, as many phone numbers are commonly written with extra characters, for example +44 (0) 208 123 1234.

As mobile phones "know" their own number, we expect that most mobile phones will be able to do things like autocompleting these entry fields. None currently do this, although the iPhone brings up a telephone number input screen (**Figure 3.8**).

FIGURE 3.8 The iPhone's keypad for completing `<input type=tel>`.

The color input type

`<input type=color>` allows the user to input a colour value via a picker. So far, it's only implemented on the BlackBerry (**Figure 3.9**) and Opera.

FIGURE 3.9 `<input type=color>` on the BlackBerry.

Don't forget the name attribute!

Just because new client-side validation is built into browsers, don't forget to give your input fields (and groups of radio buttons) unique values for the name attribute, because that's how you access these values on the server that the form submits to. Older versions of Opera require this before the new HTML5 validation is performed, as that's what the spec said at the time.

As older versions of IE can get the id and name tangled up when you do getElementByID, we recommend using the same unique value for the id and name of each field, thereby making your form more accessible, too:

```
<label for=f-email>Email address</label>
<input id=f-email name=f-email type=email>
```

New attributes

As well as new input types, the `<input>` element has several new attributes to specify behaviour and constraints: autocomplete, min, max, multiple, pattern, and step. There's also a new attribute, list, that hooks up with a new element to allow a new data input method.

The list attribute and <datalist>

The combination of an `<input>` with a list attribute and a `<datalist>` is a combo box—a combination of a drop-down list and a single-line textbox, that allows users to enter their own text if they don't want to choose one of the predefined options.

The list is contained in a new `<datalist>` element, the `id` of which is referenced in the value of the list attribute:

```
<input id=form-person-title  type=text list=mylist>
      <datalist id=mylist>
            <option label=Mr value=Mr>
            <option label=Ms value=Ms>
            <option label=Prof value="Mad Professor">
      </datalist>
```

`<datalist>` has no rendering of its own, but instead shows up as values in a select-like field.

The previous example uses type=text to allow free-form input, but you can use `<datalist>` with url and email.

Many have asked why the `<input>`/`<datalist>` pair isn't combined into a single new element like `<select>` is. The answer lies with backwards compatibility: the `<input>`/`<datalist>` pairing degrades to `<input type=text>` in legacy browsers, so the user can at least enter something, and so you can easily fake the full implementation with JavaScript for those browsers as well.

Jeremy Keith has a good example of this backwards compatibility at **http://adactio.com/journal/4272/** (reproduced with his permission):

```
<label for="source">How did you hear about us?</label>
<datalist id="sources">
      <select name="source">
            <option>please choose...</option>
            <option value="Television">Television</option>
            <option value="Radio">Radio</option>
            <option value="Newspaper">Newspaper</option>
            <option>Other</option>
      </select>
      If other, please specify:
</datalist>
<input id="source" name="source" list="sources">
```

Notice how we've wrapped the `<option>` elements in an additional `<select>`, making the contents of the datalist mimic the markup of an old-school dropdown selection. Browsers that understand `<datalist>` will ignore anything other than `<option>` elements, so the nested `<select>` is invisible to them. The text "If other, please specify" is also ignored. Nonconforming browsers, on the other hand, don't see the <datalist> element, and will instead fall back to showing what they see as a standard <select>. They also display the "If other" text and the input field that the datalist is attached to.

In other words, browsers that understand <datalist> see each <option> as being part of the datalist, and see nothing else. Browsers that don't support <datalist> see each <option> as being part of a <select> and see the additional text "If other, please specify," and the input that is hooked onto the datalist via the list attribute degrades to a simple text input field (**Figure 3.10**).

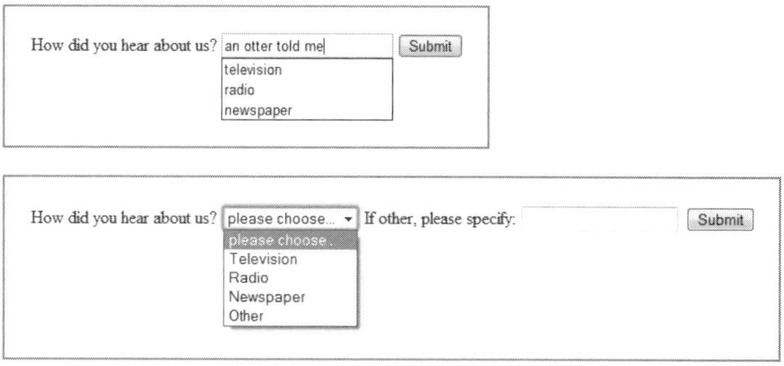

FIGURE 3.10 <datalist> in Opera (top) and gracefully degrading in Safari (bottom).

> **NOTE** The Working Group is considering removing this method of graceful degradation through markup, on the somewhat shaky grounds that web authors don't use it much and it's hard to specify and implement (what to do about <script> elements inside a <datalist>?)

If it is removed, we'll note it on **www.introducinghtml.com** and you'll have to rely on scripting to make <datalist> degradable in older browsers. Which would be a shame.

This is an excellent pattern that will become part of your day-to-day form-coding arsenal—unless the Working Group decides to take it away from us, see Note!

Like me, this ain't pretty, but it does work (although not so far in IE10 Platform Preview 2, where it degrades into the select + input) and it demonstrates how the new features can degrade gracefully.

The autofocus attribute

The autofocus boolean provides a declarative way to focus a form control when a page is loaded. Previously, a developer had to write JavaScript that triggered the control's focus(). method onload. Now the browser can do clever things like not actually focusing the control if the user is already typing elsewhere (a common problem of old-school JavaScript onload focus scripts).

There should be only one such input field on a page. From a usability perspective, this attribute should be used with care. We recommend only using it on pages that have a form field as their central purpose—a search form page, for example.

The placeholder attribute

A usability trick employed regularly by developers is placing text in an input field as a hint for the user, removing the text when the user focuses on the field, and restoring the text when focus leaves the field. This used to require JavaScript. However, it can now be done declaratively with the `placeholder` attribute. The specification says, "For a longer hint or other advisory text, the title attribute is more appropriate."

This is generally rendered in a lighter shade of the input's font colour. It can be styled using ::-webkit-input-placeholder, :-moz-placeholder and -ms-input-placeholder. For future compatibility, also add –o-input-placeholder. This is experimental and not in the official CSS spec.

It's important to note that placeholder does not replace form `<label>`s.

The required attribute

The new `required` attribute can be used on `<textarea>` and most input fields (except when the type attribute is hidden, image, or some button types such as submit). Modern browsers will not allow the user to submit the form if required fields are empty and report an error.

We recommend also adding the ARIA attribute `aria-required` to such input fields for assistive technology. (See the discussion of ARIA in Chapter 2.)

The multiple attribute

`<input type=file>` is not new in HTML5, but when used in conjunction with the new `multiple` attribute, the user can now upload multiple files:

`<input type=file multiple>`

This was impossible to do in HTML4, so web authors used Java applets or Flash to achieve the same effect:

multiple can also be used with other input types: for example, `<input type=email multiple>` allows the user to enter comma-separated email addresses.

The pattern attribute

Some of the input types mentioned previously—email, number, url, and so on—are really "baked-in" regular expressions, as the browser just checks if the values entered look like they should.

NOTE If regular expressions scare you but you want to learn more, or you're keen to fuel your regular expression ninja skills, take a gander at Steven Levithan's blog (http://blog.stevenlevithan.com) which talks about them almost exclusively.

Suppose you want to match against a different template? The `pattern` attribute allows you to specify a custom regular expression that the input must match. So, if the user must always enter a single digit plus three uppercase alphabetic characters, the regular expression would be one number [0–9] and three letters [A–Z]{3}, all in uppercase, and the input would be coded

```
<input pattern="[0-9][A-Z]{3}" name=part
       ¬title="A part number is a digit followed by three
       ¬uppercase letters.">
```

You could also add a `placeholder="1ABC"` or something similar as a short hint.

The specification explains that the regular expressions in the pattern attribute match the syntax of regular expressions in JavaScript, except that there's an implied ^(:? at the beginning and)$ at the end.

So if you're accustomed to working with regular expressions, you're already familiar with what you need to do. If not, you've got the fun world of regular expressions to explore!

The Internet is littered with JavaScript regular expressions that match this, that, and the other, so it's likely that you'll find what you're looking for. However, regular expressions, when kept simple, are relatively easy to get working.

For example, to match a ZIP code in the format of 99999 or 99999-9999 (assuming the 9s are all kinds of numbers), you can use:

```
<input pattern="[0-9]{5}(\-[0-9]{4})?" title="A zip code in
¬the format of 99999 or 99999-9999">
```

This regular expression looks for a numerical sequence of five, with an optional suffix of a dash followed by another sequence of four numbers.

We could extend this pattern to also validate UK post codes (using a simplified post code match):

```
<input required pattern="[0-9]{5}(\-[0-9]{4})?|[a-zA-Z]
¬{1,2}\d{1,2}\s?\d[a-zA-Z]{1,2}" name=part title="A valid
¬zip code or UK postcode">
```

Now our regular expression has become much more complicated and it can be quite tricky to test this pattern on a big form in a web page. Since the pattern's regular expression matches the syntax of a JavaScript regular expression, we can test this in a browser console such as Firebug or Opera Dragonfly, using pure JavaScript to determine whether the pattern will work. In the example below, I'm just testing the UK post code match, and using the JavaScript test method to experiment. Note that I've also wrapped my tests with the leading ^(:? and trailing)$ as the HTML5 spec states:

```
/^(:?[a-zA-Z]{1,2}\d{1,2}\s?\d[a-zA-Z]{1,2})$/.test
¬("bn14 8px")
> true
/^(:?[a-zA-Z]{1,2}\d{1,2}\s?\d[a-zA-Z]{1,2})$/.test
¬("bn149 8px")
> false
```

Those results are correct, since "bn149" isn't a legal part of a post code (or certainly not for this contrived example!). Finally, it's worth noting that the pattern attribute is case sensitive, and since we have no way to switch to case *insensitive* mode, we need to match on lowercase and uppercase explicitly in this example (hence the [a-zA-Z]).

The autocomplete attribute

Most browsers have some kind of autocomplete functionality. HTML has an `autocomplete` attribute which lets you control how this works. Although it's newly standardized in HTML5, it's not a new feature; it was a non-standard feature of IE5.

The default state is for the input to inherit the autocomplete state of its form owner. Forms have autocomplete on by default.

If the autocomplete attribute of a form element is set to on, the field is fine for autocompletion.

I'll quote the wry humour of the specification's description of the off state: "The off state indicates either that the control's input data is particularly sensitive (for example, the activation code for a nuclear weapon); or that it is a value that will never be reused (for example, a one-time-key for a bank login) and the user will therefore have to explicitly enter the data each time."

The min and max attributes

As we've seen with `<input type=number>`, these `min` and `max` attributes constrain the range of values that can be entered in an input; you can't submit the form with a number smaller than `min` or larger than `max`. But they can also be used with other input types—for example, `<input type=date min=2010-01-01 max=2010-12-31>` will only accept a date that's in the year 2010. It's trivial to make the server write HTML that has a `min` of today, so only future days are allowed (for a flight booking site, for example) or a `max` of today (for a field collecting date of birth, for example).

The step attribute

The `step` attribute controls the level of granularity of input. So if you want the user to enter a percentage between 0 and 100, but only to the nearest 5, you can specify

`<input type=number mix=0 max=100 step=5>`

and the spinner control will increment in steps of 5.

Taking the example of a time control, you can also use `step=any`. This allows any time in the day to be selected, with any accuracy (for example, thousandth-of-a-second accuracy or more); normally, time controls are limited to an accuracy of one minute.

`<input name=favtime type=time step=any>`

The form attribute

Traditionally, form controls all needed to be inside a `<form>` element. If, for whatever reason—design, styling, or the like—authors wanted to have a form somewhere on the page and some other related controls somewhere else, they would (in the worst case) wrap the entire page up in a form element.

But—brave new world!—in HTML5, a number of elements that were previously required to be within a form element (`<button>`, `<fieldset>`, `<input>`, `<label>`, `<select>`, `<textarea>`, plus `<object>` and the new elements like `<keygen>`, `<meter>`, `<output>`, and `<progress>`) can now be anywhere on the page and associated with a form using a `form` attribute pointing at the `id` of its *form owner.*

Consider this example:

```
<form id=foo>
<input type="text">
...
</form>
<textarea form=foo></textarea>
```

The `<input>` is owned by the form foo, as it is contained within it and does not have a form attribute overriding that ownership. The `<textarea>` is outside the form, but is still owned by it, as its form attribute points to the id of its form owner.

This gives a lot more flexibility with styling when you want those elements to appear visually (and structurally) outside the parent forms.

The form attribute is supported in Opera, Firefox, and Chrome. As Safari shares a codebase with Chrome, it's likely to appear there soon, too. IE has no support currently, and at the time of writing, none has been announced for IE10.

`<progress>`, `<meter>` elements

The `<progress>` element is used to represent a "progress meter," to indicate the completion of a task—downloading a file, for example. It has two attributes: max, which specifies how much work the task requires in total, and value, which specifies how much of the task has been completed. The units are arbitrary and not specified:

```
<progress value=5 max=20>5</progress>
```

In supporting browsers, this is replaced with a progress meter graphic (**Figure 3.11**).

FIGURE 3.11 `<progress>` in Chrome (left) and Opera (right). Chrome's progress meter is slightly animated; Opera's is static.

`<meter>` is very similar (many have questioned whether there needs to be two separate elements at all). The spec says that `<meter>` "represents a scalar measurement within a known range, or a fractional value; for example disk usage, the relevance of a query result, or the fraction of a voting population to have selected a particular candidate."

It takes the following floating-point attributes:

- value—the "measured" value shown by meter
- min—the lower bound of the range for the meter
- low—the point that marks the upper boundary of the "low" segment of the meter
- high—the point that marks the lower boundary of the "high" segment of the meter
- max—the upper bound of the range for the meter
- optimum—the point that marks the "optimum" position for the meter

Only value is required. If min and max are missing, the range 0 to 1 is assumed

Opera and Chrome (the two browsers that support `<progress>` and `<meter>` at the time of this writing) colour the meter differently if the value is between the low to high values.

In older browsers, the text content of the elements is displayed as fallback content.

Putting all this together

It's pretty confusing to work out which attributes go with which input types when you're meeting them all at once as we are here. But it's actually quite straightforward when you start using them. For example, you can't use `min` and `max` on a `<textarea>`, because that wouldn't make sense, but you can use `required`.

A blog comments form

Let's look at a classic form example that most of us are already familiar with. Nearly all blogs have a comment section, with fields for the commenter's name (required), her email address (required), URL (optional), and the comment (required). That would need a fair bit of JavaScript if we were to do our form validation by hand.

In HTML5, however, we need only use some new form types. We also add a submit button—currently browsers only show validation messages when a form is actually submitted.

```
<form>
 <label for=form-name>Name</label>
 <input name=form-name id=form-name type=text required>
 <label for=form-email>Email</label>
 <input name=form-email id=form-email type=email required>
 <label for=form-url>URL</label>
 <input name=form-url id=form-url type=url>
 <label for=form-comment>Comment</label>
 <textarea name=form-comment id=form-comment required>
 </textarea>
 <input type=submit>
</form>
```

Hey, Presto! We now have a sexy comment form that validates user input...no JavaScript required!

A slider, with scripted output

We've seen `<input type=range>` earlier in this chapter. Notice that, by default, browsers show the slider, but don't give any indication of the minimum, maximum, or current value of the slider, so let's code up an example that actually shows the user the range allowed by the slider by automatically indicating the minimum and maximum values, and dynamically outputting the slider's current value.

The slider will go from 1 to 11, as all good controls should (be they for guitar amps or otherwise). The step will be 1, which is the default, so we can omit that attribute:

```
<input type=range min=1 max=11 name=tap>
```

To show the user the minimum and maximum values, we can use generated content (which doesn't work on sliders in WebKit browsers):

```
input[type=range]::before {content: attr(min);}
input[type=range]::after {content: attr(max);}
```

This will show the values, and style them as defined in CSS. For example, **Figure 3.12** renders

```
input[type=range]{width:500px; color:red; font-family:
¬ cursive; font-size:2em;}
```

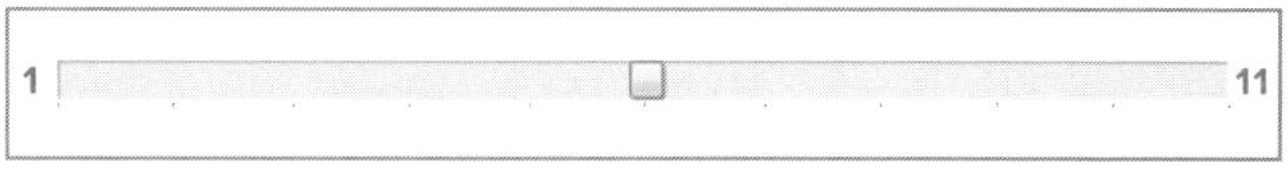

FIGURE 3.12 Opera's rendering of `<input type=range>` with min and max values generated.

We'll echo the current value of the slider with the new output element.

The `<output>` element

The `<output>` element is for showing results of some calculation or other with script. It can have a form owner, either by being inside a form or via a form attribute. The new `<progress>` and `<meter>` elements discussed earlier can be similarly associated with a form to provide feedback to the user.

We tie it to the slider by the name of the slider (name=tap), and use the oninput event on the containing form. When the output's form owner receives input (as the slider is moved), we'll echo back the value of that input:

```
// this example assumes variable output contains the DOM
¬ output element
// and the variable slider contains the DOM input range
¬ element
<form oninput="output.value=slider.value">
    <input id=slider type=range min=1 max=5 value=5>
    <output id=output>5</output>
</form>
```

> NOTE The first edition of this book used onforminput rather than the oninput event, but that's deprecated. Markup history buffs can read www.useragentman.com/ blog/2011/05/10/is-onforminput-deprecated-in-html5-forms-and-why-should-i-care-anyways/ for more.

The actual contents of the output element (in this case, "5") is only there as a starting value, to be shown before the slider is actually changed. In this simple example, we simply put the "5" in the markup, as it's the same starting value as the input type=range. You could, of course, use a script that runs onload and programmatically prefills the output with the value of its associated input.

Using WAI-ARIA for transitional accessibility

Although we said that `<input type=range>` removed responsibility for accessibility from the developer, that's true only when HTML5 is widely supported and assistive technology understands this new type of form input.

During this transitional time, if you want to use HTML5 sliders, add some WAI-ARIA information, which for the time being will result in some duplication:

```
<input id=tap
name=tap
type=range
min=1
max=11
value=0
aria-valuemin=1
aria-valuemax=11
aria-valuenow=0>
```

> **NOTE** In the first edition of this book, I added a `role=slider` attribute to tell assistive technology how to map the control to operating system controls. I was wrong, or at least premature. In an ideal world of full browser support (one day, dear reader, one day), this would be fine. But for now, don't do it declaratively; do it in JavaScript after seeing if input type=range is supported. (See the "Backwards compatibility with legacy browsers" section below.) In browsers that don't support type=range, setting it declaratively adds a role of slider on a plain text input which would be wrong and very confusing to an assistive technology user.

Update `aria-valuenow` with JavaScript when the slider position is changed. In this case, you'll want to bind to the change event on the slider; in our example, we'll just use the onchange attribute. Unfortunately, we can't use the property syntax to update the `aria-valuenow` value; we have to update the DOM attribute for the value to update correctly:

```
<input id=tap
name=tap
type=range
min=1
max=11
value=0
aria-valuemin=1
aria-valuemax=11
aria-valuenow=0
onchange="this.setAttribute('aria-valuenow',
¬this.value)">
```

This will update the value of the `aria-valuenow` attribute, and can be tested if you inspect the element using a DOM inspector.

Backwards compatibility with legacy browsers

The big question is: What can we do for legacy browsers? The answer is that you don't retire your pre-existing JavaScript validation or fancy DHTML datepickers just yet, but you leave them as a fallback after doing some feature detection.

As we've seen before, browsers will fall back to using input type=text whenever they encounter a type that they don't support. So, a legacy browser, faced with input type=email, will simply change it to an input type=text. This change also happens in the DOM and, by checking the type of the input, we can programmatically determine if the browser supports the new fancy elements, and act accordingly if not.

For instance, to detect whether `<input type=email>` is supported, you can make a new `<input type=email>` with JavaScript, but don't add it to the page. Then, interrogate your new element to find out what its type attribute is. If it's reported back as "email," then the browser supports the new feature—so let it do its work and don't bring in any JavaScript validation. If it's reported back as "text," it's fallen back to the default, indicating that it's not supported. So your code should load an alternative validation library, ideally through a *lazy load* technique.

```
var i = document.createElement("input");
i.setAttribute("type", "email");
return i.type !== "text";
```

You can test attributes, too:

```
return 'autofocus' in document.createElement("input");
```

So what does this buy you? First and foremost, you're making your forms usable and accessible, providing easy entry mechanisms like datepickers and validating user input before it even goes on a roundtrip to the server. Secondly, you're doing it in a resource-friendly way, using the browser's built-in capabilities (if they already understand client-side validation and the new html5 types/attributes) or, for legacy browsers, gracefully patching in support with traditional JavaScript libraries.

See Chapter 12 for a methodology and discussion of how to shoehorn support into older browsers.

Styling new form fields and error messages

Whenever we present the new intelligent form fields at conferences, someone asks us how to style these new fields and error messages.

You can do some basic styling on most of the new controls: fonts, colours, and the like. With some controls, however, using current CSS is more problematic. For example, with a `type=range` slider, what does `color` refer to and what would `background-color` style? What would `border-radius` affect? How would you change the colour of the "track" that the slider runs along?

The natural home for adding new CSS hooks for styling form fields is the enticingly named CSS Basic User Interface Module (**http://www.w3.org/TR/css3-ui/**). This has been around since 2004 and—now that browsers have caught up with it—this specification is being updated by Tantek Çelik.

There already are some useful ideas that you can implement right now—for example, you can use the `:invalid` pseudo-class to style a form field to show that its contents are invalid, so the user gets that feedback immediately, without having to hit submit. This CSS styles invalid form fields with a red border, and valid inputs green:

```
input:invalid {border:2px solid red;}
input:valid { border: 2px solid green; }
```

Unfortunately, this presents several usability problems. A required input, for example, is invalid at page load (because it's required but is blank) and therefore the styles will be set, which is off-putting to the user. An `input type=email` will be invalid the moment the user starts typing, until the first character after "@" is entered, because until that time it's not a valid email address.

The mighty Patrick Lauke (one of this book's technical editors) suggests using a combination of `:focus`, to mitigate the problem and only show the styling when the user is interacting with that particular form field:

```
input:focus:invalid {border:2px solid red;}
input:focus:valid {border: 2px solid green;}
```

This works, but only for the currently focussed input. We want something more: we want the invalid fields to be styled differently only after users have entered some content.

Because of these problems, Firefox uses an alternative pseudo-class called `-moz-ui-invalid` which provides a much better user experience, as the Mozilla Developer Center describes: "If the control is valid when the user starts interacting with it, the validity styling is changed only when the user shifts focus to another control. However, if the user is trying to correct a previously flagged value, the control shows immediately when the value becomes valid. Required items have the pseudo-class applied only if the user changes them or attempts to submit an unchanged valid value."

Other pseudo-classes available include `:in-range` and `:out-of-range` and `:indeterminate` (the latter would apply to a number input with min/max that is currently empty).

While we wait for a fully specified, properly sanctioned way of consistently styling all the other things in all browsers, there are a few vendor-specific tweaks and tricks that can be used. We've already seen Mozilla's `ui-invalid`, for example. WebKit offers us ways in which to style the validation error message bubbles (see Figure 3.2):

- `::-webkit-validation-bubble{}`
- `::-webkit-validation-bubble-top-outer-arrow{}`
- `::-webkit-validation-bubble-top-inner-arrow{}`
- `::-webkit-validation-bubble-message{}`

Currently, there aren't many cross-browser methods of changing the look and feel of HTML forms. This isn't necessarily a bad thing. Your branding people will, of course, lament that placeholder text isn't in corporate purple and orange. But it's a usability and accessibility win; although it's tempting to style the stuffing out of your form fields, whatever your branding people say, it's better to leave forms as close to the browser defaults as possible. A browser's slider and date pickers will be the same across different sites, making it much more comprehensible to users. It's much better that a date picker on site X looks and behaves the same as a date picker on site Y or site Z.

And, by using native controls rather than faking sliders and date pickers with JavaScript, your forms are much more likely to be accessible to users of assistive technology.

Overriding browser defaults

Built-in validation messages are great, but what if you want to customise these error messages? What if it's Talk Like a Pirate Day? Perhaps I want to change all the validation messages to speak like an angry pirate, too.

It's possible, with a bit of JavaScript via `setCustomValidity`. However, by setting a custom message, it causes the field to be invalid in the first place, so the workaround is to first set the custom validity to an empty string—clearing any custom error—perform a validity check manually in the code, and then set the custom message so that it's then presented to the user.

So instead of reading:

humptydumpty is not a legal email address

We'll change the validation to read the following in "traditional" pirate speak:

humptydumpty be not a legal email address

The setCustomValidity method allows me to specify my own validation message:

```
<!DOCTYPE html>
<title>custom validity</title>
<form>
<input type=email id=foo name=foo>
<input type=submit>
</form>
<script>
var email = document.getElementById('foo');
email.form.onsubmit = function () {
  // reset any previously specified custom validity - let
  ¬the browser run its validation logic
  email.setCustomValidity('');
  // now, after the browser tested if the value entered is
  ¬actually an email address, inject custom validation
  ¬message if the validation turns out false (i.e. it's
  ¬not an email address)
  if (!email.validity.valid) {
    email.setCustomValidity(email.value + " be not a legal
    ¬email address");
  }
};
</script>
```

Figure 3.13 shows a custom validation message.

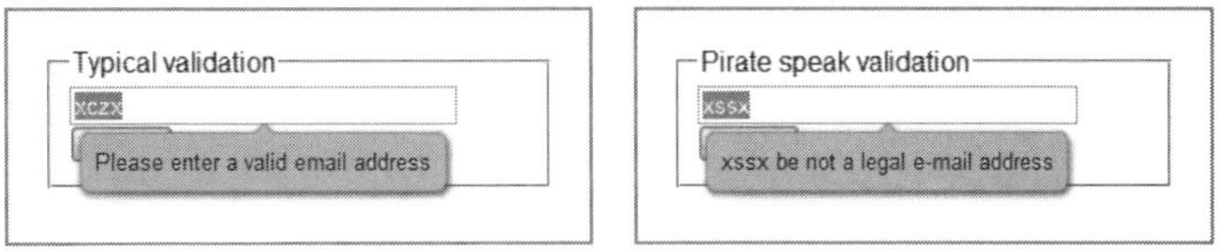

FIGURE 3.13 Opera rendering
the default validation message
for email (left) and our custom
"speak like an angry pirate day"
validation (right).

Unfortunately, as it stands today, only Opera supports this properly. In fact, it's questionable that the submit event should even
fire if the field is invalid. Perhaps we should be listening for the
invalid event on the element? But if we set the custom valid
message, when the error is corrected, the field remains marked
as invalid because we've set our custom error. So it runs the
invalid test again, removing the custom error—but at this point
the user has to hit submit *twice* just to get the form to be submitted when there was a corrected error.

In fact, the only appropriate way of setting a custom message is,
on every key press to check the validity of the field. Personally, I
find this odd that we would have to poll the input element, but in
a way, it behaves the same way the :invalid CSS pseudo selector works. So our example from above changes to:

```
<!DOCTYPE html>
<title>custom validity</title>
<form>
<input type=email id=foo name=foo>
<input type=submit>
</form>
<script>
var email = document.getElementById('foo');
email.oninput = function () {
  // reset any previously specified custom validity - let
  ¬the browser run its validation logic
  email.setCustomValidity('');
  // now, after the browser tested if the value entered is
  ¬actually an email address, inject custom validation
  ¬message if the validation turns out false (i.e. it's
  ¬not an email address)
  if (!email.validity.valid) {
    email.setCustomValidity(email.value + " be not a legal
    ¬email address");
  }
};
</script>
```

However, if the way the custom validation messages work isn't your bag, then there is a way to roll your own validation behaviour, to make it feel more integral to your application. When we run setCustomValidity it sets the read-only DOM attribute called validationMessage. We can use this if we manage validation ourselves, which we'll look at in the next section.

Note that if you like single-vendor markup, you can override the error messages in Firefox using the proprietary x-moz-errormessage attribute

```
<input type=email x-moz-errormessage="Please specify a
¬ valid email address.">
```

Using JavaScript for DIY validation

So far we've seen how we can use a little JavaScript to customise the message the user sees when validation errors occur. If you want to spice things up further, you can use JavaScript to completely handle all the validation and feedback to the user.

Using the JavaScript Web Forms API, we can control how we present validation feedback to our visitor, but we can still defer all the actual validation heavy lifting code to the new forms, APIs. We can also use the API to determine exactly why a particular form field failed to validate.

Forcing element validation

All form elements and input elements (including <select> and <textarea>) include a checkValidity method on the DOM node. You'd be forgiven for thinking this is the method you'd want to use to override the browser's default validation and feedback process.

The checkValidity method returns true or false depending on the success of the validation checks, but at the same time it's *telling* the browser to run through its checks, and displaying the error messages if required. If you want to take control of the presentation of validation feedback, then you *don't* want to use this method.

Element validity

Individual form fields, along with having the checkValidity method, also have a validity DOM attribute that returns a ValidityState object. There are a number of state attributes on the validity object, but the simplest and most important is the `valid` attribute. This value can be tested using JavaScript to drive a bespoke validation feedback system.

> **NOTE** It's worth noting that `<fieldset>` elements also have the validity attribute, but they don't do anything. The validity attribute is always true. You can also call the checkValidity method on fieldsets, but again, nothing happens in the current browsers that support custom validation.

If we hook into the submit event handler on our form, we can manually loop through all the input fields and check the validity object. But what happens if the field *has no* validation rules? You're in luck: The API provides a `willValidate` attribute that we can test to see whether we should or shouldn't try to validate this particular field. Here's a (contrived) example:

```
var email = document.getElementById('email');
if (email.willValidate) {
  if (!email.validity.valid) {
    alert("Yarr, ye old email be invalid");
  }
}
```

Once you have the individual form field's validation state, you could pull in any custom messages set via element. validationMessage or test the different validity states, which also include valueMissing, typeMismatch, patternMismatch, tooLong, rangeUnderflow, rangeOverflow, stepMismatch, and customError.

What's particularly important is that you disable the native browser's validation behaviour. By adding the novalidate attribute to the form element, as you'll see next, it disables the validation feedback, but in fact the JavaScript API is still available and you are still able to check the validity state on the fields. This means you can have full control of the error feedback process.

Avoiding validation

The last question we need to answer is: What if you want to submit the form—but you *don't* want the browser to validate it? This is possible, too. But why on earth would you want to do this? What if you have a multistage registration form, either for sign-up or for submitting some content? For long forms it could be useful to split the form into stages (as eBay might do when you're selling an item). You might even want to allow your visitors to save the *state* of their submission, even if the form isn't currently complete and valid.

There are two levels of control for *not* validating. This can apply to the individual input control or to the entire form. The `novalidate` attribute can only be set on a form element and prevents validation for that particular field. As we saw in the previous section, if you want to disable the native validation feedback (that is, the little bubbles that appear under the input elements) but still have the JavaScript API available—which still returns true or false for the valid states on the fields—then this bad boy is for you.

The second method, `formnovalidate`, which is practical and available today, is allowed on individual input elements and button elements (though probably only makes sense on `type="submit"` and `type="button"`). The `formnovalidate` attribute allows the form to be submitted and bypass all the validation that has been set on the form fields. The following example snippet of code would allow you to have a save session button with each fieldset to allow the user to save his progress without triggering the validation rules from running until he hits the final submit button:

```
<form>
  <fieldset>
    <legend>Some bits about you</legend>
    <div>
      <label for="email">Email:</label>
      <input id="email" name="email" type="email"
      ¬ required />
    </div>
    <div>
      <label for="url">Homepage:</label>
      <input id="url" type="url" name="url" />
    </div>
    <input type="submit" value="save session"
    ¬formnovalidate />
  </fieldset>
```

You could even hook into the save session button to trigger JavaScript-based validation based on only those fields inside the fieldset via the `HTMLFieldSetElement.elements` property (though this is a new property in the HTML5 spec, so you may have to rely on `fieldset.getElementsByTagName` and find all the form fields).

The "whenever anything changes" event

> **NOTE** In the first edition of this book, we talked about `onforminput`, but since then the event handler has been deprecated. But fear not, this section remains valid, because the very similar `oninput` event handler is part of HTML5 and we can use it in a very similar way to `onforminput`.

One almost insignificant change to the `<form>` element is a new event called oninput. In fact, this is a useful event that fires on the form element when any of the form fields within the form change. This saves you having to attach lots of onchange handlers to each form control.

For instance, if I were to create a colour picker that gives me both RGBA and HSLA, typically I would have to hook event listeners to each of the value sliders. By using the oninputchange event, I'm able to hook a single event listener to the form and recalculate my RGBA and HSLA values using a single method.

Whether I'm attaching lots of event listeners or just a single one, the result is very similar. However, this feels a lot cleaner and better designed, as there's no duplication of event listeners.

When a slider is changed, it generates the RGBA and HSLA and update the preview colour. The code listing below is just the JavaScript required:

```
form.oninput = function () {
  var i = this.length, values = [], value = 0;
  while (i--, value = this[i].value) {
    if (this[i].type == 'range') {
      switch (this[i].name) {
        // alpha_channel is between 0-1
        case 'alpha_channel': values.push(value / 100);
        ¬break;
        // hue is a plain value from 0-360
        case 'hue': values.push(value); break;
        // default includes saturation & luminance as a
        ¬percentage
        default: values.push(value + '%');
      }
    }
  }
  hsla.value = 'hsla(' + values.reverse().join(', ') + ')';
  preview.style.backgroundColor = hsla.value;
  rgba.value = getComputedStyle(preview, null).
  ¬backgroundColor;
};
```

My final colour picker makes use of the range input type, the new oninput event, and the new output elements to show the value (though this could easily use .innerHTML). The final result is shown in **Figure 3.14**.

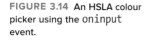

What's particularly important about the oninput event is that unlike the onchange, which fires only when the element is *blurred* (although historically some browsers got this wrong, and fired during input—strangely this wasn't IE getting it wrong for a change!), oninput fires when the user is inputting to the form and whilst the changes are happening immediately.

Summary

Hopefully you've seen that HTML5 forms offer a huge productivity boost for developers and a consistent experience for users. They offer a ton of features right out of the box that previously would have required a lot of custom coding (such as form validation, or creating slider controls). Implementation is at varying, but increasing, levels in Opera, the WebKit browsers (Safari and Chrome), and beginning in Firefox and IE10. The lack of implementation in IE9 can be faked with JavaScript, as the new features are designed to degrade gracefully.

Now, let's move on to even sexier subjects.

CHAPTER 4

Video and Audio

Bruce Lawson and Remy Sharp

A LONG TIME AGO, in a galaxy that feels a very long way away, multimedia on the Web was limited to tinkling MIDI tunes and animated GIFs. As bandwidth got faster and compression technologies improved, MP3 music supplanted MIDI and real video began to gain ground. All sorts of proprietary players battled it out—Real Player, Windows Media, and so on—until one emerged as the victor in 2005: Adobe Flash, largely because of its ubiquitous plugin and the fact that it was the delivery mechanism of choice for YouTube.

HTML5 provides a competing, open standard for delivery of multimedia on the Web with its native video and audio elements and APIs. This chapter largely discusses the `<video>` element, as that's sexier, but most of the markup and scripting are applicable to `<audio>` as well.

Native multimedia: why, what, and how?

In 2007, Anne van Kesteren wrote to the Working Group:

"Opera has some internal experimental builds with an imple-mentation of a <video> element. The element exposes a simple API (for the moment) much like the Audio() *object:* play()*,* pause()*,* stop()*. The idea is that it works like* <object> *except that it has special* <video> *semantics much like* <img> *has image semantics."*

While the API has increased in complexity, van Kesteren's origi-nal announcement is now implemented in all the major brows-ers, including Internet Explorer 9.

An obvious companion to a <video> element is an <audio> element; they share many similar features, so in this chapter we discuss them together and note only the differences.

<video>: Why do you need a <video> element?

Previously, if developers wanted to include video in a web page, they had to make use of the <object> element, which is a generic container for "foreign objects." Due to browser incon-sistencies, they would also need to use the previously invalid <embed> element and duplicate many parameters. This resulted in code that looked much like this:

```
<object width="425" height="344">
<param name="movie" value="http://www.youtube.com/
¬ v/9sEI1AUFJKw&hl=en_GB&fs=1&"></param>
<param name="allowFullScreen"
value="true"></param>
<param name="allowscriptaccess"
value="always"></param>
<embed src="http://www.youtube.com/
¬ v/9sEI1AUFJKw&hl=en_GB&fs=1&"
type="application/x-shockwave-flash"
allowscriptaccess="always"
allowfullscreen="true" width="425"
height="344"></embed>
</object>
```

This code is ugly and ungainly. Worse still is the fact that the browser has to pass the video off to a third-party plugin; hope that the user has the correct version of that plugin (or has the rights to download and install it, and the knowledge of how to do so); and then hope that the plugin is keyboard accessible—along with all the other unknowns involved in handing the content to a third-party application.

Plugins can also be a significant cause of browser instability and can create worry for less technical users when they are prompted to download and install newer versions.

Whenever you include a plugin in your pages, you're reserving a certain drawing area that the browser delegates to the plugin. As far as the browser is concerned, the plugin's area remains a black box—the browser does not process or interpret anything that happens there.

Normally, this is not a problem, but issues can arise when your layout overlaps the plugin's drawing area. Imagine, for example, a site that contains a movie but also has JavaScript or CSS-based drop-down menus that need to unfold over the movie. By default, the plugin's drawing area sits on top of the web page, meaning that these menus will strangely appear behind the movie.

Problems and quirks can also arise if your page has dynamic layout changes. Resizing the dimensions of the plugin's drawing area can sometimes have unforeseen effects—a movie playing in the plugin may not resize, but instead simply may be cropped or display extra white space. HTML5 provides a standardised way to play video directly in the browser, with no plugins required.

> **NOTE** `<embed>` is finally standardised in HTML5; it was never part of any previous flavour of (X)HTML.

One of the major advantages of the HTML5 video element is that, finally, video is a full-fledged citizen on the Web. It's no longer shunted off to the hinterland of `<object>` or the nonvalidating `<embed>` element.

So now, `<video>` elements can be styled with CSS. They can be resized on hover using CSS transitions, for example. They can be tweaked and redisplayed onto `<canvas>` with JavaScript. Best of all, the innate hackability that open web standards provide is opened up. Previously, all your video data was locked away; your bits were trapped in a box. With HTML5 multimedia, your bits are free to be manipulated however you want.

What HTML5 multimedia isn't good for

Regardless of the sensationalist headlines of the tech journalists, HTML5 won't "kill" all plugins overnight. There are use-cases for plugins not covered by the new spec.

> **NOTE** If you're really, really anxious to do DRM, check out **http://lists.whatwg. org/htdig.cgi/whatwg-whatwg. org/2010-July/027051.html** for Henri Sivonen's suggested method, which requires no changes to the spec.

Copy protection is one area not dealt with by HTML5—unsurprisingly, given that it's a standard based on openness. So people who need digital rights management (DRM) are probably not going to want to use HTML5 video or audio, as they'll be as easy to download to a hard drive as an `<img>` is now. Some browsers offer simple context-menu access to the URL of the video, or even let the user save the video. Developers can view source, find the reference to the video's URL, and download it that way. (Of course, you don't need us to point out that DRM is a fool's errand, anyway. All you do is alienate your honest users while causing minor inconvenience to dedicated pirates.)

HTML5 can't give us adaptive streaming either. This is a process that adjusts the quality of a video delivered to a browser based on changes to network conditions to ensure the best experience. It's being worked on, but it isn't there yet.

Plugins currently remain the best cross-browser option for accessing the user's webcam or microphone and then transmitting video and audio from the user's machine to a web page such as Daily Mugshot or Chatroulette, although `getUserMedia` and WebRTC are in the cards for Chrome, Opera, and Firefox—see "Video conferencing, augmented reality" at the end of this chapter. After shuddering at the unimaginable loneliness that a world without Chatroulette would represent, consider also the massive amount of content already out there on the web that will require plugins to render it for a long time to come.

Anatomy of the video and audio elements

At its simplest, to include video on a page in HTML5 merely requires this code:

```
<video src=turkish.webm></video>
```

The .webm file extension is used here to point to a WebM-encoded video.

Similar to `<object>`, you can put fallback markup between the tags for older web browsers that do not support native video. You should at least supply a link to the video so users can download it to their hard drives and watch it later on the operating system's media player. **Figure 4.1** shows this code in a modern browser and fallback content in a legacy browser.

```
<h1>Video and legacy browser fallback</h1>
<video src=leverage-a-synergy.webm>
   Download the <a href=leverage-a-synergy.webm>How to
   ¬leverage a synergy video</a>
</video>
```

FIGURE 4.1 HTML5 video in a modern browser and fallback content in a legacy browser.

However, this example won't actually do anything just yet. All you can see here is the first frame of the movie. That's because you haven't told the video to play, and you haven't told the browser to provide any controls for playing or pausing the video.

autoplay

While you can tell the browser to play the video or audio automatically once the web page is loaded, you almost certainly shouldn't, as many users (and particularly those using assistive technology, such as a screen reader) will find it highly intrusive. Users on mobile devices probably won't want you using their bandwidth without them explicitly asking for the video. Nevertheless, here's how you do it:

```
<video src=leverage-a-synergy.webm autoplay>
   <!-- your fallback content here -->
</video>
```

controls

> **NOTE** Browsers have different levels of keyboard accessibility. Firefox's native controls are right and left arrows to skip forward/back (up and down arrows after tabbing into the video), but there is no focus highlight to show where you are, and so no visual clue. The controls don't appear if the user has JavaScript disabled in the browser; so although the contextual menu allows the user to stop and start the movie, there is the problem of discoverability.

Opera's accessible native controls are always present when JavaScript is disabled, regardless of whether the `controls` attribute is specified.

IE9 has good keyboard accessibility. Chrome and Safari appear to lack keyboard accessibility. We anticipate increased keyboard accessibility as manufacturers iron out teething problems.

Providing controls is approximately 764 percent better than autoplaying your video. See **Figure 4.2**. You can use some simple JavaScript to write your own (more on that later) or you can tell the browser to provide them automatically:

```
<video src=leverage-a-synergy.webm controls>
</video>
```

Naturally, these differ between browsers, as the spec doesn't prescribe what the controls should look like or do, but most browsers don't reinvent the wheel and instead have stuck to what has become the general norm for such controls—there's a play/pause toggle, a seek bar, and volume control.

Browsers have chosen to visually hide the controls, and only make them appear when the user hovers or sets focus on the controls via the keyboard. It's also possible to move through the different controls using only the keyboard. This native keyboard accessibility is already an improvement on plugins, which can be tricky to tab into from surrounding HTML content.

If the `<audio>` element has the `controls` attribute, you'll see them on the page. Without the attribute, you can hear the audio but nothing is rendered visually on the page at all; it is, of course, there in the DOM and fully controllable via JavaScript and the new APIs.

FIGURE 4.2 The default controls in Firefox. (These are similar in all modern browsers.)

poster

The `poster` attribute points to an image that the browser will use while the video is downloading, or until the user tells the video to play. (This attribute is not applicable to `<audio>`.) It removes the need for additional tricks like displaying an image and then removing it via JavaScript when the video is started.

If you don't use the `poster` attribute, the browser shows the first frame of the movie, which may not be the representative image you want to show.

The behavior varies somewhat on mobile devices. Mobile Safari does grab the first frame if no `poster` is specified; Opera Mobile conserves bandwidth and leaves a blank container.

muted

The `muted` attribute, a recent addition to the spec (read: "as yet, very little support"), gives a way to have the multimedia element muted by default, requiring user action to unmute it. This video (an advertisement) autoplays, but to avoid annoying users, it does so without sound, and allows the user to turn the sound on:

```
<video src="adverts.cgi?kind=video" controls autoplay loop
¬ muted></video>
```

height, width

The `height` and `width` attributes tell the browser the size of the video in pixels. (They are not applicable to `<audio>`.) If you leave them out, the browser uses the intrinsic width of the video resource, if that is available. Otherwise it uses the intrinsic width of the poster frame, if that is available. If neither is available, the browser defaults to 300 pixels.

If you specify one value but not the other, the browser adjusts the size of the unspecified dimension to preserve the video's aspect ratio.

If you set both `width` and `height` to an aspect ratio that doesn't match that of the video, the video is not stretched to those dimensions but is rendered letterboxed inside the video element of your specified size while retaining the aspect ratio.

loop

The `loop` attribute is another Boolean attribute. As you would imagine, it loops the media playback. Support is flaky at the moment, so don't expect to be able to have a short audio sample and be able to loop it seamlessly. Support will get better—browsers as media players is a new phenomenon.

preload

Maybe you're pretty sure that the user wants to activate the media (she's drilled down to it from some navigation, for example, or it's the only reason to be on the page), but you don't want to use autoplay. If so, you can suggest that the browser preload the video so that it begins buffering when the page loads in the expectation that the user will activate the controls.

```
<video src=leverage-a-synergy.ogv controls preload>
</video>
```

There are three spec-defined values for the `preload` attribute. If you just say `preload`, the user agent can decide what to do. A mobile browser may, for example, default to not preloading until explicitly told to do so by the user. It's important to remember that a web developer can't control the browser's behavior: `preload` is a hint, not a command. The browser will make its decision based on the device it's on, current network conditions, and other factors.

- preload=auto (or just preload)

  This is a suggestion to the browser that it should begin downloading the entire file.

- preload=none

  This state suggests to the browser that it shouldn't preload the resource until the user activates the controls.

- preload=metadata

  This state suggests to the browser that it should just prefetch metadata (dimensions, first frame, track list, duration, and so on) but that it shouldn't download anything further until the user activates the controls.

> **NOTE** So long as the http endpoint is a streaming resource on the Web, you can just point the `<video>` or `<audio>` element at it to stream the content.

src

As on an `<img>`, the `src` attribute points to audio or video resource, which the browser will play if it supports the specific codec/container format. Using a single source file with the `src` attribute is really only useful for rapid prototyping or for intranet sites where you know the user's browser and which codecs it supports.

However, because not all browsers can play the same formats, in production environments you need to have more than one source file. We'll cover this in the next section.

Codecs—the horror, the horror

Early drafts of the HTML5 specification mandated that all browsers should have built-in support for multimedia in at least two codecs: Ogg Vorbis for audio and Ogg Theora for movies. Vorbis is a codec used by services like Spotify, among others, and for audio samples in games like Microsoft Halo.

However, these requirements for default format support were dropped from the HTML5 spec after Apple and Nokia objected, so the spec makes no recommendations about codecs at all. This leaves us with a fragmented situation, with different browsers opting for different formats, based on their ideological and commercial convictions.

Currently, there are two main container/codec combinations that developers need to be aware of: the new WebM format (**www.webmproject.org**) which is built around the VP8 codec that Google bought for $104 million and open licensed, and the ubiquitous MP4 format that contains the royalty-encumbered H.264 codec. H.264 is royalty-encumbered because, in some circumstances, you must pay its owners if you post videos that use that codec. We're not lawyers so can't give you guidance on which circumstances apply to you. Go to **www.mpegla.com** and have your people talk to their people's people.

In our handy cut-out-and-lose chart (**Table 4.1**), we also include the Ogg Theora codec for historical reasons—but it's really only useful if you want to include support for older versions of browsers with initial `<video>` element support like Firefox 3.x and Opera 10.x.

NOTE At time of writing, Chrome still supports H.264 but announced it will be discontinued. Therefore, assume it won't be supported.

TABLE 4.1 Video codec support in modern browsers.

	WEBM (VP8 CODEC)	MP4 (H.264 CODEC)	OGV (OGG THEORA CODEC)
Opera	Yes	No	Yes
Firefox	Yes	No	Yes
Chrome	Yes	Yes—see Note, *support will be discontinued*	Yes
IE9 +	Yes (but codec must be installed manually)	Yes	No
Safari	No	Yes	No

Marvel at the amazing coincidence that the only two browsers that support H.264 are members of the organization that collects royalties for using the codec (**www.mpegla.com/main/ programs/AVC/Pages/Licensors.aspx**).

A similarly fragmented situation exists with audio codecs, for similar royalty-related reasons (see **Table 4.2**).

TABLE 4.2 Audio codec support in modern browsers.

	.OGG/ .OGV (VORBIS CODEC)	MP3	MP4/ M4A (AAC CODEC)	WAV
Opera	Yes	No	No	Yes
Firefox	Yes	No	No	Yes
Chrome	Yes	Yes	Yes	Yes
IE9 +	No	Yes	Yes	No
Safari	No	Yes	Yes	Yes

NOTE It's possible to polyfill MP3 support into Firefox. JSmad (jsmad.org) is a JavaScript library that decodes MP3s on the fly and reconstructs them for output using the Audio Data API, although we wonder about performance on lower-spec devices. Such an API is out-of-the-scope of this book—though we've included things like geolocation which aren't part of HTML5, single-vendor APIs are stretching the definition too far.

The rule is: provide both a royalty-free WebM *and* an H.264 video, and both a Vorbis and an MP3 version of your audio, so that nobody gets locked out of your content. Let's not repeat the mistakes of the old "Best viewed in Netscape Navigator" badges on sites, or we'll come round and pin a "n00b" badge to your coat next time you're polishing your FrontPage CD.

Multiple <source> elements

To do this, you need to encode your multimedia twice: once as WebM and once as H.264 in the case of video, and in both Vorbis and MP3 for audio. Then, you tie these separate versions of the file to the media element.

What's the "best" codec?

Asking what's "better" (WebM or MP4) starts an argument that makes debating the merits of Mac or PC seem like a quiet chat between old friends.

To discuss inherent characteristics, you need to argue about macroblock type in B-frames and six-tap filtering for derivation of half-pel luma sample predictions—for all intents and purposes, "My flux capacitor is bigger than yours!"

Suffice it to say that for delivering video across the Web, both WebM and MP4 offer good-enough quality at web-friendly compression. Ogg Theora is less web-friendly.

The real differences are royalty encumbrance and hardware acceleration. Some people need to pay if they have MP4/H.264 video on their website.

There are many chips that perform hardware decoding of H.264, which is why watching movies on your mobile phone doesn't drain the battery in seconds as it would if the video were decoded in software. At the time of this writing (July 2011, a year after WebM was open sourced), hardware-decoding chips for WebM are just hitting the market.

Previously, we've used the `<video src="...">` syntax to specify the source for our video. This works fine for a single file, but how do we tell the browser that there are multiple versions (using different encoding) available? Instead of using the single src attribute, you nest separate `<source>` elements for each encoding with appropriate type attributes inside the `<audio>` or `<video>` element and let the browser download the format that it can display. Faced with multiple `<source>` elements, the browser will look through them (in source order) and choose the first one it finds that it thinks it can play (based on the type attribute—which gives explicit information about the container MIME type and the codec used—or, missing that, heuristic based on file extension). Note that in this case we do not provide a src attribute in the media element itself:

1. `<video controls>`

2. `<source src=leverage-a-synergy.mp4 type='video/mp4;`
   `¬ codecs="avc1.42E01E, mp4a.40.2"'>`

3. `<source src=leverage-a-synergy.webm type='video/webm;`
   `¬ codecs="vp8, vorbis"'>`

4. `<p>Your browser doesn't support video.`

5. `Please download the video in <a href=leverage-a-`
   `¬ synergy.webm>webM</a> or <a href=leverage-a-`
   `¬ synergy.mp4>MP4</a> format.</p>`

6. `</video>`

Line 1 tells the browser that a video is to be inserted and gives it default controls. Line 2 offers an MP4 version of the video. We've put the mp4 first, because some old versions of Mobile Safari on the iPad have a bug whereby they only look at the first <source> element, so that if it isn't first, it won't be played. We're using the type attribute to tell the browser what kind of container format is used (by giving the file's MIME type) and what codec was used for the encoding of the video and the audio stream. If you miss out on the type attribute, the browser downloads a small bit of each file before it figures out that it is unsupported, which wastes bandwidth and could delay the media playing.

Notice that we used quotation marks around these parameters—the spec uses 'video/mp4; codecs="avc..."' (single around the outside, double around the codec). Some browsers stumble when it's the other way around. Line 3 offers the WebM equivalent. The codec strings for H.264 and AAC are more complicated than those for WebM because there are several profiles for H.264 and AAC, to cater for different categories of devices and connections. Higher profiles require more CPU to decode, but they are better compressed and take less bandwidth.

We could also offer an Ogg video here for older versions of Firefox and Opera, after the WebM version, so those that can use the higher-quality WebM version pick that up first, and the older (yet still HTML5 <video> element capable) browsers fall back to this.

Inside the <video> element is our fallback message, including links to *both* formats for browsers that can natively deal with neither video type but which is probably on top of an operating system that can deal with one of the formats, so the user can download the file and watch it in a media player outside the browser.

OK, so that's native HTML5 video for users of modern browsers. What about users of legacy browsers—including Internet Explorer 8 and older?

Video for legacy browsers

Older browsers can't play native video or audio, bless them. But if you're prepared to rely on plugins, you can ensure that users of older browsers can still experience your content in a way that is no worse than they currently get.

> **NOTE** The content between the tags is fallback content only for browsers that do not support the `<video>` element at all. A browser that understands HTML5 video but can't play any of the formats that your code points to will not display the "fallback" content between the tags, but present the user with a broken video control instead. This has bitten me on the bottom a few times. Sadly, there is no video record of that.

Remember that the contents of the `<video>` element can contain markup, like the text and links in the previous example? Here, we'll place an entire Flash video player movie into the fallback content instead (and of course, we'll also provide fallback for those poor users who don't even have that installed). Luckily, we don't need to encode our video in yet another format like FLV (Flash's own legacy video container); because Flash (since version 9) can load MP4 files as external resources, you can simply point your custom Flash video player movie to the MP4 file. This combination should give you a solid workaround for Internet Explorer 8 and older versions of other browsers. You won't be able to do all the crazy video manipulation stuff we'll see later in this chapter, but at least your users will still get to see your video.

The code for this is as hideous as you'd expect for a transitional hack, but it works anywhere that Flash Player is installed—which is almost everywhere. You can see this nifty technique in an article called "Video for Everybody!" by its inventor, Kroc Camen (**http://camendesign.com/code/video_for_everybody**).

Alternatively, you could host the fallback content on a video hosting site and embed a link to that between the tags of a video element:

```
<video controls>

    <source src=leverage-a-synergy.mp4 type='video/mp4;
    ¬ codecs="avc1.42E01E, mp4a.40.2"'>
    <source src=leverage-a-synergy.webm type='video/webm;
    ¬ codecs="vp8, vorbis"'>
<embed src="http://www.youtube.com/v/cmtcc94Tv3A&hl=
¬ en_GB&fs=1&rel=0" type="application/x-shockwave-flash"
¬ allowscriptaccess="always" allowfullscreen="true"
¬ width="425" height="344">
</video>
```

You can use the HTML5 Media Library (**http://html5media.info**) to hijack the `<video>` element and automatically add necessary fallback by adding one line of JavaScript in the page header.

Encoding royalty-free video and audio

Ideally, you should start the conversion from the source format itself, rather than recompressing an already compressed version which reduces the quality of the final output. If you already have a web-optimised, tightly compressed MP4/H.264 version, don't convert that one to WebM/VP8, but rather go back to your original footage and recompress that if possible.

For audio, the open-source audio editing software Audacity (**http://audacity.sourceforge.net/**) has built-in support for Ogg Vorbis export.

For video conversion, there are a few good choices. For WebM, there are only a few encoders at the moment, unsurprisingly for such a new codec. See **www.webmproject.org/tools/** for the growing list.

For Windows and Mac users we can highly recommend Miro Video Converter (**www.mirovideoconverter. com**), which allows you to drag a file into its window for conversion into WebM, Theora, or H.264 optimised for different devices such as iPhone, Android Nexus One, PS2, and so on.

The free VLC (**www.videolan.org/vlc/**) can convert files on Windows, Mac, and Linux.

For those developers who are not afraid by a bit of command-line work, the open-source FFmpeg library (**http://ffmpeg.org**) is the big beast of converters. `$ ffmpeg -i video.avi video.webm` is all you need.

The conversion process can also be automated and handled server-side. For instance, in a CMS environment, you may be unable to control the format in which authors upload their files, so you may want to do compression at the server end. ffmpeg can be installed on a server to bring industrial-strength conversions of uploaded files (maybe you're starting your own YouTube killer?).

If you're worried about storage space and you're happy to share your media files (audio and video) under one of the various CC licenses, have a look at the Internet Archive (**www.archive.org/create/**), which will convert and host them for you. Just create a password and upload, and then use a `<video>` element on your page but link to the source file on their servers.

Another option for third-party conversion and hosting is vid.ly. The free service allows you to upload any video up to 2GB via the website, after which they will convert it. When your users come to the site, they will be served a codec their browser understands, even on mobile phones.

Sending differently compressed videos to handheld devices

Video files tend to be large, and sending very high-quality video can be wasteful if sent to handheld devices where the small screen sizes make high quality unnecessary. There's no point in sending high-definition video meant for a widescreen monitor to a handheld device screen, and most users of smartphones and tablets will gladly compromise a little bit on encoding quality if it means that the video will actually load over a mobile connection. Compressing a video down to a size appropriate for a small screen can save a lot of bandwidth, making your server and—most importantly—your mobile users happy.

HTML5 allows you to use the `media` attribute on the `<source>` element, which queries the browser to find out screen size (or number of colours, aspect ratio, and so on) and to send different files that are optimised for different screen sizes.

> **NOTE** We use `min-device-width` rather than `min-width`. Mobile browsers (which vary the reported width of their viewport to better accommodate web pages by zooming the viewport) will then refer to the nominal width of their physical screen.

This functionality and syntax is borrowed from the CSS Media Queries specification **www.w3.org/TR/css3-mediaqueries** but is part of the markup, as we're switching source files depending on device characteristics. In the following example, the browser is "asked" if it has a min-device-width of 800 px—that is, does it have a wide screen. If it does, it receives `hi-res.webm`; if not, it is sent `lo-res.webm`:

```
<video controls>
    <source src=hi-res.webm ... media="(min-device-width:
    ¬ 800px)">
    <source src=lo-res.webm>
    ...
</video>
```

Also note that you should still use the `type` attribute with `codecs` parameters and fallback content previously discussed. We've just omitted those for clarity.

Rolling custom controls

One truly spiffing aspect of the `<video>` and `<audio>` media elements is that they come with a super easy JavaScript API. The API's events and methods are the same for both `<audio>` and `<video>`. With that in mind, we'll stick with the sexier media element: the `<video>` element for our JavaScript discussion.

As you saw at the start of this chapter, Anne van Kesteren has spoken about the new API and about the new simple methods such as `play()`, `pause()` (there's no stop method: simply pause and move to the start), `load()`, and `canPlayType()`. In fact, that's *all* the methods on the media element. Everything else is events and attributes.

Table 4.3 provides a reference list of media attributes, methods, and events.

TABLE 4.3 Media Attributes, Methods, and Events

ATTRIBUTES	METHODS	EVENTS
error state	load()	loadstart
error	canPlayType(type)	progress
network state	play()	suspend
src	pause()	abort
currentSrc	addTrack(label, kind, language)	error
networkState		emptied
preload		stalled
buffered		play
ready state		pause
readyState		loadedmetadata
seeking		loadeddata
controls		waiting
controls		playing
volume		canplay
muted		canplaythrough
tracks		seeking
tracks		seeked
playback state		timeupdate
currentTime		ended
startTime		ratechange
duration		
paused		
defaultPlaybackRate		
playbackRate		
played		
seekable		
ended		
autoplay		
loop		
width [video only]		
height [video only]		
videoWidth [video only]		
videoHeight [video only]		
poster [video only]		

Using JavaScript and the new media API, you have complete control over your multimedia—at its simplest, this means that you can easily create and manage your own video player controls. In our example, we walk you through some of the ways to control the video element and create a simple set of controls. Our example won't blow your mind—it isn't nearly as sexy as the <video> element itself (and is a little contrived!)—but you'll get a good idea of what's possible through scripting. The best bit is that the UI will be all CSS and HTML. So if you want to style it your own way, it's easy with just a bit of web standards knowledge—no need to edit an external Flash Player or similar.

Our hand-rolled basic video player controls will have a play/pause toggle button and allow the user to scrub along the timeline of the video to skip to a specific section, as shown in **Figure 4.3**.

FIGURE 4.3 Our simple but custom video player controls.

NOTE Some browsers, in particular Opera, will show the native controls even if JavaScript is disabled; other browsers, mileage may vary.

Our starting point will be a video with native controls enabled. We'll then use JavaScript to strip the native controls and add our own, so that if JavaScript is disabled, the user still has a way to control the video as we intended:

```
<video controls>
    <source src="leverage-a-synergy.webm" type="video/webm" />
    <source src="leverage-a-synergy.mp4" type="video/mp4" />
    Your browser doesn't support video.
    Please download the video in <a href="leverage-a-
    ¬ synergy.webm">WebM</a> or <a href="leverage-a-
    ¬ synergy.mp4">MP4</a> format.
</video>
<script>
var video = document.getElementsByTagName('video')[0];
video.removeAttribute('controls');
</script>
```

Play, pause, and toggling playback

Next, we want to be able to play and pause the video from a custom control. We've included a button element that we're going to bind a click handler and do the play/pause functionality from. Throughout my code examples, when I refer to the play object it will refer to this button element:

```
<button class="play" title="play">&#x25BA;</button/>
```

We're using ►, which is a geometric XML entity that *looks* like a play button. Once the button is clicked, we'll start the video and switch the value to two pipes using ▐, which looks (a little) like a pause, as shown in **Figure 4.4**.

For simplicity, I've included the button element as markup, but as we're progressively enhancing our video controls, all of these additional elements (for play, pause, scrubbing, and so on) should be generated by the JavaScript.

In the play/pause toggle, we have a number of things to do:

1. If the user clicks on the toggle and the video is currently paused, the video should start playing. If the video has previously finished, and our playhead is right at the end of the video, then we also need to reset the current time to 0, that is, move the playhead back to the start of the video, before we start playing it.

2. Change the toggle button's value to show that the next time the user clicks, it will toggle from pause to play or play to pause.

3. Finally, we play (or pause) the video:

```
playButton.addEventListener('click', function () {
  if (video.paused || video.ended) {
    if (video.ended) {
      video.currentTime = 0;
    }
    this.innerHTML = ''; // &#x2590;&#x2590; doesn't
    ¬ need escaping here
    this.title = 'pause';
    video.play();
  } else {
    this.innerHTML = ''; // &#x25BA;
    this.title = 'play';
    video.pause();
  }
}, false);
```

▶ ►

▮▮ ▐ (twice)

FIGURE 4.4 Using XML entities to represent play and pause buttons.

The problem with this logic is that we're relying entirely on our own script to determine the state of the play/pause button. What if the user was able to pause or play the video via the native video element controls somehow (some browsers allow the user to right click and select to play and pause the video)? Also, when the video comes to the end, the play/pause button would still show a pause icon. Ultimately, we need our controls always to relate to the state of the video.

Eventful media elements

The media elements fire a broad range of events: when play-back starts, when a video has finished loading, if the volume has changed, and so on. So, getting back to our custom play/pause button, we strip the part of the script that deals with changing its visible label:

```
playButton.addEventListener('click', function () {
   if (video.ended) {
      video.currentTime = 0;
   }
   if (video.paused) {
      video.play();
   } else {
      video.pause();
   }
}, false);
```

> **NOTE** In these examples, we're using the addEventListener DOM level 2 API, rather than the attachEvent, which is specific to Internet Explorer up to version 8. IE9 supports video, but it thankfully also supports the standardised addEventListener, so our code will work there, too.

In the simplified code, if the video has ended we reset it, and then toggle the playback based on its current state. The label on the control itself is updated by separate (anonymous) functions we've hooked straight into the event handlers on our video element:

```
video.addEventListener('play', function () {
   play.title = 'pause';
   play.innerHTML = '';
}, false);
video.addEventListener('pause', function () {
   play.title = 'play';
   play.innerHTML = '';
}, false);
video.addEventListener('ended', function () {
   this.pause();
}, false);
```

Whenever the video is played, paused, or has reached the end, the function associated with the relevant event is now fired, making sure that our control shows the right label.

Now that we're handling playing and pausing, we want to show the user how much of the video has downloaded and therefore how much is playable. This would be the amount of *buffered* video available. We also want to catch the event that says how much video has been played, so we can move our visual slider to the appropriate location to show how far through the video we are, as shown in **Figure 4.5**. Finally, and most importantly, we need to capture the event that says the video is *ready* to be played, that is, there's enough video data to start watching.

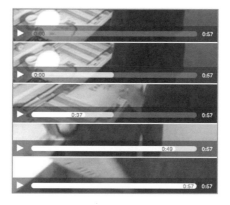

FIGURE 4.5 Our custom video progress bar, including seekable content and the current playhead position.

Monitoring download progress

The media element has a "progress" event, which fires once the media has been fetched but potentially before the media has been processed. When this event fires, we can read the `video.seekable` object, which has a `length`, `start()`, and `end()` method. We can update our seek bar (shown in **Figure 4.5** in the second frame with the whiter colour) using the following code (where the buffer variable is the element that shows how much of the video we can seek and has been downloaded):

```
video.addEventListener('progress', updateSeekable, false);
function updateSeekable() {
  var endVal = this.seekable && this.seekable.length ?
  ¬ this.seekable.end() : 0;
  buffer.style.width = (100 / (this.duration || 1) *
  ¬ endVal) + '%';
}
```

The code binds to the progress event, and when it fires, it gets the percentage of video that can be played back compared to the length of the video. Note the keyword `this` refers to the video element, as that's the context in which the updateSeekable function will be executed. The `duration` attribute is the length of the media in seconds.

However, there's some issues with Firefox. In previous versions the seekable length didn't match the actual duration, and in the latest version (5.0.1) seekable seems to be missing altogether. So to protect ourselves from the seekable time range going a little awry, we can also listen for the progress event and default to the duration of the video as backup:

```
video.addEventListener('durationchange', updateSeekable,
¬ false);
video.addEventListener('progress', updateSeekable, false);
function updateSeekable() {
  buffer.style.width = (100 / (this.duration || 1) *
    (this.seekable && this.seekable.length ? this.seekable.
    ¬ end() : this.duration)) + '%';
}
```

It's a bit rubbish that we can't reliably get the seekable range. Alternatively we could look to the `video.buffered` property, but sadly since we're only trying to solve a Firefox issue, this value in Firefox (currently) doesn't return *anything* for the `video.buffered.end()` method—so it's not a suitable alternative.

When the media file is ready to play

When your browser first encounters the video (or audio) element on a page, the media file isn't ready to be played just yet. The browser needs to download and then decode the video (or audio) so it can be played. Once that's complete, the media element will fire the canplay event. *Typically* this is the time you would initialise your controls and remove any "loading" indicator. So our code to initialise the controls would *typically* look like this:

```
video.addEventListener('canplay', initialiseControls,
¬ false);
```

Nothing terribly exciting there. The control initialisation enables the play/pause toggle button and resets the playhead in the seek bar.

However, sometimes this event won't fire right away (or when you're expecting it to). Sometimes the video suspends download because the browser is trying to prevent overwhelming your system. That can be a headache if you're expecting the `canplay` event, which won't fire unless you give the media element a bit of a kicking. So instead, we've started listening for the `loadeddata` event. This says that there's some data that's been loaded, though not necessarily all the data. This means that the metadata is available (height, width, duration, and so on) and *some* media content—but not *all* of it. By allowing the user to start playing the video at the point in which `loadeddata` has fired, browsers like Firefox are forced to go from a suspended state to downloading the rest of the media content, which lets them play the whole video.

You may find that in most situations, if you're doing something like creating a custom media player UI, you might not need the actual video data to be loaded—only the metadata. If that's the case, there's also a `loadedmetadata` event which fires once the first frame, duration, dimensions, and other metadata is loaded. This may in fact be all you need for a custom UI.

So the correct point in the event cycle to enable the user interface is the `loadedmetadata`:

```
video.addEventListener('loadedmetadata', initialiseControls,
¬ false);
```

> **NOTE** The events to do with loading fire in the following order: `loadstart`, `durationchange`, `loadedmetadata`, `loadeddata`, `progress`, `canplay`, `canplaythrough`.

Media loading control: preload

Media elements also support a `preload` attribute that allows you to control how much of the media is loaded when the page renders. By default, this value is set to `auto`, but you can also set it to `none` or `metadata`. If you set it to `none`, the user will see either the image you've used for the poster attribute, or nothing at all if you don't set a poster. Only when the user tries to play the media will it even request the media file from your server.

By setting the `preload` attribute to `metadata`, the browser will pull down required metadata about the media. It will also fire the `loadedmetadata` event, which is useful if you're listening for this event to set up a custom media player UI.

A race to play video

Here's where I tell you that as much as native video and audio smells of roses, there's a certain pong coming from somewhere. That somewhere is a problem in the implementation of the media element that creates what's known as a "race condition."

A race, what now?

In this situation, the race condition is where an expected sequence of events fires in an unpredicted order. In particular, the events fire *before* your event handler code is attached.

The problem is that it's possible, though not likely, for the browser to load the media element before you've had time to bind the event listeners.

For example, if you're using the `loadedmetadata` event to listen for when a video is ready so that you can build your own fancy-pants video player, it's possible that the native video HTML element may trigger the events *before* your JavaScript has loaded.

Workarounds

There are a few workarounds for this race condition, all of which would be nice to avoid, but I'm afraid it's just something we need to code for defensively.

WORKAROUND #1: HIGH EVENT DELEGATION

In this workaround, we need to attach an event handler on the `window` object. This event handler *must* be above the media element. The obvious downside to this approach is that the script element is above our content, and risks blocking our content from loading (best practice is to include all script blocks at the end of the document).

Nonetheless, the HTML5 specification states that media events should bubble up the DOM all the way to the window object. So when the `loadedmetadata` event fires on the window object, we check where the event originated from, via the `target` property, and if that's our element, we run the setup code. Note that in the example below, I'm only checking the `nodeName` of the element; you may want to run this code against all audio elements or you may want to check more properties on the DOM node to make sure you've got the right one.

```
<script>
function audioloaded() {
  // setup the fancy-pants player
}

window.addEventListener('loadedmetadata', function (event) {
    if (event.target.nodeName === 'AUDIO') {
      // set this context to the DOM node
      audioloaded.call(event.target);
    }
}, true);

</script>

<audio src="hanson.mp3">
  <p>If you can read this, you can't enjoy the soothing
  ¬ sound of the Hansons.</p>
</audio>
```

WORKAROUND #2: HIGH AND INLINE

Here's a similar approach using an inline handler:

```
<script>
function audioloaded() {
  // setup the fancy-pants player
}
</script>

<audio src="hanson.mp3" onloadedmetadata=
¬ "audoloaded.call(this)">
  <p>If you can read this, you can't enjoy the soothing
  ¬ sound of the Hansons.</p>
</audio>
```

Note that in the inline event handler I'm using .call(this) to set the this keyword to the audio element the event fired upon. This means it's easier to reuse the same function later on if browsers (in years to come) do indeed fix this problem.

By putting the event handler inline, the handler is attached as soon as the DOM element is constructed, therefore it is in place *before* the loadedmetadata event fires.

WORKAROUND #3: JAVASCRIPT GENERATED MEDIA

Another workaround is to insert the media using JavaScript. That way you can create the media element, attach the event handlers, and *then* set the source and insert it into the DOM.

Remember: if you do insert the media element using JavaScript, you need to either insert all the different source elements manually, or detect the capability of the browser, and insert the src attribute that the browser supports, for instance WebM/video for Chrome.

I'm not terribly keen on this solution because it means that those users without JavaScript don't get the multimedia at all. Although a lot of HTML5 is "web applications," my gut (and hopefully yours, too) says there's something fishy about resorting to JavaScript *just* to get the video events working in a way that suits our needs. Even if your gut isn't like mine (quite possible), big boys' Google wouldn't be able to find and index your amazing video of your cat dancing along to Hanson if JavaScript was inserting the video. So let's move right along to workaround number 4, my favourite approach.

WORKAROUND #4: CHECK THE READYSTATE

Probably the best approach, albeit a little messy (compared to a simple video and event handler), is to simply check the readyState of the media element. Both audio and video have a readyState with the following states:

- HAVE_NOTHING = 0;
- HAVE_METADATA = 1;
- HAVE_CURRENT_DATA = 2;
- HAVE_FUTURE_DATA = 3;
- HAVE_ENOUGH_DATA = 4;

Therefore if you're looking to bind to the loadedmetadata event, you only want to bind if the readyState is 0. If you want to bind before it has enough data to play, then bind if readyState is less than 4.

Our previous example can be rewritten as:

```
<audio src="hanson.mp3">
  <p>If you can read this, you can't enjoy the soothing
  ¬ sound of the Hansons.</p>
</audio>

<script>
function audioloaded() {
  // setup the fancy-pants player
}

var audio = document.getElementsByTagName('audio')[0];

if (audio.readyState > 0) {
  audioloaded.call(audio);
} else {
  audio.addEventListener('loadedmetadata', audioloaded,
  ¬ false);
}
</script>
```

This way our code can sit nicely at the bottom of our document, and if JavaScript is disabled, the audio is still available. All good in my book.

Will this race condition ever be fixed?

Technically I can understand that this issue has always existed in the browser. Think of an image element: if the load event fires *before* you can attach your load event handler, then nothing is going to happen. You might see this if an image is cached and loads too quickly, or perhaps when you're working in a development environment and the delivery speed is like Superman on crack—the event doesn't fire.

Images don't have ready states, but they do have a complete property. When the image is being loaded, complete is false. Once the image is done loading (note this could also result in it *failing* to load due to some error), the complete property is true. So you could, before binding the load event, test the complete property, and if it's true, fire the load event handler manually.

Since this logic has existed for a long time for images, I would expect that this same logic is being applied to the media element, and by that same reasoning, *technically* this isn't a bug, as buggy as it may appear to you and me!

Fast forward, slow motion, and reverse

The spec provides an attribute, `playbackRate`. By default, the assumed playbackRate is 1, meaning normal playback is at the intrinsic speed of the media file. Increasing this attribute speeds up the playback; decreasing it slows it down. Negative values indicate that the video will play in reverse.

Not all browsers support playbackRate yet (only WebKit-based browsers and IE9 support it right now), so if you need to support fast forward and rewind, you can hack around this by programmatically changing currentTime:

```
function speedup(video, direction) {
  if (direction == undefined) direction = 1; // or -1 for
  ¬ reverse

  if (video.playbackRate != undefined) {
    video.playbackRate = direction == 1 ? 2 : -2;
  } else { // do it manually
    video.setAttribute('data-playbackRate', setInterval
    ¬ ((function playbackRate () {
      video.currentTime += direction;

return playbackRate; // allows us to run the
¬ function once and setInterval
    })(), 500));
  }
}

function playnormal(video) {
  if (video.playbackRate != undefined) {
    video.playbackRate = 1;
  } else { // do it manually
    clearInterval(video.getAttribute('data-playbackRate'));
  }
}
```

As you can see from the previous example, if playbackRate is supported, you can set positive and negative numbers to control the direction of playback. In addition to being able to rewind and fast forward using the playbackRate, you can also use a fraction to play the media back in slow motion using video.playbackRate = 0.5, which plays at half the normal rate.

Full-screen video

For some time, the spec prohibited full-screen video, but it's obviously a useful feature so WebKit did its own proprietary thing with `WebkitEnterFullscreen();`. WebKit implemented its API in a way that could only be triggered by the user initiating the action; that is, like pop-up windows, they can't be created unless the user performs an action like a click. The only alternative to this bespoke solution by WebKit would be to stretch the video to the browser window size. Since *some* browsers have a full-screen view, it's possible to watch your favourite video of Bruce doing a Turkish belly dance in full screen, but it would require the user to jump through a number of hoops—something we'd all like to avoid.

In May 2011, WebKit announced it would implement Mozilla's full-screen API (**https://wiki.mozilla.org/Gecko:FullScreenAPI**). This API allows any element to go full-screen (not only `<video>`)—you might want full-screen `<canvas>` games or video widgets embedded in a page via an `<iframe>`. Scripts can also opt in to having alphanumeric keyboard input enabled during full-screen view, which means that you could create your super spiffing platform game using the `<canvas>` API and it could run full-screen with full keyboard support.

As Opera likes this approach, too, we should see something approaching interoperability. Until then, we can continue to fake full-screen by going full-window by setting the video's dimensions to equal the window size.

Multimedia accessibility

We've talked about the keyboard accessibility of the video element, but what about transcripts and captions for multimedia? After all, there is no `alt` attribute for video or audio as there is for `<img>`. The fallback content between the tags is meant only for browsers that can't cope with native video, not for people whose browsers can display the media but can't see or hear it due to disability or situation (for example, being in a noisy environment or needing to conserve bandwidth).

There are two methods of attaching synchronized text alternatives (captions, subtitles, and so on) to multimedia, called *in-band* and *out-of-band*. In-band means that the text file is included in the multimedia container; an MP4 file, for example, is actually a container for H.264 video and AAC audio, and can hold other metadata files too, such as subtitles. WebM is a container (based on the open standard Matroska Media Container format) that holds VP8 video and Ogg Vorbis audio. Currently, WebM doesn't support subtitles, as Google is waiting for the Working Groups to specify the HTML5 format: "WHATWG/W3C RFC will release guidance on subtitles and other overlays in HTML5 <video> in the near future. WebM intends to follow that guidance". (Of course, even if the container can contain additional metadata, it's still up to the media player or browser to expose that information to the user.)

Out-of-band text alternatives are those that aren't inside the media container but are held in a separate file and associated with the media file with a child <track> element:

```
<video controls>
<source src=movie.webm>
<source src=movie.mp4>
<track src=english.vtt kind=captions srclang=en>
<track src=french.vtt kind=captions srclang=fr>
<p>Fallback content here with links to download video
¬files</p>
</video>
```

This example associates two caption tracks with the video, one in English and one in French. Browsers will have some UI mechanism to allow the user to select the one she wants (listing any in-band tracks, too).

The <track> element doesn't presuppose any particular format, but the browsers will probably begin by implementing the new WebVTT format (previously known as WebSRT, as it's based on the SRT format) (**www.whatwg.org/specs/web-apps/current-work/multipage/the-video-element.html#webvtt**).

This format is still in development by WHATWG, with lots of feedback from people who really know, such as the BBC, Netflix, and Google (the organisation with probably the most experience of subtitling web-delivered video via YouTube). Because it's still in flux, we won't look in-depth at syntax here, as it will probably be slightly different by the time you read this.

WebVTT is just a UTF-8 encoded text file, which looks like this at its simplest:

```
WEBVTT

00:00:11.000 --> 00:00:13.000
Luftputefartøyet mitt er fullt av ål
```

This puts the subtitle text "Luftputefartøyet mitt er fullt av ål" over the video starting at 11 seconds from the beginning, and removes it when the video reaches the 13 second mark (not 13 seconds later).

No browser currently supports WebVTT or <track> but there are a couple of polyfills available. Julien Villetorte (@delphiki) has written Playr (**www.delphiki.com/html5/playr/**), a lightweight script that adds support for these features to all browsers that support HTML5 video (**Figure 4.6**).

FIGURE 4.6 Remy reading Shakespeare's Sonnet 155, with Welsh subtitle displayed by Playr.

WebVTT also allows for bold, italic, and colour text, vertical text for Asian languages, right-to-left text for languages like Arabic and Hebrew, ruby annotations (see Chapter 2), and positioning text from the default positioning (so it doesn't obscure key text on the screen, for example), but only if you need these features.

The format is deliberately made to be as simple as possible, and that's vital for accessibility: *If it's hard to write, people won't do it*, and all the APIs in the world won't help video be accessible if there are no subtitled videos.

> **NOTE** Scott Wilson's VTT Caption Creator (http://scottbw.wordpress.com/2011/06/28/creating-subtitles-and-audio-descriptions-with-html5-video/) is a utility that can help author subtitles to be used as standalone HTML, or a W3C Widget.

Let's also note that having plain text isn't just important for people with disabilities. Textual transcripts can be spidered by search engines, pleasing the Search Engine Optimists. And, of course, text can be selected, copied, pasted, resized, and styled with CSS, translated by websites, mashed up, and all other kinds of wonders. As Shakespeare said in Sonnet 155, "If thy text be selectable/'tis most delectable."

Synchronising media tracks

HTML5 will allow for alternative media tracks to be included and synchronised in a single `<audio>` or `<video>` element .

You might, for example, have several videos of a sporting event, each from different camera angles, and if the user moves to a different point in one video (or changes the playback rate for slow motion), she expects all the other videos to play in sync. Therefore, different media files need to be grouped together.

This could be a boon for accessibility, allowing for sign-language tracks, audio description tracks, dubbed audio tracks, and similar additional or alternative tracks to the main audio/video tracks.

MediaElement.js, King of the Polyfills

MediaElement.js (**www.mediaelementjs.com**) is a plugin developed by John Dyer (**http://j.hn**), a web developer for Dallas Theological Seminary.

Making an HTML5 player isn't rocket surgery. The problem comes when you're doing real world video and you need to support older browsers that don't support native multimedia or browsers that don't have the codec you've been given.

Most HTML5 players get around this by injecting a completely separate Flash Player. But there are two problems with this approach. First, you end up with two completely different playback UIs (one in HTML5 and one in Flash) that have to be skinned and styled independently. Secondly, you can't use HTML5 Media events like "ended" or "timeupdate" to sync other elements on your page.

MediaElement.js takes a different approach. Instead of offering a bare bones Flash player as a fallback, it includes a custom player that mimics the entire HTML5 Media API. Flash (or Silverlight, depending on what the user has installed) renders the media and then bubbles fake HTML5 events up to the browser. This means that with MediaElement.js, even our old chum IE6 will function as if it supports <video> and <audio>. John cheekily refers to this as a fall "forward" rather than a fallback.

On mobile systems (Android, iOS, WP7), MediaElement.js just uses the operating system's UI. On the desktop, it supports all modern browsers with true HTML5 support and upgrades older browsers. Additionally, it injects support using plugins for unsupported codecs support. This allows it to play MP4, Ogg, and WebM, as well as WMV and FLV and MP3.

MediaElement.js also supports multilingual subtitles and chapter navigation through <track> elements using WebVTT, and there are plugins for Wordpress, Drupal, and BlogEngine.net, making them a no-brainer to deploy and use on those platforms.

A noble runner-up to the crown is LeanBack Player **http://dev.mennerich.name/showroom/html5_video/** with WebVTT polyfilling, no dependency on external libraries, and excellent keyboard support.

NOTE On 25 August 2011, the American Federal Communications Commission released FCC 11-126, ordering certain TV and video networks to provide video description for certain television programming.

Providing descriptions of a program's key visual elements in natural pauses in the program's dialogue is a perfect use of mediagroup and the associated API.

This can be accomplished with JavaScript, or declaratively with a `mediagroup` attribute on the `<audio>` or `<video>` element:

```
<div>
  <video src="movie.webm" autoplay controls
  ¬ mediagroup=movie></video>
  <video src="signing.webm" autoplay
  ¬ mediagroup=movie></video>
</div>
```

This is very exciting, and very new, so we won't look further: the spec is constantly changing and there are no implementations.

Video conferencing, augmented reality

As we mentioned earlier, accessing a device's camera and microphone was once available only to web pages via plugins. HTML5 gives us a way to access these devices straight from JavaScript, using an API called getUserMedia. (You might find it referred to as the <device> element on older resources. The element itself has been spec'd away, but the concept has been moved to a pure API.)

An experimental build of Opera Mobile on Android gives us a glimpse of what will be possible once this feature is widely available. It connects the camera to a `<video>` element using JavaScript by detecting whether getUserMedia is supported and, if so, setting the stream coming from the camera as the `src` of the `<video>` element:

NOTE getUserMedia is a method of the navigator object according to the spec. Until the spec settles down, though, Opera (the only implementors so far) are putting it on the opera object.

```
<!DOCTYPE html>
<h1>Simple web camera display demo</h1>
<video autoplay></video>
<script type="text/javascript">
var video = document.getElementsByTagName('video')[0],
      heading = document.getElementsByTagName('h1')[0];
```

```
if(navigator.getUserMedia) {
  navigator.getUserMedia('video', successCallback,
  ¬ errorCallback);
  function successCallback( stream ) {
    video.src = stream;
  }
  function errorCallback( error ) {
    heading.textContent =
        "An error occurred: [CODE " + error.code + "]";
  }
```

```
} else {
  heading.textContent =
      "Native web camera streaming is not supported in
      ¬ this browser!";
}
</script>
```

Once you've done that, you can manipulate the video as you please. Rich Tibbett wrote a demo that copies the video into canvas (thereby giving you access to the pixel data), looks at those pixels to perform facial recognition, and draws a moustache on the face, all in JavaScript (see **Figure 4.7**).

FIGURE 4.7 Remy Sharp, with a magical HTML5 moustache. (Photo by Julia Gosling)

Norwegian developer Trygve Lie has made demos of getUserMedia that use Web Sockets (see Chapter 10) to send images from an Android phone running the experimental Opera Mobile build to a desktop computer. See **https://github.com/trygve-lie/demos-html5-realtime** for the source code and a video demonstrating it.

Obviously, giving websites access to your webcam could create significant privacy problems, so users will have to opt-in, much as they have to do with geolocation. But that's a UI concern rather than a technical problem.

Taking the concept even further, there is also a Peer-to-Peer API being developed for HTML, which will allow you to hook up your camera and microphone to the <video> and <audio> elements of someone else's browser, making it possible to do video conferencing.

In May 2011, Google announced WebRTC, an open technology for voice and video on the Web, based on the HTML5 specifications. WebRTC uses VP8 (the video codec in WebM) and two audio codecs optimised for speech with noise and echo cancellation, called iLBC, a narrowband voice codec, and iSAC, a bandwidth-adaptive wideband codec (see **http://sites.google. com/site/webrtc/**).

As the project website says, "We expect to see WebRTC support in Firefox, Opera, and Chrome soon!"

Summary

You've seen how HTML5 gives you the first credible alternative to third-party plugins. The incompatible codec support currently makes it harder than using plugins to simply embed video in a page and have it work cross-browser.

On the plus side, because video and audio are now regular elements natively supported by the browser (rather than a "black box" plugin) and offer a powerful API, they're extremely easy to control via JavaScript. With nothing more than a bit of web standards knowledge, you can easily build your own custom controls, or do all sorts of crazy video manipulation with only a few lines of code. As a safety net for browsers that can't cope, we recommend that you also add links to download your video files outside the `<video>` element.

There are already a number of ready-made scripts available that allow you to easily leverage the HTML5 synergies in your own pages, without having to do all the coding yourself. jPlayer (**www.jplayer.org**) is a very liberally licensed jQuery audio player that degrades to Flash in legacy browsers, can be styled with CSS, and can be extended to allow playlists. For video, you've already met Playr, MediaElement.js and LeanBack Player which are my weapons of choice, but many other players exist. There's a useful video player comparison chart at **http://praegnanz.de/ html5video/**.

Accessing video with JavaScript is more than writing new players. In the next chapter, you'll learn how to manipulate native media elements for some truly amazing effects, or at least our heads bouncing around the screen—and who could conceive of anything more amazing than that?

CHAPTER 5

Canvas

Remy Sharp

IF THE VIDEO ELEMENT is the poster boy of HTML5, the canvas element is definitely the Han Solo of HTML5. It's one of the larger parts of the HTML5 specification, and in fact the canvas API, the *2D drawing context*, has been split into a separate document, though the canvas element itself *is* still part of the official HTML5 spec.

The canvas element provides an API for two-dimensional drawing—lines, fills, images, text, and so on. The API has already been used in a huge range of situations, including (interactive) backgrounds to websites, navigation elements, graphing tools, full-fledged applications, games, and emulators. Who knew Super Mario canvas-based games would open the eyes of so many developers!

If you think back to the days of the version of MS Paint that came with Windows 95, you can imagine some of the functionality of canvas. In fact, Paint has been replicated using the canvas element, as shown in **Figure 5.1**. Applications that aim to become full-fledged vector drawing suites (**Figure 5.2**) are popping up all over the Web (whereas Scalable Vector Graphics [SVG] would be a better choice—see the "When to use Canvas, when to use SVG" sidebar later in this chapter). As these applications are based on Open Web technology, they work in a browser on more devices, too. The Harmony application shown in **Figure 5.3** even works on mobile devices, including the iPhone and Android phones.

The 2D API is large enough that I suspect we'll see entire books dedicated to the subject. Since I have only one chapter to talk about it, I'll primarily show you the basics. But I'll also include some of the funky stuff you can do with the canvas element, like capturing frames from a video or processing individual pixels from an image inside the canvas. I'll even show you how to export to files ready to be saved to your desktop. And I'll show you how to create your first animation, which might even hark back to the days of BASIC computing.

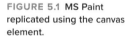

FIGURE 5.1 **MS Paint replicated using the canvas element.**

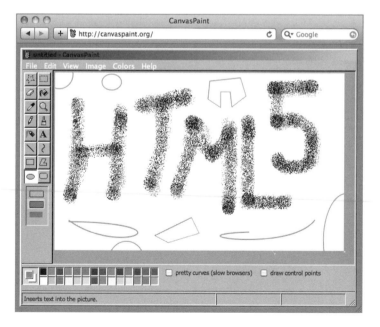

FIGURE 5.2 More advanced drawing applications are emerging using canvas.

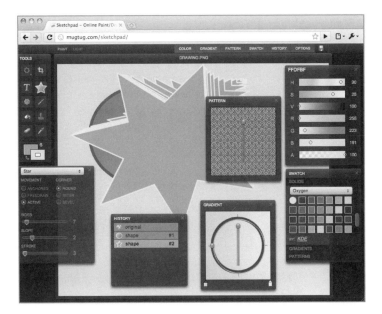

FIGURE 5.3 The canvas drawing demo Harmony also works, unmodified, on mobile browsers.

Canvas basics

The *hello world* of any canvas demo starts with putting the canvas element on your page. Initially the canvas is completely invisible and by default it is 300 pixels wide by 150 pixels high:

```
<!DOCTYPE html>
<title>canvas hello world</title>
<canvas></canvas>
```

The canvas element is now in place. Use JavaScript to get the 2D context to allow you to draw:

```
var ctx = document.querySelector('canvas').
¬ getContext('2d');
```

Now that you have the context, you have access to the full API to draw as you please. For instance, you can add simple shapes to your canvas (**Figure 5.4**):

```
ctx.fillRect(10, 20, 50, 50);
```

FIGURE 5.4 A filled rectangle using the default settings on a canvas.

What about browser support?

Browser support is fairly good for the canvas element; four of the big five browsers support canvas in the latest versions of the browser (and in fact its support is fairly good in previous versions of the browsers, too). "What about Internet Explorer?" is the question that is perpetually asked.

For versions of IE that don't support canvas (IE8 and below), you can shim canvas support in a few ways. The first is FlashCanvas which looks to be the most promising. It does have to rely on Flash as the backup, but it should read all the canvas code and translate it for you to a Flash graphics layer: http://flashcanvas.net.

Similarly, there is a method using Silverlight and a library called html5canvas (http://blogs.msdn.com/ delay/archive/2009/08/24/using-one-platform-to-build-another-html-5-s-canvas-tag-implemented-using- silverlight.aspx); and finally there is a library called excanvas (http://code.google.com/p/explorercanvas/), which translates the canvas API to Microsoft's VML.

These libraries don't cover *the entirety* of the 2D API, but they do cover most of the commonly used methods. Several demos show comparisons from examples in the wild. Out of these options, the web community appears pretty positive about the FlashCanvas polyfill. It's just a little ironic to me that we're relying on Flash (again) for a technology that's touted as replacing Flash. But, hey, this is the way of the web.

It's worth pointing out and being wary that these polyfills won't have the same performance as native canvas. Without seeing charts upon charts upon charts, I would expect the FlashCanvas to perform the best of the lot, but it won't be a like for like performance, particularly compared to when the browser has hardware-accelerated canvas rendering as IE9 does.

FIGURE 5.5 **Using fill styles and rectangle strokes.**

> **NOTE** querySelector and querySelectorAll are new DOM methods that accept a CSS selector and return the elements it matches. Currently available in all the latest browsers, querySelector returns the first DOM node it finds, whereas querySelectorAll returns a NodeList object that you'll need to iterate over.

The arguments to fillRect are x, y, width, and height. The x and y coordinates start in the top left. As shown in Figure 5.4, the default colour is black. Let's add some colour and draw an outline around the canvas so that the canvas looks like **Figure 5.5**:

```
ctx.fillStyle = 'rgb(0, 255, 0)';
ctx.fillRect(10, 20, 50, 50); // creates a solid square
ctx.strokeStyle = 'rgb(0, 182, 0)';
ctx.lineWidth = 5;
ctx.strokeRect(9, 19, 52, 52); // draws an outline
```

In the previous code listing, you're drawing twice on the canvas: once with fillRect and once with strokeRect. When you're not drawing, you're setting the colour and style of the 2D context which must happen before the fill or stroke happens, otherwise the default colour of black is used. Along with CSS colours (for example, RGB, hex, RGBA, and so on), fillStyle and strokeStyle also accept gradients and patterns generated using the 2D API.

Painting gradients and patterns

Using the context object, you can generate a linear gradient, radial gradient, or a pattern fill, which in turn can be used as the fillStyle on the canvas. Gradients and radial gradients work similar to CSS gradients, in that you specify a start point and colour stops for the gradient.

Patterns, on the other hand, allow you to point to an image source and then specify how the pattern should repeat, again similar to the repeat process on a CSS background image. What makes createPattern really interesting is that the image source can be an image, another canvas, or a video element (though using video as a source isn't yet implemented at the time of writing).

Creating a simple gradient is easy and possibly even faster than starting up Photoshop:

```
var canvas = document.querySelector('canvas'),
    ctx = canvas.getContext('2d'),
    gradient = ctx.createLinearGradient(0, 0, 0, canvas.
    ¬ height);
gradient.addColorStop(0, '#fff');
gradient.addColorStop(1, '#000');
ctx.fillStyle = gradient;
ctx.fillRect(0, 0, canvas.width, canvas.height);
```

FIGURE 5.6 **A vertical gradient on a canvas element.**

The code in the previous listing uses the 2D context object to generate a linear gradient object to which you can then apply colour stops. The arguments are the starting point of the gradient, x1 and y1, and the endpoint of the gradient, x2 and y2. In this example, I'm telling the gradient to start in the top left and finish at the bottom left of the canvas. This creates a gradient that runs vertically (**Figure 5.6**).

Radial gradients are very similar, except the createRadialGradient takes the radius after each coordinate:

```
var canvas = document.querySelector('canvas'),
    ctx = canvas.getContext('2d'),
    gradient = ctx.createRadialGradient(canvas.width/2,
      canvas.height/2, 0,
      canvas.width/2, canvas.height/2, 150);
gradient.addColorStop(0, '#fff');
gradient.addColorStop(1, '#000');
ctx.fillStyle = gradient;
ctx.fillRect(0, 0, canvas.width, canvas.width);
```

FIGURE 5.7 **This radial gradient starts and ends at the same point, but the ending radius is much greater, causing a smooth, circular gradient.**

The only difference is the kind of gradient that's created. In this example, I've moved the first point of the gradient to start in the centre of the canvas starting with a radius of zero. The gradient uses a radius of 150 pixels, but notice that it also starts in the same place: canvas.width/2, canvas.height/2. This is so my example creates a smooth, circular gradient (**Figure 5.7**).

Patterns are even easier to use. You need a source, and then you can drop the source element into the createPattern method and use the result as the fillStyle. The only caveat is that the element, in the case of images and videos, must have finished loading to capture the source properly.

To create the effect shown in **Figure 5.8** (a tiled image across the back of the canvas), first stretch the canvas over the size of the window. Then dynamically create an image and, when it fires the load event, use the image as the source of a repeating pattern:

```
var canvas = document.querySelector('canvas'),
    img = document.createElement('img'),
    ctx = canvas.getContext('2d');
canvas.width = window.innerWidth;
canvas.height = window.innerHeight;
img.onload = function () {
```

```
      ctx.fillStyle = ctx.createPattern(this, 'repeat');
      ctx.fillRect(0, 0, canvas.width, canvas.height);
};
img.src = 'remysharp_avatar.jpg';
```

FIGURE 5.8 Tiling an
image on a canvas using the
createPattern method.

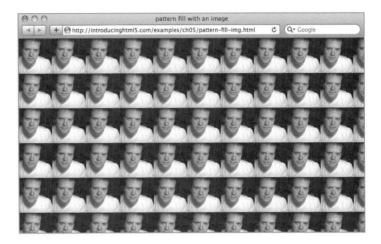

In this example I've created an image on the fly using document. createElement. Only after the onload event fires do I continue to build the pattern fill. You need to wait until all the image data has loaded before you can begin to use it.

Now that the image is loaded, I'm able to set the fillStyle using createPattern. I've used createPattern(this, 'repeat'), and this refers to the image that fired the load event, but I can just as easily use another canvas as the source. The string 'repeat' follows the same syntax as CSS background-repeat, in that repeat-x, repeat-y, and no-repeat also work.

If you use CSS to change the canvas element's size, this will simply *stretch* the canvas. This doesn't actually do anything to the pixels in the canvas, only the canvas DOM node as you can see in **Figure 5.9**. If you were to draw something to the canvas and change the canvas element's height or width property (say you wanted to change the default 300x150 dimensions) it will blank out the contents of the canvas, and also reset the state of your drawing fill styles, stroke styles, line width, and so on. This effectively does a reset on your canvas, a trick or a problem depending on your point of view.

FIGURE 5.9 When a canvas stretches after it's finished drawing, so do the contents of the canvas.

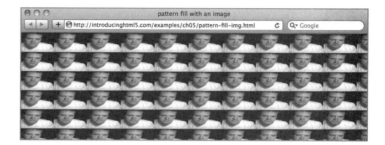

Drawing paths

FIGURE 5.10 My contrived stick man drawing using the path API.

Within the 2D API is a path API that allows you to move around the canvas and draw lines or shapes. The contrived example in **Figure 5.10** shows a stick man drawn using the path API.

I won't take you through all the code used to produce the stick man, just the highlights so you can see what methods I used. To draw the stick man, you must specify the x, y coordinates around the canvas that you want to draw, painstakingly specifying each individual line. To draw the stick man head, run the following code:

```
ctx.beginPath();
ctx.arc(100, 50, 30, 0, Math.PI*2, true); // head
ctx.fill();
```

Getting from degrees to radians

The arc, bezier, and quadratic methods use radians, so if you're used to working with degrees, you'll need to convert them to radians. Here's the JavaScript you need to go from degrees to radians:

```
var radians = degrees * Math.PI / 180;
```

It's also common to pass 360 degrees to the drawing methods, which is simply `Math.PI * 2`, and equally 180 degrees is `Math.PI`.

This gives you a solid, filled head. I've given the x, y coordinates of 100, 50, respectively, and a radius of 30 pixels. The next arguments are the start and endpoints in radians. In this example, I want a complete circle, so I start at zero and end at `Math.PI*2`, which is equal to 360 degrees in radians. Finally the sixth argument is the direction to draw the arc: clockwise or counterclockwise. In this case it doesn't matter, but it's still required.

FIGURE 5.11 An example of
how a continued path causes
an error in the final drawing.

Once the head is drawn, I want to draw a face. The eyes
and smile will be in red (well, grey in the figure). When I draw
the facial features, I need to use beginPath again. **Figure 5.11**
shows what the result would be if I didn't use beginPath. This
is because the previous arc line I drew would be included in
the final face path, and because I'm starting a new arc for the
mouth, as you'll see in the following code listing. I could fix the
line joining the edge of the head to the mouth by using moveTo,
which is effectively *lifting the pen* from the canvas to begin
drawing someplace else, but I don't want the coloured outline
around the head.

```
ctx.beginPath();
// draw the smile
ctx.strokeStyle = '#c00';
ctx.lineWidth = 3;
ctx.arc(100, 50, 20, 0, Math.PI, false);
ctx.stroke();
```

The previous code listing gives me a nice semicircle for the
smile with a new stroke colour and width. For the head I used
fill, but for the face I need to use stroke, which will draw the
line rather than a solid shape. Next the eyes:

```
ctx.beginPath();
ctx.fillStyle = '#c00';
// start the left eye
ctx.arc(90, 45, 3, 0, Math.PI*2, true);
ctx.fill();
ctx.moveTo(113, 45);
// draw the right eye
ctx.arc(110, 45, 3, 0, Math.PI*2, true);
ctx.fill();
ctx.stroke(); // thicker eyes
```

I started a new path again, which means I can start drawing the
arc for the eyes without using moveTo (as I did when making the
smile). However, once I filled the arc, creating a solid-looking eye,
I *lift* the pen with moveTo(113, 45) to draw the right eye. Notice
that I moved to the right by the arc's first x coordinate plus the
radius value to create a solid line, which ensures that the starting
point of the arc matches where I put the pen down. Finally I use
the stroke method to give the eyes a bit more thickness.

The code goes on to move the drawing point around and finally
end up with an image of our stick man.

There are other path methods, which are beyond the scope of this chapter, that you can use for finer control over the lines and shapes you draw, including `quadraticCurveTo`, `bezierCurveTo`, `arcTo`, `rect`, `clip`, and `isPointInPath`.

When to use Canvas, when to use SVG

Canvas and SVG are both very good drawing APIs, but for different reasons, and, as with anything, you want to use the right tool for the job. SVG is a *retained-mode API*, and the 2D canvas API is an *immediate-mode API*.

SVG is vector based, so it handles scaling much better; canvas produces a bitmap-based image—it doesn't scale, it just zooms. SVG maintains a tree that represents the current state of all the objects drawn on-screen (similar to the regular DOM tree that represents the current document). As this tree is available, it makes it a great candidate for interactivity because you can bind to specific objects in the tree and listen for click or touch events and even do easy hit detection for games. You can write SVG by hand as it's just XML—and now all the latest browsers have full support for SVG (except, oddly, Andriod WebKit browsers) both externally linked and inline alongside HTML5. But if wrestling XML isn't your cup of tea, desktop tools such as Adobe Illustrator and Inkscape can export and import SVG graphics which makes life a little easier.

If you need some convincing of the almighty awesome power of SVG, have a look at Raphaël, the JavaScript library by Dmitry Baranovskiy (**http://raphaeljs.com**). It uses SVG exclusively and is able to create some very impressive drawings and animations.

Canvas is effectively an array of pixels that's very well suited to lots of animations and highly JavaScript-centric applications. It's a lower-level API when compared to SVG, which means that it's better for when there *isn't* mouse interaction. This is because there's no tree maintaining the state of the canvas because you can't hook an event handler to objects you draw on a canvas—you would have to calculate the position of the mouse interaction and maintain all the coordinates of painted objects in memory. Since canvas is JavaScript centric, in your processing loop you can handle keyboard events on the document level. Finally, as the canvas is pixel orientated, as illustrated by the screenshots at the start of this chapter, it's great for pixel pushing.

Each of these technologies has its strengths and weaknesses. As the developer, it's your job to understand the requirements of your application and pick the right one. Good luck!

Using transformers: pixels in disguise

As well as being able to move the pen around the canvas using methods like moveTo and drawing shapes and lines, you can adjust what happens to the canvas *under* the pen using transformations.

Transformation methods include rotation, scaling, transformation, and translation (all similar to their CSS counterparts).

In **Figure 5.12**, I've drawn a spiral; the aim is to have it rotate in a circle, giving a quasi-Twilight Zone effect. Ideally I would keep the function that draws the spiral the same, not changing any positions, starting points, or anything else. This would keep the code much easier to manage. So to ensure that the spiral code remains simple, I can rotate the canvas under the pen, and then redraw the exact same spiral, except the result is rotated slightly in one direction.

FIGURE 5.12 **An animated spiral going around, and around, and around.**

The rotate method rotates from the top left (0, 0) position by default. This wouldn't do at all, and if I rotated the canvas from this position, the spiral would circulate offscreen, as if it were on a pendulum. Instead I need to rotate from the centre of the spiral, which I'll place in the centre of the canvas. Therefore I need to rotate from the centre of the canvas.

The translate method can help me here. It moves the 0, 0 coordinate to a new position. **Figure 5.13** shows that I've drawn a dot and also shows the arguments I passed to translate. Each time translate runs it sets the new coordinates to 0, 0. Note that the translate doesn't rotate or move the canvas in a way that's presented to the user; it's translating the underlying coordinate system that subsequent drawing functions refer to.

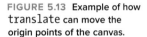

FIGURE 5.13 Example of how translate can move the origin points of the canvas.

Now to achieve my rotating spiral I need to initialise the canvas using translate, and then use setInterval to redraw my spiral (note that drawSpiral is my own function, rather than a native method, that draws the path for a spiral with a series of stroke calls):

```
ctx.translate(ctx.canvas.width/2, ctx.canvas.height/2);
drawSpiral(); // the complicated magic mathematics

setInterval(function () {
  ctx.clearRect(-ctx.canvas.width/2, -ctx.canvas.height/2,
              ctx.canvas.width, ctx.canvas.height);
  ctx.rotate(Math.PI / 180 * 0.5) // 1/2 a degree
  drawSpiral();
}, 10);
```

The only caveat I have to deal with is clearing the canvas. I would normally use clearRect(0, 0, width, height), but since translate has moved the 0, 0 position to the centre of the canvas, I need to manually specify the top left, as seen in the previous code listing.

Capturing images

As well as drawing lines and shapes, you can copy images from other sources, specifically images, videos, and other canvas elements. I've already shown that you can use images as the source of a `createPattern` fill. You can also draw images straight onto your canvas. You can even crop and manipulate the images as they're copied:

```
var ctx = document.getElementById('mycanvas').
getContext('2d'),
    img = new Image();

img.onload = function () {
  ctx.canvas.height = 500;
  ctx.canvas.width = 500;
  ctx.drawImage(this, 10, 10, 100, 100, 0, 0, 500, 500);
};
img.src = 'bruce-and-remy-promo-pics.jpg';
```

The code above is a simple example of how I can dynamically create an image on the fly, and once it's loaded I can draw a section of it in to my canvas. As we'll see in a moment you have a few ways of using the `drawImage` method, and here what I've done is take a 100x100 pixel crop from 10 pixels left and 10 pixels right, and stretch it in to the canvas over 500 pixels wide and tall.

Since you can also capture an image from a video element, this makes for some interesting opportunities. There's already lots of demos out in the wild, showing some interesting effects like dynamically injecting content into video, green screen replacement for video, and facial recognition—all using combinations of canvas and video, all written in JavaScript.

The capturing and drawing is done entirely through the `drawImage` method, which needs a reference to the source (an image, video, or canvas element), a target position (the top/left coordinates of where you want to draw the image in your canvas), and a few optional arguments that allow you to crop and scale the image:

- `drawImage(image, dx, dy)`
- `drawImage(image, dx, dy, dw, dh)`
- `drawImage(image, sx, sy, sw, sh, dx, dy, dw, dh)`

where d is the destination position and s is the source. For example, if I took Bruce's synergy video from Chapter 4, and

TIP All 2D drawing contexts have a back reference to the canvas which they draw against. This means you don't have to pass around two variables to functions, you can just pass the context and get the back reference to the canvas element if you wanted to change the height, width, or get the data url.

wanted to run a repeating thumbnail of him bashing the banana across the top of my website, I could do it by drawing a cropped and scaled version of the video using the `drawImage` method.

The components I need are:

* A canvas fixed across the top of my site

* A *hidden* video running the synergies video

* A way to loop just the bit of the video I want

* A method to capture what's on the video and transfer it to the canvas

The reason I'm using a hidden video is because this will be the source for my canvas, but I don't want it to be seen. I just want to keep grabbing the video frame and putting it on the canvas.

I *just* want the part of Bruce smashing the banana with the mallet (the part from 0:49 to 0:52), so I need to tell the video to play only that part. There's no content attribute I can use to tell it to start from a particular point, so I'll just force the `currentTime` to second 49. Then on the `timeupdate` event, I'll force the `currentTime` back to 49 if it goes above 52 seconds. So my time range is the window of 49 to 52 seconds in the video. Due to some browsers trying to hold back data and missing support for the `video.seekable` property, for this example I'll use a timer to try to force the start time:

```
var jumpTimer = setInterval(function () {
  try {
    // if the data isn't available, setting currentTime
    ¬will throw an error
    video.currentTime = start;
    clearInterval(jumpTimer);
    video.play();
  } catch (e) {}
}, 100);


video.addEventListener('timeupdate', function () {
  if (this.currentTime > 52) this.currentTime = 49;
}, false);
```

The previous code keeps trying to set the `video.currentTime` value, but doing so before the video data is ready throws a JavaScript error. If the error is thrown, the code doesn't reach `clearInterval`. If successful, the `setInterval` is cleared and the video is played.

Now that the video loop is in place, I can start grabbing frames from the video element. I *could* use the `timeupdate` event to draw the canvas, but I know that the effect doesn't perform anywhere nearly as well as if I run the canvas drawing in its own timer. I could speculate that this is because the browser is trying to do the hard work to render the video element; separating it in a timer gives the browser some room to breathe.

Once the `loadeddata` event fires on the video, I'll initialise the canvas so it's the same width as the window (otherwise our image would stretch, as you saw in Figure 5.9). Then I'll mute the video (to avoid being too annoying!) and calculate the shortest edge because I want to crop a square from the video and repeat it across the canvas:

```
video.addEventListener('loadeddata', function () {
  var size = 78; // thumbnail size
  canvas.width = window.innerWidth;
  video.volume = 0;
  shortestEdge = video.videoHeight > video.videoWidth ?
    video.videoWidth :
    video.videoHeight;

  // kick off our drawing loop
  setInterval(function () {
    for (var i = 0, w = canvas.width; i < w; i += size) {
    // arguments have been broken into multi lines
      ctx.drawImage(
        video,
        (video.videoWidth - shortestEdge)/2, // sx
        (video.videoHeight - shortestEdge)/2, // sy
        shortestEdge, // sw
        shortestEdge, // sh
        i, // dx
        0, // dy
        size, // dh
        size // dy
      );
    }
  }, 67); // 67 is approximately 15fps
}, false);
```

All the magic happens inside the `setInterval`, which triggers every 67/1000th of a second (JavaScript measures seconds by 1000 milliseconds; therefore 1000 milliseconds/15 frames per second = about 67, or approximately 15 fps—equally 25fps would be 1000/25), which should be good enough for faking video playback. Once inside the `setInterval`, I'll loop over the width of the canvas, incrementing by the size of the thumbnail I'm drawing to fill the canvas horizontally.

The mapping for the arguments to the `drawImage` method is shown in **Figure 5.14**.

FIGURE 5.14 **A visual representation of arguments passed to** `drawImage`.

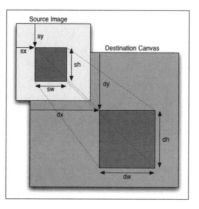

Using a simple crop for the height and width, and using the shortest edge, I can then easily scale the crop to the thumbnail size and let the canvas do all the hard work for me. The result: Bruce bashing a banana across the top of my site (**Figure 5.15**).

FIGURE 5.15 **An animated banner across my site using canvas and video.**

Pushing pixels

One very cool feature of the canvas API is its ability to interrogate individual pixels, something that isn't possible with SVG, which is vector-based, and not really aimed at pixel-level operations. You can get every pixel from the 2D context object broken down into four colour channels: red, green, blue, and the alpha transparency channel (rgba). For example:

```
var ctx = document.querySelector('canvas').
¬ getContext('2d'),
    img = document.createElement('img');
```

```
// wait until the image has loaded to read the data
img.onload = function () {
  ctx.drawImage(img, 0, 0);
  var pixels = ctx.getImageData(0, 0, img.width,
  ¬ img.height);
};
```

The variable pixels is a CanvasPixelArray, which contains the height, width, and data properties. data is an array of the pixel data, which is made up as follows

```
[ r1, g1, b1, a1, r2, g2, b2, a2, r3, g3, b3, a3, ... ]
```

> **NOTE** To use the source of another image in the **drawImage** method, it must be served through http (not a local file system).

where r1, g1, b1, a1 makes up the first pixel, r2, g2, b2, a2 makes up the second pixel, and so on. This means that data. length is the number of pixels captured from the getImageData (in the previous example this will be the same size as the image) multiplied by 4, as there are 4 channels to each pixel. Note that the pixel arrangement in the CanvasPixelArray is from top-left to bottom-right, going row by row for the area selected.

Since you have access to this data, you can do pixel-level processing. So you *could* create custom image filters for applications like the image editors shown in Figure 5.2 or perhaps scan the image for particular colour ranges or even write a web app that does facial recognition.

Paul Rouget and Tristan Nitot of Mozilla showed off a demo early in 2009 (see **Figure 5.16**) that uses a video drawn onto a canvas and injects dynamic content on top of it. As each video frame is drawn on the canvas, the pixel data is read and searched for a solid block of white (where the pixel is 255, 255, 255), which is used as an anchor point to draw another visual element on the canvas. In Figure 5.16, another canvas element has been dynamically injected. You can play with the demo here: **http://people.mozilla.com/~prouget/demos/DynamicContentInjection/play.xhtml**.

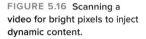

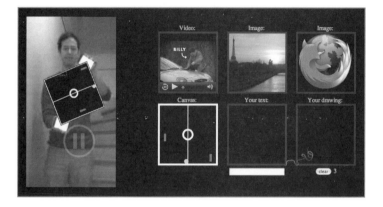

In the following code example, I load an image into the canvas and invert all the pixels, creating a strange X-ray version of Bruce and me (**Figure 5.17**):

```
var ctx = document.querySelector('canvas').
¬getContext('2d'),
    img = document.createElement('img');

// wait until the image has loaded
img.onload = function () {
  ctx.canvas.width = img.width;
  ctx.canvas.height = img.height;
  ctx.drawImage(img, 0, 0);
  var pixels = ctx.getImageData(0, 0, img.width,
  ¬img.height);

  for (var i = 0, n = pixels.data.length; i < n; i += 4) {
    pixels.data[i+0] = 255 - pixels.data[i+0]; // red
    pixels.data[i+1] = 255 - pixels.data[i+2]; // green
    pixels.data[i+2] = 255 - pixels.data[i+1]; // blue
    // i + 3 is the alpha channel which we don't need
  }
  ctx.putImageData(pixels, 0, 0);
};
img.src = 'authors.jpg';
```

In the previous code listing, I wait until the image has loaded before trying to copy it to the canvas. I draw it into the canvas and immediately read out the pixel data to invert the image.

In the for loop, I'm using i += 4, which ensures I'm iterating over *each pixel* and not the pixel channels. By setting the pixel bit to 255 minus the current value, I get an inverted colour.

Finally, I put the modified pixels back into the canvas using putImageData, passing in the CanvasPixelArray object and the x/y start point.

FIGURE 5.17 If you were to X-ray Bruce and Remy, you'd see they look just as strange.

> **NOTE** For security, the canvas element contains an internal origin-clean flag that's set to true by default. This flag will flip to false if an image or video is used whose origin does not match that of the document that owns the canvas. The same goes for using a canvas as an image source if it already has the origin-clean flag set to false. If the flag is false, you won't be able to use the getImageData or toDataURL methods. This remains the case even if you change the size of your canvas or draw on the canvas after the flag is set to false.

Saving to file

You've made the next best thing since sliced bread? Want to save your beautiful drawing to your desktop? You want to export it in multiple formats? No problem. Canvas has you covered.

The canvas *element* (*not* the 2D context) supports exporting the current state of the canvas to a data URL.

What's a data URL?

Most browsers support Base64 encoded assets, such as an image. Web applications like Gmail use Base64 encoded images in their CSS to reduce the number of requests being made over the wire (even though it actually makes the CSS file larger as all the image data is embedded). The URL scheme looks like this:

data:image/png;base64,iVBORw0KGgoAAAANSUhEUgAAAAoAAAAK...

It starts with data, then the mime type, then the encoding, Base64, and then the raw data (which roughly speaking is 30 percent larger than the source image). This raw data is what's exported by the canvas element, and browsers are able to decode the data in to real assets (sadly, this doesn't include IE7 or previous incarnations of IE). In addition, IE8 only supports data URLs up to a length of 32 KB—something to watch out for!

Exporting is very easy. The canvas has the `toDataURL` method, which can be invoked with the format in which you want your image. Only PNG support is required by the canvas specification, but browsers can support other types if they choose. For example, Safari supports GIF, PNG, and JPG. Trying to get the data URL for an unsupported TIFF format returns exclusively the letter *A* multiple times and no data:<mime-type>. Opera supports only PNG, but on requesting a JPG or GIF, it still returns a PNG (ignoring the file format). Old versions of Firefox (on a Mac) supported only PNG, throwing an error on all other types (which was a little severe if you ask me). The lesson here is that once you have your data URL back, ensure that it starts with data:<*your-mime-type*> to ensure that they match up and that you get back the image in the format you asked for.

The following example generates a drawing similar to our *hello world* example and immediately saves it to a PNG by redirecting the browser to the rendered data URL:

```
var ctx = document.querySelector('canvas').
¬ getContext('2d');
ctx.fillStyle = 'rgb(0, 0, 255)';
ctx.fillRect(0, 0, ctx.canvas.width, ctx.canvas.height);
ctx.fillStyle = 'rgb(0, 255, 0)';
ctx.fillRect(10, 20, 50, 50); // little square
window.location = ctx.canvas.toDataURL('image/png');
```

Finally, the toDataURL also takes an optional second argument that is available only if image/jpg has been implemented to allow you to specify the quality level of the generated image. This value would be between 0.0 and 1, with 1 being the highest quality available—but be careful, as this will affect the size of the final image, and, in our case, the size of the Base64 data string generated by the toDataURL method.

Animating your canvas paintings

You've seen some basic animations using canvas throughout this chapter, but I wanted to explain some of the concepts in detail here.

Simple animation is mostly about clearing the current canvas state and drawing the whole thing again. This is very quick to do, as the canvas is a native drawing API. I'll show you a demo that takes Bruce's bouncy head and bounces it around the canvas area. This example is based on the canvas breakout tutorial by Bill Mill, but I jazzed it up with Bruce's mug bouncing instead of a solid black ball.

The Processing JavaScript Library

As you'll find out, it's a blast to navigate around the canvas with a pen drawing lines and filling shapes, but there are already some libraries available that make working with the canvas much easier. One such library is called processing.js (**http://processingjs.org/**), written by the author of jQuery, John Resig.

It's not actually a library designed to ease working with canvas, but it in fact interprets the Processing language in JavaScript, which is in turn drawn on the canvas element. In many ways, processing.js is a great tool for visualisation and abstracts away a lot of the more complicated drawing and animation procedures in the 2D drawing API.

The code used for **Figure 5.18** is relatively simple and breaks down as follows:

1. Initialise the canvas and objects you want to draw.

2. Clear the canvas.

3. Draw the ball on the canvas.

To add extra spice, I rotate Bruce's face in circles whilst he bounces around. So I'll have to do some rotation on the canvas, too.

FIGURE 5.18 While away the hours whilst you watch Bruce's face bounce around a canvas animation.

Since I'm going to rotate Bruce's face, I'll let *another* canvas handle that task (so I can keep my main canvas free from rotation and translations). This keeps my tasks simple in that I'm rotating an image of Bruce in one canvas while I'm working out the position of his face and drawing in the second.

```
var ctx = document.querySelector('canvas').
¬ getContext("2d"),
    ballctx,
    x = 100, // arbitrary start points
    y = 50,
    dx = 2,
    dy = 4,
    width = ctx.canvas.width,
    height = ctx.canvas.height;

// load the image
ballImg = document.createElement('img');
ballImg.src = 'bruce-ball.png';

// once loaded, start the ball bouncing
ballImg.onload = function () {
  var ball = document.createElement('canvas');
```

```
    ball.height = 50;
    ball.width = 50;

    ballctx = ball.getContext('2d');
    // translate to centre to rotate properly
    ballctx.translate(25, 25);

    setInterval(draw, 10);
};


function draw() {
    ctx.clearRect(0, 0, width, height);

    ballctx.rotate(Math.PI/180*5); // 5 degrees

    // draw at the 0,0 position
    ballctx.drawImage(ballImg, 0, 0, ballImg.width,
    ¬ballImg.height, -25, -25, 50, 50);

    // copy the rotated source
    ctx.drawImage(ballctx.canvas, x, y);

    if (x + dx > width || x + dx < 0)
        dx = -dx;
    if (y + dy > height || y + dy < 0)
        dy = -dy;

    x += dx;
    y += dy;
}
```

All the action is happening in the draw function, but only after I've finished setting up. In the setup, the code dynamically creates a new canvas for the ball but doesn't put it inside the DOM. This canvas is then translated so the rotation of Bruce's face happens in the centre of the canvas. I can still use the 2D context of this "unattached" canvas and I explicitly give this canvas a height and width (otherwise it's automatically set to 300x150px).

The draw function then runs every 1/100th of a second (10 milliseconds), constantly incrementing the x and y position and redrawing the ball canvas on the main canvas, but not before the blanket *clearing* of the canvas with ctx.clearRect(0, 0, width, height), which is effectively resetting the entire effect.

So that's it. Animation. Probably most akin to a flip-book animation.

Saving and restoring drawing state

There is a little more hope built into the 2D API: drawing state. There are two methods on the context object: save and `restore`, which manage the current stack of drawing states. The save method *pushes* the current state on to the stack, whereas `restore` *pops* from the top of the stack.

Drawing states don't cover *everything* you do to the canvas, but they do include the following:

- Transformations

- Clipping regions (not covered in this book)

- Current values for the following attributes: `fillStyle`, `font`, `globalAlpha`, `globalCompositeOperation`, `lineCap`, `lineJoin`, `lineWidth`, `miterLimit`, `shadowBlur`, `shadowColor`, `shadowOffsetX`, `shadowOffsetY`, `strokeStyle`, `textAlign`, and `textBaseline`.

> **NOTE** Save and restore do not affect the current paths or current bitmap on the canvas (you can't restore to a previous state of the image on the canvas).

For example, the following code snippet from the Mozilla canvas composition tutorial shows how it would draw 50 stars on a canvas in random positions. It sets the position using the translate method. But at the end of each iteration of the loop, it restores the original state of the canvas, thus moving the top/left of the canvas to the real top left, rather than the position of the last translate:

```
for (var j=1;j<50;j++){
  ctx.save();
  ctx.fillStyle = '#fff';
  ctx.translate(75-Math.floor(Math.random()*150),
                75-Math.floor(Math.random()*150));
  drawStar(ctx,Math.floor(Math.random()*4)+2);
  ctx.restore();
}
```

Rendering text

canvas allows you to render text and specify fonts, sizes, alignment, and baselines. You can also fill text (as normal text might appear) and stroke text (around the outline). The old Bespin project was a great example of how custom text rendering can be used to create a fully functional code editor written entirely with the canvas API (it's since been superceded by Ace by the nice folks at Ajax.org—but their version doesn't use a canvas).

Drawing text requires the string and coordinates. For example, to show you how to use `translate`, I used an annotated canvas (shown in **Figure 5.19** and earlier in Figure 5.13). I used `fillText` to annotate the new centre point of the canvas to label the dots I had placed around the canvas (whose height and width are hard coded to 300x300 for this example):

```
function dot(string) {
  ctx.beginPath();
  ctx.arc(0,0,5,0,Math.PI*2,true); // draw circle
  ctx.fill();
  ctx.fillText(string, 5, 10); // render text
}
```

Now I can translate the canvas and call the dot function, passing the string I want printed next to the dot:

```
dot('1. no translate'); // show dot
ctx.translate(150, 150);
dot('2. (150, 150)'); // show dot
ctx.translate(-100, 20);
dot('3. (-100, 20)'); // show dot
```

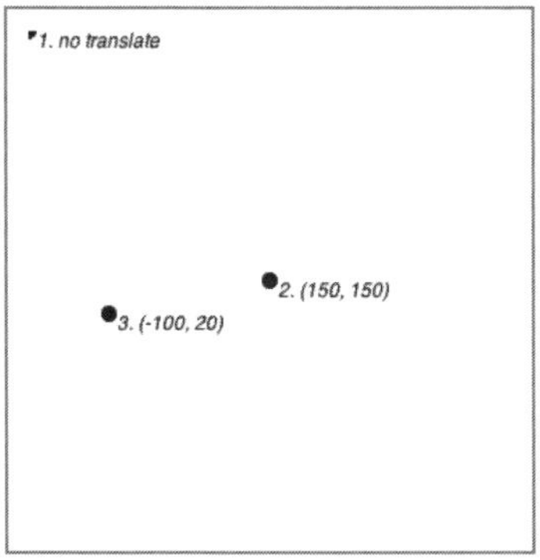

FIGURE 5.19 Using `fillText` to annotate a canvas.

By default, the `fillText` method uses a 10 pixel tall sans serif as the selected font. You can change this to your own font style by setting the font property on the context using the same syntax as CSS fonts (for example, `ctx.font = 'italic 400 12px/2 helvetica neue, sans-serif'`). You can even use CSS3 web fonts, provided they've been fully loaded before you use them. When I call `fillText`, the text rendering uses the same `fillStyle` that I set earlier (or uses the canvas default). Equally `strokeText` uses the current `strokeStyle`.

Accessibility within the canvas element

> **NOTE** JIT means Just in Time compilation, a technique used to improve the runtime performance of a program.

One reason that canvas is so fast on today's optimised *JIT* JavaScript interpreters is that it keeps no DOM: it really is just a big bunch of pixels, with no information stored about which geometric shapes, text, or images have been thrown at them (compare this to SVG, which does maintain all those as separate objects in a DOM structure). So, for example, if you need any kind of collision detection, you need to do all the bookkeeping yourself. There is no representation of what objects have been drawn that JavaScript can interrogate.

This also causes difficulty for accessibility. If your games are keyboard- *and* mouse-accessible, that goes a long way to meeting the needs of many. But for users with visual impairments, there is nothing for assistive technology to hook into. Canvas text is the same: bringing text into canvas means it ceases to be text and is just pixels. It's even worse than <img> because at least that can take alt text. Although the contents of the element (the text between the canvas tags) can be changed with script to reflect the canvas text you're inserting with JavaScript, I'm not optimistic that developers will do this.

> **NOTE** Filament Group's jQuery Visualize plugin uses jQuery to inject a canvas element to a page that graphs the information from a data table in the markup. Assistive technologies have access to the raw data table, while the information is supplemented with visual graphs for sighted users.

An accessibility task force of the Working Group is looking at ways to enhance the accessibility of canvas. It's not impossible: Flash 5 managed to add accessibility features. However, I recommend that, for the time being, canvas not be used for user interfaces or as the only way to communicate information. Filament Group's jQuery Visualize plugin is a good example of canvas being used to supplement accessible information (see Note).

Summary

The canvas API finally gives developers the ability to dynamically generate and manipulate graphics client-side, directly in the browser, without the need for plugin-based detours via Flash and Co. The canvas is especially powerful for pixel-level processing, and I can imagine that canvas-based applications will be pushing the boundaries of what we've historically seen on the Web.

However, you should be careful to choose the right technology for the job. Consider SVG before ploughing ahead with your next Awesome 3.0 app. And watch out for the possible accessibility implications.

CHAPTER 6

Data Storage

Remy Sharp

DATA STORAGE IS fundamental in nearly all applications, web or desktop. This can include storing a unique key to track page impressions, saving usernames and preferences, and so on. The list is endless.

Up until now, storing data in a web app required you to either store it on the server side and create some linking key between the client and the server—which means your data is split between locations—or store it in cookies on the client.

Cookies suck. Not the edible ones, the ones in the browser. They're rubbish. There's a number of issues with cookies that make them a pain to work with. On starting any new project that requires cookies, I'll immediately go hunting for my cookie JavaScript library. If I can't find that, I'll head over to Peter-Paul Koch's cookie code, and copy and paste away.

> **NOTE** Get Peter-Paul Koch's cookie code at **www.quirksmode.org/js/ cookies.html**.

Looking at how cookies work, they're overly complicated. Setting a cookie in JavaScript looks like this:

```
document.cookie = "foo=bar; path=/";
```

That's a session-based cookie. Now, if I want to store something for longer, I'll have to set it in the future, and give it a specific lifetime (and if I want it to persist, I'll have to keep setting this to be *n* days in the future):

```
document.cookie = "foo=bar; path=/; expires=Tues,
¬ 13 Sept 2010 12:00:00";
```

The time format is important too, which only causes more head-aches. Now, the icing on the horrible-tasting cookie—to delete a cookie, I need to set the value to blank:

```
document.cookie = "foo=; path=/";
```

In fact, the cookie isn't *really* deleted, it's just had the value changed and had the expiry set to the current session (that is, when the browser is shut down). Delete should really mean delete.

Cookies don't work because they're a headache. The new storage specifications completely circumvent this cumbersome approach to setting, getting, and removing data by offering a clean API.

Being British though, I feel I need to add a caveat to the "cook-ies suck" statement. But fear not—it's only a small caveat. If you need to share client-side data with the server side, cookies are the right solution because they append themselves to every request automatically. If you don't, then you want a client-side storage engine. To me, Web Storage evolved as cookies should have, but Web Storage has even more functionality, hence the evolution. So with my caveat aside, let's look at what today's browsers have in store for us (pardon the pun)!

Storage options

There are three options when it comes to storing data on the client side:

- Web Storage—supported in all the latest browsers— **http://www.w3.org/TR/webstorage/**

- Web SQL Database—supported in Opera, Chrome, and Safari— **http://www.w3.org/TR/webdatabase/**

- IndexedDB—at the time of writing, experimental support in Chrome 12, Firefox 5, and Internet Explorer 10— **http://www.w3.org/TR/Indexeddb/**

Conveniently, the name Web SQL Database instantly gives you a clue as to how it works: It uses SQL-based syntax to query a local database. You may think that's great as you already know SQL. The small potential issue is that the specification currently has a stonking great sign notifying readers that the spec is no longer being maintained. However, as it has such good support, particularly in the mobile space, I want to show you how to use the API. In addition, Google uses Web SQL Database in its mobile version of Gmail, so I'm confident the technology will remain in browsers for quite some time to come.

IndexedDB's name is less descriptive, though you'd probably be able to guess how it works. IndexedDB is a document data store, akin to today's popular "NoSQL" databases, like MongoDB. Essentially you have a key and you can store any data type against that key, rather than having a set number and type of columns as per traditional SQL databases. Interestingly, IndexedDB puts events at the core of how you work with the API. We'll talk more about that toward the end of the chapter.

Web Storage is a much simpler system in which you associate a key with a value, compared to the amount of code required when working with Web SQL Database or IndexedDB. Support for the Web Storage API is much better than the current alternatives—but this should change with time leaving us with a simple storage method (Web Storage) and larger data storage (IndexedDB as support flushes through to the rest of the browsers). I'll look at all three of these APIs, how they work, and how to debug data in each system.

Web Storage typically has a limit of 5 MB (but browsers will generally ask permission from the users if more than 5 MB is required, and ask whether they want to allow the website to go beyond the current default).

On the other side of the fence, the Web SQL Database specification doesn't talk about limits, and it's up to the author to try to gauge the total size of the database when it's created.

Then there's IndexedDB spec that doesn't mention limitations (on the other, other side of the fence?), but it appears as Chrome has a limit of 5 MB. It's unclear what the limits are in Firefox and IE10. I am sure that as this specification gets better support in the browsers, these limits will be well documented.

All data is tied to document *origins* which is made up of the protocol, plus host, plus port number (which defaults to port 80)—which means that data on **http://remysharp.com** cannot access data on the secure version on **https://remysharp.com**.

In either case, the browser will throw an exception error if the API isn't able to write the data, but I'll focus on smaller applications where the data stored is around the 100 KB mark.

Web Storage

> **NOTE** When I'm referring to windows having access, I'm referring to the window object. This is usually bound to a particular origin (protocol + host + port) and applies to browser windows and tabs. Just in case you were confused!

In a nutshell, the Web Storage API is cookies on steroids (but do refer to my caveat previously if this upsets you). One key advantage of this API is that it differentiates between session data and long-term data. If you set a "session" cookie (that is, one without expiry data), that data item is available in all windows that have access to that domain until the browser is shut down. Web Storage, on the other hand, allows you to define a `sessionStorage` that really only refers to the particular window/tab the user is currently in. Once it's closed, the data disappears, rather than sticking around until the entire browser is closed.

The storage API offers two types of storage: `sessionStorage` and `localStorage`.

> **NOTE** Cookies on steroids versus regular cookies: IE6 supports only 20 cookies per domain and a maximum size of 4 KB per cookie. Web Storage has no maximum number of items that can be stored per domain, and it limits the aggregate size to upwards of 5 MB.

If you create data in `sessionStorage`, it's available only to that window until the window is closed (when the session has ended). If you opened another window on the same domain, it wouldn't have access to that session data. This is useful to avoid having data from a session "leak" across different windows.

`localStorage` data is tied to a particular origin and spans all windows that are open on that domain. If you set some data on local storage it immediately becomes available on any other window on the same domain. It also remains available until it's explicitly deleted either by the web application or by the user. Otherwise, you can close your browser, reboot your machine, come back to it days later, and the data will still be there. Here you have persistent data without the hassle of cookies, which require you to reset the expiry again and again.

What makes Web Storage much, much better than cookies is not only the API but also the event system that comes with it. I'll talk about events toward the end of this section.

Watch out for Firefox cookie security

Firefox implements slightly different security around access to session and local storage: If cookies are disabled, accessing `sessionStorage` or `localStorage` will throw a security error. For this reason, your application should check whether it's able to set cookies before trying to access either of these two storage APIs.

```
var cookiesEnabled = (function () {
  // the id is our test value
  var id = new Date().getTime();

  // generate a cookie to probe cookie access
  document.cookie = '__cookieprobe=' + id + ';path=/';

  // if the cookie has been set, then we're good
  return (document.cookie.indexOf(id) !== -1);
})();
```

This code tries to set a cookie and then immediately read it back again. If it fails to read the cookie, it means that security is blocking you from writing and therefore you can't access the `sessionStorage` or `localStorage`. If cookies aren't enabled, the implications are that reading from `sessionStorage` or `localStorage` will cause a security warning and break your script.

Alternatively, you could just check for Web Storage support with a try/catch and polyfill support (as explained in Chapter 12 and somewhat later in this chapter) using JavaScript.

The 15-second tutorial

I'm so confident that you'll understand how to use `localStorage` immediately that I've included code below, even before I've explained how it all works, and I'm certain you'll grok the basics of Web Storage straightaway!

```
localStorage.superHero = "Remy";
localStorage.superVillain = "Bruce";
// some super hero fight occurs
delete localStorage.superVillain;
// the page is reload, browser restarted - we don't care -
¬ we're superheroes!
alert("The world's baddest badass is: " +
¬ localStorage.superHero);
```

Yep, it's *that* simple. If you shut down your browser, reboot your machine, and go back to the same domain where this data was set, it would all still be there. You could alert out the `localStorage.superHero` value and it would give you, of course, *Remy*!

An overview of the API

Since both `sessionStorage` and `localStorage` descend from the Web Storage API, they have the exact same API (from the specification):

```
readonly attribute unsigned long length;
getter DOMString key(in unsigned long index);
getter DOMString getItem(in DOMString key);
setter creator void setItem(in DOMString key, in any data);
deleter void removeItem(in DOMString key);
void clear();
```

This API makes setting and getting data very easy. The `setItem` method simply takes a key and a value. The `getItem` method takes the key of the data you want and returns the content, as shown here:

```
sessionStorage.setItem('twitter', '@rem');
alert( sessionStorage.getItem('twitter') ); // shows @rem
```

It's worth making very clear that the `getItem` method only supports strings. This is important because it means if you try to store an object, it actually returns "[Object object]." More importantly, this means numbers being stored are actually being returned as strings, which can cause errors in development.

To highlight the possible problems, here's an example: Let's say that Bruce runs a website selling videos of himself parading as a professor of science. You've added a few of these videos to your shopping basket because you're keen to learn more about "synergies." The total cost of your shopping basket is $12, and this cost is stored in `sessionStorage`. When you come to the checkout page, Bruce has to add $5 in shipping costs. At an earlier point during your application, $12 was stored in sessionStorage. This is what your (contrived) code would look like:

```
sessionStorage.setItem('cost', 12);

// once shipping is added, Bruce's site tells you the
¬total cost:
function costWithShipping(shipping) {
 alert(sessionStorage.getItem('cost') + shipping);
}

// then it shows you the cost of the basket plus shipping:
costWithShipping(5);
```

If sessionStorage had stored the value as a number, you would see an alert box showing 17. Instead, the cost of $12 was saved as a string. Because JavaScript uses the same method for concatenation as it does for addition (for example, the plus symbol), JavaScript sees this as *appending* a number to a string—so the alert box actually shows 125—much more than you'd probably be willing to pay to watch any video of Bruce! What's going on here is *type coercion*: upon storing the data in the storage API, the data type is coerced into a string.

Finally, it's worth noting that if the key doesn't exist when you call getItem, the storage API will return null. If you're planning to use the storage API to initialise values, which is quite possible, test for null before proceeding because it can throw a pretty nasty spanner in the works if you try to treat null as any other type of object.

Ways to access storage

You're probably thinking, "Hang on a minute, Remy showed me how to grok web storage in 15 seconds, but how does all this *getItem*, *setItem* stuff relate?" I'm glad you're paying attention. If you look back at the API, you'll see that getItem, setItem, and removeItem are a getter, setter, and deleter, respectively. This means that when we call delete localStorage.superVillain, JavaScript is making a call to removeItem for us. Of course, if you spotted that already, good for you. Pat yourself on the back.

An *expando* is a short and expressive way of getting, setting, and deleting data out of the storage object, and as both sessionStorage and localStorage descend from the Web Storage API, they both support this method of accessing the data.

Using our example of storing a Twitter screen name, we can do the same thing using expandos:

```
sessionStorage.twitter = '@rem';
alert( sessionStorage.twitter ); // shows @rem
```

Remember the expando method of storing values is also subject to the "stringifying" of values as we saw in the previous example, with Bruce's video website, because it's going via the setter method of setItem.

Using the key method

The API also provides the key method, which takes an index parameter and returns the associated key. This method is useful to enumerate the data stored in the storage object. For example, if you wanted to show all the keys and associated data, you wouldn't particularly know what the keys were for each of the data items, so loop through the length of the storage object and use the key method to find out:

```
for (var i = 0; i < sessionStorage.length; i++) {
  alert( sessionStorage.key(i) + '=' +
  ¬ sessionStorage.getItem( sessionStorage.key(i) ) );
}
```

Another word of warning: It's conceivable that you might be storing some value under the name of "key," so you might write some code like the following:

```
sessionStorage.setItem('key',
¬ '27152949302e3bd0d681a6f0548912b9');
```

Now there's a value stored against the name "key," and we already had a method called key on the storage object. Alarm bells are ringing, right?

Some browsers, WebKit specifically, overwrite the key method with your new value. The knock-on effect is the developer tools in WebKit make use of the key method to enumerate and display all the data associated with the storage object—so the "Storage" view for that storage type (sessionStorage, in our example) will now be broken until that value has been removed.

Other browsers such as Firefox will keep the key method and your key value stored separately. Using the expando syntax will give you the method, and using getItem('key') will give you the value.

NOTE I expect that as the browsers continue to develop, this kind of bug will be crushed—but in the meantime, do your very best to avoid using names that already exist on the storage API.

Removing data

There are three ways to remove data from the storage object programmatically: directly using the deleter, removeItem, and clear. The removeItem method takes a key, the same key used in setItem and getItem, and deletes the entry for that particular item.

Using clear removes all entries, clearing the entire storage object. For example

```
sessionStorage.setItem('remy', "Master of the Universe");
sessionStorage.setItem('bruce', "Master of the Puniverse");
alert( sessionStorage.length ); // shows 2
sessionStorage.removeItem('bruce');
alert( sessionStorage.length ); // show 1
sessionStorage.clear();
alert( sessionStorage.length ); // shows 0
```

Storing more than strings

NOTE JSON (JavaScript Object Notation) is a text based open standard for representing data. The specification found at http://json.org is so simple it actually fits on the back of a business card!

You can work around the stringifying of objects by making use of JSON. Since JSON uses text to represent a serialised JavaScript object, we can use this to store objects and convert stored data back into objects. However, it would require putting a wrapper on the set and get methods, which (depending on your application) may not be a problem at all.

All the latest browsers (either nightly or final releases) support native JSON encoding using the JSON.parse and JSON.stringify methods. For those browsers that don't have JSON support, we can include Douglas Crockford's JSON library (available at **https://github.com/douglascrockford/JSON-js**).

Now you can convert your data storage and retrieval with JSON as follows:

```
var videoDetails = {
  author: 'bruce',
  description: 'how to leverage synergies',
  rating: '-2'
};

sessionStorage.setItem('videoDetails', JSON.
stringify(videoDetails) );

// later on, as in page reloads later, we can extract the
¬ stored data
var videoDetails = JSON.parse(sessionStorage.getItem
¬ ('videoDetails'));
```

As I mentioned in the API overview section, if the key doesn't exist in the storage object, then it will return null. This isn't a problem for the native JSON parsers as `JSON.parse(null)` returns null—as you would expect. However, for Douglas Crockford's JavaScript version, passing null will throw an error. So if you know it's possible that Crockford's JSON JavaScript library is being loaded, protect against this error by using the following:

```
var videoDetails = JSON.parse(sessionStorage.getItem
¬('videoDetails') || 'null');
```

This ensures that if null is returned from the getItem method, you pass in a JSON-encoded version of null, and thus the JavaScript based JSON parser won't break.

Using debugging tools

Although there's good support for the Web Storage API, the debuggers are still maturing. So aside from inspecting the `sessionStorage` or the `localStorage` there are just a few tools available. Often from the debugging tools, you can modify keys and values and delete entries.

> **NOTE** To enable the Developer menu in Safari, go to Preferences and from the Advanced tab, check the Show Developer Menu in the Menu Bar box. Chrome's debugger is available from the "spanner," Tools menu, and Developer Tools.

WEBKIT'S DEVELOPER TOOLS

While I refer to WebKit, in this section I'm covering Safari, the nightly build of Safari (WebKit) and Google Chrome. Web-Kit's developer tools allows us to view the `localStorage` and `sessionStorage` values stored as shown in **Figure 6.1**.

FIGURE 6.1 Chrome's storage debugger (Safari has very nearly the same interface).

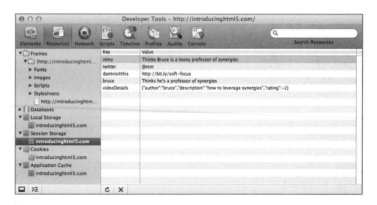

FIREFOX'S DEBUGGER

FIGURE 6.2 Firefox's built in debugger.

Using Firefox's native JavaScript console you can easily inspect the storage objects. If you enter "sessionStorage" or "localStorage" in the console command and execute the code, the storage object can now be clicked on and its details can be seen (**Figure 6.2**).

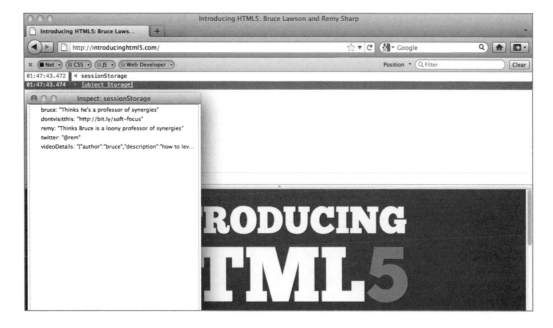

OPERA DRAGONFLY

Dragonfly comes shipped with Opera, and from the Storage tab you can access all the data stored in association with the current page. In particular, there are separate tabs for Local Storage and Session Storage to inspect all the data linked with those data stores (**Figure 6.3**).

FIGURE 6.3 Opera Dragonfly debugger to inspect storage.

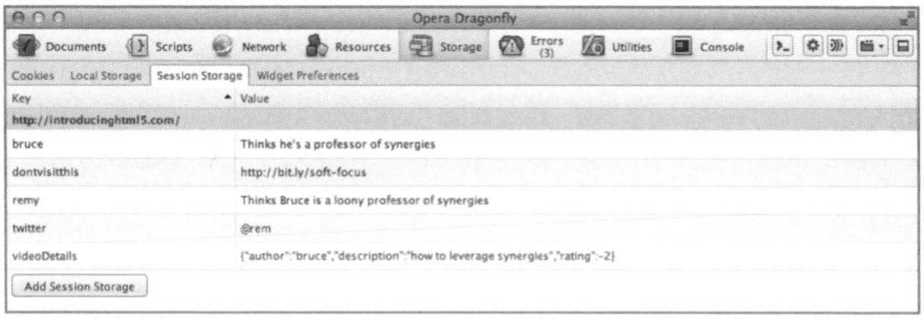

Storage Events

What makes Web Storage particularly unique is that it also comes with events that notify you of updates to the data store.

The first thing to know is that the storage event doesn't fire on the window storing the actual data. It will only fire on the *other* windows whose storage is affected.

This means that storage events only fire for `sessionStorage` on iframes on the same origin and windows that have been opened using the pop-up technique of `window.open()`, as these all share the same session. Storage events for `localStorage` fire on all windows open on the same origin, and we'll see an example of how that could be useful.

When the event fires, it also contains all the information about the data change as you can see from the storage event object below:

```
StorageEvent {
  readonly DOMString key;
  readonly any oldValue;
  readonly any newValue;
  readonly DOMString url;
  readonly Storage storageArea;
};
```

Remember that although the specification *says* it supports "any" value, it doesn't. All the browsers (currently) coerce these values to strings, so you can be sure the `oldValue` and `newValue` will be strings!

The `storageArea` points to either `localStorage` or `sessionStorage`, obviously depending on where the data was stored.

Syncing windows using storage events

Let's say we're building a radio station's website and the station had a pop-up player for the radio—but this pop-up only shows me the current song and some controls. I'm able to select music from the main window the pop-up came from (or perhaps any other window that's on this radio website, as we'll see shortly). I'm sure you've used these before when you want to listen to live music, and it's a decent way to keep the player window open the whole time.

> **NOTE** If you're young and not British there's a good chance you've never heard of Smashie and Nicey—feel free to go looking for them on YouTube!

Now we return to the website, and whilst browsing, we decide that we'd rather listen to Katy Perry and put a swift end to the live radio stream from Smashie and Nicey. But herein lies the problem: We've hit Play in the main window, but the pop-up doesn't now reflect that we're listening to "I Kissed a Girl." Storage events will save this particular website.

We can also use the storage API to work out whether the pop-up player is open already and avoid playing an audio stream more than once. (You'd not want Katy Perry competing with Smashie and Nicey at the same time—heavens no.)

From our main website, we can use the following code to track the state of the pop-up and in the pop-up code (which will follow), we listen for the event to say a new song has been selected, and we update the display.

```
function popupPlayer() {
  if (!localStorage.playerOpen) {
    // coerced to "true" but when it closes,
    // we'll remove the value.
    localStorage.playerOpen = true;

    // open popup
  }
}

function play(song) {
  localStorage.currentlyPlaying = song.title;
  // goes off and plays song in some quasi DRM,
  ¬ streaming way
}

function stop() {
  // when the song stops, or the user stops the song
  ¬ manually,
  // we want the popup player to update too
  localStorage.removeItem('currentPlaying');
}
```

Now in the pop-up, along with the code that plays the audio stream, we need to listen for the storage event that tells us the currentPlaying value has changed, and then we can start that funky new song:

```
function handleStorage(event) {
  event = event || window.event; // support IE8
  if (event.newValue === null) { // it was removed
    stopPlaying();
  } else {
    // start playing and update display
    startPlaying(event.newValue);
  }
}
```

```
window.addEventListener('storage', handleStorage, false);
window.attachEvent('storage', handleStorage);
```

Obviously there are more uses than radio, but the potential of storage events is the ability for completely separate windows on your domain to speak to each other, something that in the past would have been very fiddly indeed.

Fallback options

As the storage API is relatively simple, it's possible to replicate its functionality using alternative JavaScript methods, which could be useful if the storage API is unavailable.

> **NOTE** If you want to find out about polyfills, head over to Chapter 12; we'll wait here until you're done.

For localStorage, you could use cookies, or for better support you could use the browser specific userData methods or even a Flash object. For sessionStorage, you can use a *polyfill* that makes use of the name property on the window object. The following listing shows how you could replicate most of sessionStorage's functionality (and ensure the data remains locked to the current window, rather than leaking as cookies would) by manually implementing each of the Storage API methods. Note that the following code expects that you have JSON support in the browser, either natively or by loading Douglas Crockford's library.

```
if (typeof sessionStorage === 'undefined') {
  sessionStorage = (function () {
    var data = window.top.name ? JSON.parse(window.top..
    ¬name) : {};

    return {
      clear: function () {
        data = {};
        window.top.name = '';
      },
```

```
getItem: function (key) {
  return data[key] || null;
},
key: function (i) {
  // not perfect, but works
  var ctr = 0;
  for (var k in data) {
    if (ctr == i) return k
    else ctr++;
  }
},
removeItem: function (key) {
  delete data[key];
  window.top.name = JSON.stringify(data);
},
setItem: function (key, value) {
  data[key] = value+''; // forces the value to a
  ¬ string
  window.top.name = JSON.stringify(data);
}
};
})();
}
```

The problem with implementing sessionStorage manually (as shown in the previous code listing) is that we don't have the setters and getters (or rather IE7 and below doesn't support setters and getters and those are really the only widely deployed old browsers that lack native sessionStorage). This means you couldn't write sessionStorage.twitter = '@rem'. Although technically, the code would work, it wouldn't be registered in our storage object properly and sessionStorage.getItem('twitter') wouldn't yield a result. You could get around that particular problem, but most importantly, refreshing the browser would lose the data.

With this in mind, and depending on what browsers you are targeting (that is, whether you would need to provide a manual fallback to storage), you may want to agree with yourself for safety as to when you should stick to using the setItem and getItem methods.

Web SQL Database

Web SQL Database is another way to store and access data. As the name implies, this is a real database that you are able to query and join results. If you're familiar with SQL, then you should take like a duck to water with the database API. That said, if you're not familiar with SQL, and SQLite in particular, I'm not going to teach it in this chapter: There are bigger and uglier books that can do that, and the SQLite website (**http://sqlite.org**) is a good starting point.

The specification is a little bit grey around the size limits of these databases. When you create a new database, you, the author, get to suggest its estimated maximum size. So you could *estimate* 2 MB or you could estimate 20 MB. If you try to create a database larger than the default storage size in Safari, it prompts the user to allow the database to go over the default database size. Both Opera and Chrome simply allow the database to be created, regardless of the size. I strongly suggest that you err on the side of caution with database sizes; as I said earlier, browsers limit databases to 5 MB per domain by default. Now that you're suitably worried about SQL and database sizes, one really neat feature of the Web SQL Database API is that all the methods allow you to pass a callback that will be executed once the fandango SQL magic has completed. Callbacks are a common trait of JavaScript libraries such as jQuery. If you're not familiar with this syntax, it looks something like this (but don't worry, I'll hold your hand throughout the examples later on):

```
transaction.executeSql(sql, [], function () {
  // my executed code lives here
});
```

Due to the nature of the callback system, it also means that the database API is *asynchronous*, so you need to be careful when authoring the JavaScript to deal with the database to ensure that the sequence of events runs correctly. However, the SQL statements are queued and run in order in which they were queued, so this is one slight advantage you have over processing order: you can create tables and know that the table will be in place before you run queries on the tables.

Put plainly, if you want your code to run after the database interaction has completed, use the callback. If you don't need to wait, and you want your code to continue regardless, continue after the database API call.

Be wary of versioning!

The implementations of Web SQL Database support a slightly older version of the Web SQL Database API, and more specifically the versioning model.

Although the specification describes how you can manage and migrate from different versions of the database, this hasn't been implemented very well. The model requires you to know the version of the database on the user's machine to be able to open it. The problem is that if you have migrated through multiple versions of your database, there's no way to determine which version the visiting user is on, and opening the database with the wrong version number throws an `INVALID_STATE_ERROR`. You could wrap each of the open database attempts in a try/catch, but you'd require one for each version of your database, something that could get very messy after a few years of upgrades.

Using the Web SQL Database API

The typical database API usage involves opening the database and then executing some SQL. Note that if I were working with a database on the server side, I would typically close the database connection. This isn't required with the database API, and in fact there's no way to do this. That said, you *can* open a database multiple times without any adverse effect.

Opening and creating databases

By opening a database for the first time, the database is created. You can have only one version of your named database on the domain at any one time, so if you create version 1.0 you can't then open 1.1 without the database version having been specifically changed by your application. For the rest of this chapter, I'm going to ignore versioning and stick to one version only due to the previously stated warning.

```
var db = openDatabase('mydb', '1.0', 'My first database',
¬ 2 * 1024 * 1024);
```

The latest version of the SQL databases spec includes a fifth argument to openDatabase, but this isn't supported in any of the browsers right now. It offers a callback when the database is created for the first time. You've now created a new database called "mydb," version 1.0, with a text description of "My first database," and you've set the size of the data to 2 MB (this has to be set in bytes which is why I multiply 2 * 1024 * 1024). To ensure that the app works and detects support for the Web SQL Database API, you should also test for database support in the browser, so wrap the code with the openDatabase test:

```
var db;
if (window.openDatabase) {
  db = openDatabase('mydb', '1.0', 'My first database',
  ¬ 2 * 1024 * 1024);
}
```

It's as simple as that. Next you need to set up a new table in the database, which—like all other operations we'll be doing on this database—is done through the executeSql method.

Creating tables

When creating tables (or performing any other action on the database), you must start a database "transaction" and, within the callback, execute the relevant SQL. The transaction call-back receives an argument containing the transaction object, which allows you to run SQL statements and run the executeSql method (tx in the following example). This is done using the database object that was returned from openDatabase and by calling the transaction method:

```
var db;
if (window.openDatabase) {
  db = openDatabase('tweetdb', '1.0', 'All my tweets',
  ¬ 2 * 1024 * 1024);
  db.transaction(function (tx) {
    tx.executeSql('CREATE TABLE tweets (id, date, tweet)');
  });
}
```

The executeSql method takes four arguments, of which only the first is required:

1. SQL

2. Arguments to SQL (such as field values)

3. Success callback

4. Error callback

In the previous example, you use only the SQL parameter. Of course, if the statement to create a table runs and the table already exists, an error is triggered, but since you're not catch-ing it and it doesn't affect the program flow, in this instance you don't care.

However, the next step of this application is to load the database with tweets from Twitter, and as this has to happen once the table is in place (because of the asynchronous nature of the Web SQL Database API), you'll have to get the tweets in the "success" callback. Here's where we run into a problem: If the table exists, the transaction will fail and won't trigger the success callback. The code will run fine the first time around, but not the second. So to get around this, you'll say to create the table only if the table doesn't exist; this way the success callback fires if the table is created and if the table already exists, and the error callback is only called if there's some other problem.

```
var db;
if (window.openDatabase) {
  db = openDatabase('tweetdb', '1.0', 'All my tweets',
  ¬ 2 * 1024 * 1024);
  db.transaction(function (tx) {
    tx.executeSql('CREATE TABLE IF NOT EXISTS tweets
    ¬ (id, date, tweet)', [], function () {
      // now go and load the table up with tweets
    });
  });
}
```

Inserting and querying

Now let's say you hit Twitter for a search query for all the mentions of HTML5, you store all those tweets in your database, and then you allow the user to select the time range of tweets from the past 5 minutes, 30 minutes, 2 hours, and then all time. The time range selection will be radio buttons with click handlers, and you'll run your query to show only the tweets from that time range.

The crux of this application is split between storing the tweets in your database and showing the tweets depending on the time range.

Before any of your code runs, you must first create the database and tweets table, which will include a date column whose type is integer—which is important, as it will allow you to query the database later on in your application:

```
function setupDatabase() {
  db = openDatabase('tweets', '1.0', 'db of tweets',
  ¬ 2 * 1024 * 1024);
  db.transaction(function (tx) {
    tx.executeSql('CREATE TABLE tweets (id unique,
    ¬ screen_name, date integer, text)');
  });
  getTweets();
}
```

A few things to note about the code are

1. I'm using a global db variable. (I'm just using a global for the contrived example; global is generally bad in JavaScript.)

2. I'm telling the tweets database that the id column is unique. This means if there's a duplicate INSERT attempt, the INSERT fails.

3. If the CREATE TABLE fails, it's fine because it will fail only when the table already exists, and you're not doing anything else in that transaction.

4. Once it's done, I call getTweets, which will make the API request to Twitter, which will in turn call the storing function.

What if getTweets runs before the table gets created? It doesn't matter. That's because when we get the tweets, a new transaction is created that inserts the new SQL. Since transactions run in the order they were sent to the database, even if the create table hasn't actually run when we're creating transactions to insert new rows, we know that it's queued *ahead* of the new rows and will be there all in good time.

> **NOTE** You're creating a new transaction for each stored tweet. I'll explain transactions in more detail in the next section, but by wrapping individual **INSERT** statements you're ensuring that all the new tweets are stored, irrespective of whether you already have these in the database.

The forEach in the following code is a new JavaScript method available in all the latest browsers, allowing you to loop through an array. Mozilla's site provides simple code for implementing this in browsers that don't have it natively: **https://developer. mozilla.org/en/Core_JavaScript_1.5_Reference/Global_Objects/ Array/forEach**. Once the Twitter API call completes, it will call saveTweets, which will store each of the tweets:

```
function saveTweets(tweets) {
  tweets.results.forEach(function (tweet) {
    db.transaction(function (tx) {
      var time = (new Date(Date.parse(tweet.created_at))).
      ¬ getTime();
      tx.executeSql('INSERT INTO tweets (id, screen_name,
      ¬ date, text) VALUES (?, ?, ?, ?)', [tweet.id,
      ¬ tweet.from_user, time / 1000, tweet.text]);
```

```
                // div 1000 to get to seconds
            });
        });
    }
```

The INSERT statement is the most important part, and now you can see how the field arguments work:

```
tx.executeSql('INSERT INTO tweets (id, screen_name, date,
¬ text) VALUES (?, ?, ?, ?)', [tweet.id, tweet.from_user,
¬ time / 1000, tweet.text]);
```

Each "?" in the INSERT statement maps to an item in the array that is passed in as the second parameter to executeSql. So the first "?" maps to tweet.id, the second to tweet.from_user, and so on.

You can also see that I've divided the time by 1,000; this is because JavaScript time is counted in milliseconds, whereas SQLite wants it to be in whole seconds. This is only important for your query later on in the code where you show tweets that are 5 minutes old. This matters because you're storing dates as integers, and one second using JavaScript's getTime method gives us 1,000, whereas one second using SQLite gives us 1. So you divide by 1,000 to store seconds rather than milliseconds.

Finally, when the radio buttons are clicked, you call the show function with the amount of time as the argument:

```
var tweetEl = document.getElementById('tweets');
function show(amount) {
    db.transaction(function (tx) {
        tx.executeSql('SELECT * FROM tweets' + (amount !=
        ¬ 'all' ? ' WHERE date > strftime("%s", "now", "-' +
        ¬ amount + ' minutes")' : ''), [], function
        ¬ (tx, results) {
            var html = [],
                len = results.rows.length;

            for (var i = 0; i < len; i++) {
                html.push('<li>' + results.rows.item(i).text +
                ¬ '</li>');
            }
            tweetEl.innerHTML = html.join('');
        });
    });
}
```

This code may initially look complicated, but there are actually only a couple of things happening here:

1. Start a new transaction.

2. Run a single SQL statement, whose structure is determined by whether you want "all" or not.

Loop through the results constructing the HTML, and then set it to the tweetEl (a <ul> element) innerHTML.

There are two states the SQL query can be:

```
SELECT * FROM tweets
```

or

```
SELECT * FROM tweets WHERE date > strftime("%s", "now",
¬ "-5 minutes")
```

Where I've put -5 minutes, this can change to -30 minutes or any number that's passed in to the show function. The strftime SQLite function is generating the number of seconds from 1-Jan-1970 until "now" minus *N* minutes. Since the "date" field is being stored as an integer, you can now grab all the rows that were tweeted within the last *N* minutes.

Now you've used the third argument to the executeSql method, the success callback. The success callback receives a transaction object (just as the transaction callback does, so you could run another executeSql if you wanted), and more importantly, the result set. The result set contains three attributes:

- insertId (set only if you've inserted one or more rows)— I didn't use this in this example.

- rowsAffected—Since this is a SELECT statement, this value is 0.

- rows—This *isn't* an array, it's a collection, that *does* contain a length and item getter method. You make use of the rows object, and run a for loop from 0 to the length of the rows, and use results.rows.item(i) to get the individual rows. The individual row is an object representing the different column names, so results.rows.item(0).screen_name gives us the screen_name field from the first row.

Finally, once you have looped through all the rows that match, you can set a <ul> element to the HTML you've built up. In this example, the <ul> is stored in the variable called tweetEl.

Here is the complete code including the database support detection and the click handler code for the radio buttons:

```html
<!DOCTYPE html>
<html lang="en">
<head>
<meta charset=utf-8 />
<title>HTML5 tweet time range</title>
<style>
  body { font-family: helvetica, arial;}
</style>
</head>
<body>
  <form>
    <fieldset>
    <legend>Select a time range of recent HTML5 tweets</
    ¬legend>
    <input type="radio" value="5" id="t5m" name="timerange"
    ¬/><label for="t5m">5 minutes</label>
    <input type="radio" value="30" id="t30m" name=
    ¬"timerange" /><label for="t30m">30 minutes</label>
    <input type="radio" value="120" id="t2h" name=
    ¬"timerange" /><label for="t2h">2 hours</label>
    <input type="radio" value="all" id="tall" name=
    ¬"timerange" checked="checked" /><label for="tall">
    ¬all time</label>
    </fieldset>
  </form>
  <ul id="tweets"></ul>
<script>
var tweetEl = document.getElementById('tweets');
var db;

function setupDatabase() {
  if (!window.openDatabase) {
    tweetEl.innerHTML = '<li>Web SQL Database API is not
    ¬available in this browser, please try nightly Opera,
    ¬Webkit or Chrome.</li>';
    return;
  }
  db = openDatabase('tweets', '1.0', 'db of tweets',
  ¬2 * 1024 * 1024);
```

```
  db.transaction(function (tx) {
    tx.executeSql('CREATE TABLE tweets (id unique,
    ¬ screen_name, date integer, text)');
  });
  getTweets();
}

function getTweets() {
  var script = document.createElement('script');
  script.src = 'http://search.twitter.com/search.
  ¬ json?q=html5 -RT&rpp=100&callback=saveTweets';
  document.body.appendChild(script);
}

// our Twitter API callback function
function saveTweets(tweets) {
  tweets.results.forEach(function (tweet) {
    db.transaction(function (tx) {
      var time = (new Date(Date.parse(tweet.created_at))).
      ¬ getTime();
      tx.executeSql('INSERT INTO tweets (id, screen_name,
      ¬ date, text) VALUES (?, ?, ?, ?)', [tweet.id,
      ¬ tweet.from_user, time / 1000, tweet.text]);
      ¬ // divide by 1000 to get to seconds
    });
  });
}


function show(amount) {
  db.transaction(function (tx) {
    tx.executeSql('SELECT * FROM tweets' + (amount !=
    ¬ 'all' ? ' WHERE date > strftime("%s", "now", "-' +
    ¬ amount + ' minutes")' : ''), [], function
    ¬ (tx, results) {
      var html = [],
          len = results.rows.length;

      for (var i = 0; i < len; i++) {
        html.push('<li>' + results.rows.item(i).text +
        ¬ '</li>');
      }
      tweetEl.innerHTML = html.join('');
```

```
    });
  });
}

// bind the click handlers for the radio buttons
[].forEach.call(document.querySelectorAll('input
¬[type=radio]'), function (el) {
  el.onclick = function () {
    show(this.value);
  }
});

// go!
setupDatabase();

</script>
</body>
</html>
```

Creating transactions— and what they're good for

I've skipped over transactions so far. They're more than meets the eye. They're not just the way to run queries; they serve a particularly useful purpose. Transactions are like closed environments in which you can run your queries. You can run just one query or a group of queries within a transaction. In fact, you *can't* run a query *without* being inside a transaction, since the executeSql method is *only* available from the SQLTransaction object.

Possibly the most important aspect of transactions is this: If something fails inside the transaction (vanilla code or SQL statements), then the whole transaction (including any insertion, modifications, or deletions) is rolled back. This means it's as if the whole transaction block of code never happened.

The transaction method takes two arguments. The first is the content of the transaction; the second, optional, is the error handler. Below is a contrived example that shows how a failed transaction gets rolled back:

```
var db = openDatabase('foo', '1.0', 'foo', 1024);
db.transaction(function (tx) {
  tx.executeSql('CREATE TABLE foo (id unique, text)');
```

```
    tx.executeSql('INSERT INTO foo (id, text) VALUES
    ¬ (1, "foobar")');
  });

  db.transaction(function (tx) {
    tx.executeSql('DROP TABLE foo');

    // known to fail - so should rollback the DROP statement
    tx.executeSql('INSERT INTO foo (id, text) VALUES
    ¬ (1, "foobar")');
  }, function (error) {
    // error.message is "no such table: foo"
    alert('Rollback triggered, the table "foo" was never
    ¬ dropped due to: ' + error.message);
  });

  db.transaction(function (tx) {
    tx.executeSql('SELECT * FROM foo', [], function (tx,
    ¬ results) {
      alert('found ' + results.rows.length + ' row');
    }, function (tx, error) {
      // this will never execute
      alert('something went wrong: ' + error.message);
    });
  });
```

The steps in the previous code are:

1. Start a transaction that creates the table foo and then inserts a single row.

2. Start a transaction that drops the table foo and then incorrectly tries to insert a new row in foo.

3. The transaction fails, and rolls back the statements (that is, it's as if Step 2 never happened).

4. Start a transaction that selects all the rows from foo and alerts the number of rows.

5. The SQL query succeeds and shows "found 1 row."

Transactions are used to ensure that an atomic block of queries executes and that if any part fails, it rolls back.

IndexedDB

IndexedDB was being talked about when the first edition of this book was published, but there were no implementations at the time. Today there are only vendor-prefixed implementations at this point, but I suspect it won't be long before most, if not all, browsers support IndexedDB.

IndexedDB is a document object store. It's like a database, but it doesn't come with all SQL and relational database gubbins.

In IndexedDB, you create a new database and give it a name and a version so you can reopen it later. Then you create an object store, which is very much like a filing cabinet with indices that allow you to quickly skim through and find the right document. Once the store is ready, you can store any kind of object against the index you're filing with. It doesn't matter what it contains, and it doesn't have to have the same properties as the other objects either. This is where SQL often becomes a problem. You have a huge table, you need to add one teeny, inconspicuous new column, and so begins the pain. You have none of those woes with IndexedDB.

Using IndexedDB before it's out of beta

IndexedDB may still be in the vendor-prefix stage by the time you read this chapter.

If that's the case, you can still use IndexedDB, but you will need to either create forks in your code to handle the different naming convention, or just copy the vendor-prefixed version into the *real* name:

```
function importIndexedDB(prefix) {
  var indexedDB = window[prefix + 'IndexedDB'],
      IDBTransaction = window[prefix + 'IDBTransaction'];

  if (indexedDB !== undefined) {
    window.indexedDB = indexedDB;
  }
  if (IDBTransaction !== undefined) {
    window.IDBTransaction = IDBTransaction;
  }
}

// try all the vendor prefixes
'moz webkit o ms'.split(' ').forEach(function (vendor) {
  importIndexedDB(vendor);
});
```

Creating new IndexedDBs

To kick things off you need to open a new indexed database. You'll use the return value to create object stores and handle any errors, similar to Web SQL Database where you receive a database object and then open the database.

However, with IndexedDB every process is a *request*. As with Web SQL Database, all communication is asynchronous. It's common to see the return value called request, so that's what we'll use:

```
var request = indexedDB.open('videos');

request.onerror = function () {
  console.log('failed to open indexedDB');
};

request.onsuccess = function (event) {
  // handle version control
  // then create a new object store
};
```

Now that the database is open, assuming there wasn't an error, the onsuccess event will fire. Before we can create the new object store we need to begin by doing two things:

• Store the actual database handle, so we can perform transactions to get and store data.

• Set the version on the database; if there's no version, it means the database has just been created for the first time (and a version will need to be set as we'll see in the following examples).

The success event handler passes along an event object much like the event object you'd receive if you were listening for a click event. Inside this event we find a property called target, and inside of that is the result. The result contains—as I hope you've guessed—the result of the particular function call. In this specific case, the event.target.result contains the open database handle to our "video" database.

So the onsuccess handler is updated as such:

```
var db = null;

request.onsuccess = function (event) {
  // cache a copy of the database handle for the future
  db = event.target.result;
```

```
    // handle version control
    // then create a new object store
};

request.onerror = function (event) {
    alert('Something failed: ' + event.target.message);
};
```

Notice the error handler. In IndexedDB, errors bubble up from the request up to transaction and up to the database itself. This means that if an error occurs at any point during any kind of request, you'll see this alert box. But remember: Alert boxes are ugly and are not friends with the browser—particularly when in production; they make the salesmen angry. Make sure you change the alert box to something like a beautiful, rounded-corners message that gracefully handles the error. Now, on to initialising the database.

Version control

The first thing we do once we've opened the database connection is to handle version control. You can use any string as your version number, but if you use some logic in how you increment your versions it might save you a bit of trouble in the future. Let's call this application version "0.1." If we make an upgrade, we can compare "0.1" (the string), which will be the database version, against "0.2" which would be our upgraded code. Since this is the first time any of our code has run, and therefore we've even tried to open a new database, let's check the version and if it doesn't match, set the version and create the object stores. I should add that this isn't version control like something like SVN or Git—if you want to change the number of object stores in the database, you need to request a version change.

```
var db = null,
    version = '0.1';

request.onsuccess = function (event) {
    // cache a copy of the database handle for the future
    db = event.target.result;

    // handle version control
    if (version != db.version) {
        // set the version to 0.1
        var verRequest = db.setVersion(version);
```

```
    verRequest.onsuccess = function (event) {
      // now we're ready to create the object store!
    };
    verRequest.onerror = function () {
      console.log('unable to set the version :(');
    };
  }
};
```

Once the success event fires we can create our new object stores using the setVersion method.

Creating object stores

Inside the version control success event handler, create new object stores as follows:

```
var verRequest = db.setVersion(version);
verRequest.onsuccess = function (event) {
  var store = db.createObjectStore('blockbusters', {
    keyPath: 'title',
    autoIncrement: false
  });
  // at this point we would notify our code
  // that the object store is ready
};
```

For this application we've created a single object store, but in our next version we might choose to add an object store for directors of the movies in our video database. What's important in the createObjectStore method is the options argument we passed. This tells the object store that there should be an index (used to retrieve the blockbuster movie) and that its ID should not automatically increment; in fact, the autoIncrement flag is false by default; I've included it simply to show you how it could be used.

When it comes to storing new objects now, I must ensure the video has a unique title property, which will be indexed by IndexedDB for fast retrieval later.

Perhaps we're going to store the director name in the blockbuster video data, and not in a separate object store. In addition, I want to be able to search by director, so we add another index to our datastore:

```
store.createIndex('director', 'director', { unique: false });
```

With this we have now given the index a name (the first argument), and then the name of the property (in our case, 'director') we want indexed when new objects are stored. Finally, we'll allow more than one film by the same director by indicating that we don't expect the values to be unique.

This all means I can store and easily retrieve a blockbuster entry looking like this:

```
{
 title: "Belly Dance Bruce - Final Strike",
 date: (new Date).getTime(), // released TODAY!
 director: "Bruce Awesome",
 length: 169, // in minutes
 rating: 10,
 cover: "/images/wobble.jpg"
}
```

So let's add some videos to our blockbuster collection.

Adding and putting objects in stores

Okay, "adding and putting." No doubt you're thinking: ambiguous! There are two methods for inserting data: add and put. The first adds *new* data and requires that the data not exist in the first place. The second puts an *updated* object in the store, and if the object isn't already stored, it will insert it as new.

For the purpose of our video store database, we're going to throw caution to the wind, and just use put. If you're not feeling as callous as I am, and there's a risk of duplicate objects (if, say, the title was the same but another field was different, it would leave us with two objects when we're only expecting one for each title), be sure you use add and put with appropriate validation and checks.

```
var video = {
   title: "Belly Dance Bruce - Final Strike",
   date: (new Date).getTime(),
   director: "Bruce Awesome",
   length: 169,
   rating: 10,
   cover: "/images/wobble.jpg" },
 READ_WRITE = IDBTransaction.READ_WRITE

var transaction = db.transaction(['blockbusters'],READ_WRITE),
    store = transaction.objectStore('blockbusters'),
    request = store.put(video);
```

This code is actually doing quite a lot on the last three lines, and if you're like me, you might think there's some unnecessary repetition.

We're performing three separate tasks, outlined below.

1. Create the transaction

```
transaction = db.transaction(['blockbusters'], READ_WRITE)
```

The first task is to create a new transaction with read and write permission to the named object stores. A transaction can be bound to more than one object store, which is why we're passing in an array here. In practice I've found that I could pass null or even an empty string in the object store name argument. I'm not sure that's valid, or if it should really work, but like I said: IndexedDB is new and still in vendor-prefix mode, so it's best to stick to what the spec suggests.

Also, if we were just planning to execute read operations in the transaction, we could use `IDBTransaction.READ_ONLY`.

A day in the short life of a transaction

Transaction objects have a very short lifetime linked to the event loop in a browser. If you create a transaction and don't use it and return to the event loop, the transaction will be dead and unusable.

If, however, you run the request immediately, and if the request is successful, you can choose to place a subsequent request on the transaction and be safe in the knowledge that it will still be alive. You can continue to do this so long as you don't break for the event loop.

If you've ever used a `setTimeout(fn, 0)` in your code, you've released to the event loop—maybe to allow the browser to repaint the page, maybe for something else.

This is a fairly unique concept that I've not seen before, so definitely experiment with the transaction lifetime. Once you've got a good handle on when it's alive and when it's dead, you'll be able to make the transaction last longer than a zombie.

2. Get a reference to the store

```
store = transaction.objectStore('blockbusters')
```

This is where we get a hard fix on the object store we want to work with, and here we have to name the store. This could be any of the stores we listed in our transaction. Now, with our reference to the store, we can perform our actions, like add, put, and even get, which we'll see in a moment.

3. Save the data

```
request = store.put(video)
```

The request variable will receive a success or error event on the object. Maybe I care whether it's been stored, maybe I want my code to continue and let the spotty 15-year-old clerk continue adding the pile of Bruce Awesome videos to our database. That's the nice thing about the *asynchronous-ness* of IndexedDB—I can let my website carry on without being interrupted as the data is stored.

Now that you've stored some data, what about getting it out?

Whipping it out again

If you've followed the process for storing data, the process of getting data back out is very similar and simple.

We still need to create a transaction. Since we're only getting data, we could ask for that transaction to be read-only, but it doesn't matter in this case if we use a read/write permission. We still get the object store, and instead of adding or putting, we *get*:

```
var transaction = db.transaction(['blockbusters'],READ_WRITE),
    store = transaction.objectStore('blockbusters'),
    request = store.get(key);
```

The important part is that the key variable we pass to the get method is compared against the keyPath we defined when the object store was created. In our video example, we said that blockbusters have their key based on the video title.

What if you wanted to get *all* the videos out of the store? Using the get method won't cut it. We need to iterate through the entire data store:

```
var transaction = db.transaction(['blockbusters'],READ_WRITE),
    store = transaction.objectStore('blockbusters'),
    data = [];

var request = store.openCursor();

request.onsuccess = function (event) {
  var cursor = event.target.result;
  if (cursor) {
    // value is the stored object
    data.push(cursor.value);
    // get the next object
    cursor.continue();
  } else {
    // we've got all the data now, call
    // a success callback and pass the
    // data object in.
  }
};
```

In this code block, we're opening up our object store as usual, but instead of executing a *get* we open a *cursor*. This allows us to cycle through each stored object. We could easily use this process to find all the videos with a rating of five or more stars by adding a nested check against cusor.value.rating before pushing the current stored object onto our data array of results.

For example:

```
function find(filter, callback) {
  // READ_WRITE was declared earlier on in our code
  var transaction = db.transaction(['blockbusters'],
  ¬READ_WRITE),
      store = transaction.objectStore('blockbusters'),
      data = [];

  var request = store.openCursor();

  request.onsuccess = function (event) {
    var cursor = event.target.result;
    if (cursor) {
      if (filter(cursor.value) === true) {
```

```
      // value is the stored object
      data.push(cursor.value);
    }
    // get the next object
    cursor.continue();
  } else {
    callback(data);
  }
  };
}

// example usage
find(function (data) {
  return data.rating > 5;
}, function (found) {
  alert('Found ' + found.length + ' videos with a high
  ¬ rating');
});
```

Deleting and dropping data like a hot potato

What if you made a mistake or want to remove data? Maybe you've had complaints about Bruce's latest film, *Banana Smash, Pink Fury*, and you need to delete it.

The process is exactly the same as the get method, except we call the delete method when passing in the key (note that for this, you'll need write permissions too):

```
var transaction = db.transaction(['blockbusters'],READ_WRITE),
    store = transaction.objectStore('blockbusters'),
    request = store.delete(key);
```

There's also a method for clearing an entire object store: clear. The clear method doesn't take any arguments and the process, again, is exactly the same.

There are two more ways of clearing data: deleteObjectStore and deleteDatabase. The method names are fairly self-explanatory, but they're not as simple to use.

deleteObjectStore can only run from a transaction. The method sits on the database object (the result of the indexedDB.open method). However, you can't delete the object store using a regular transaction. You can *only* delete the object store from a set version transaction. Remember earlier on in this section, when I showed you how to create object stores—the `setVersion` success handler is the only time you can both add and remove stores.

Finally, there's `deleteDatabase`. As handy as this would be for debugging, unfortunately it doesn't appear to be implemented in any browsers right now. I expect this will change as the specification matures and isn't vendor-prefixed, but for the time being it does make debugging difficult because it's hard to get back to the reset position.

Deleting an IndexedDB database in Chrome

There are probably ways of doing this in each browser, but I've discovered a way of removing the database, if you're happy poking around in Chrome.

Navigate to ~/Library/Application Support/Google/Chrome/Default/IndexedDB on a Mac and C:\Users\<you>\AppData\Local\Google\Chrome\User Data\Default\IndexedDB\ on Windows 7 (other system paths can be located at **http://goo.gl/v702q**).

Once you're in the IndexedDB directory, you can see databases listed by their domain. If you want to clear that database, make sure Chrome is closed, and just delete that file.

Do so at your own risk though—don't come running to me when your browser blows up all over your machine. That said, it's worked just fine for me so far!

Debugging

Debugging is *hard*. At the time of writing there are two key components missing from IndexedDB:

- **There are no debugging tools.** Web SQL Database and Web Storage both have visual tools in the browser web inspectors (like ChromeDevTools or Opera Dragonfly). There are currently none for IndexedDB, making it quite difficult to debug. It's not impossible—just tricky!

- **There's no way to delete a database.** As only Firefox and Chrome have IndexedDB at this time, and both still have vendor prefixes, I suspect this is only something that needs to be added. Since a necessary step during development is to reset the current state of the application, not being able to delete the database is fairly limiting. You can get around this by manually deleting all the object stores and then resetting the version, but it's really not the same!

However, it's still early days, and as a developer, the simplicity of working with IndexedDB has a much nicer feeling than Web SQL Database—or certainly for this developer it does.

Summary

In this chapter, you learned about three different APIs for storing data locally in the browser that beat the pants off using cookies.

These storage APIs allow you to store a lot more data than the traditional cookie and make the associated programming a lot easier than before. On top of that, the Web Storage API has really good support in all the latest browsers (and older browsers can be supported using JavaScript).

In this humble author's opinion, although Web SQL Database is depreciated, it'll be here for some time—mostly because web giant's like Google use this technology in Gmail *and* they make browsers.

However, IndexedDB is very close to stable implementations and support could well overthrow Web SQL Database altogether. That said, if there's a limit of only 5 MB in IndexedDB and there's no way to increase that—Web Storage has 5 MB too, and it's dirt easy to develop with.

Whichever API you choose, it means you can drop the awful and stale cookies of today!

CHAPTER 7

Offline

Remy Sharp

HOW MANY TIMES have I been working on a train, desperately trying to get a 3G connection with my cheap dongle, and failed to navigate a web application because we went into a tunnel (and thus lost all connectivity)? A lot, that's how many. Computing with no Internet or with a choppy connection has always been common with mobile computing, but now you are more likely to be trying to work in a hosted application. Sometimes, you may simply chose to go offline, what then? As we become more mobile with our computers, being able to use a website outside of reception becomes more and more important.

We're used to creating web apps that rely absolutely on the Web. Our websites run in browsers, which are designed to be a viewport onto the Web. The offline web applications part of the HTML5 spec takes the "web" out of "web app." The browser will manage a local cache so our application will work without an Internet connection.

Pulling the plug: going offline

> **NOTE** In the context of the offline spec, the manifest is a list of files that defines what files should be included for your offline application.

To work offline, an application need only a *manifest* telling the browser what it needs to store in its local cache. The manifest can be as simple as a list of files and you'll be done. Once the browser has stored the cache of assets, CSS, JavaScript, images, and so on, when the page is reloaded the browser uses these local assets to drive the website.

Along with telling the browser what to cache, you can also tell it what *not* to cache, ensuring that requests to that particular URL always go via the Web. Finally, HTML5 gives you a way to manage fallback cases. In the situation where you're currently without a connection and you try to access a resource that isn't in your local (offline) cache, the fallback can be used to serve a *different* resource (which is also cached by the browser). For example, going to the chat part of your application could fall back to a page saying this feature is available only whilst online.

The first part of an offline application is down to the manifest, which tells the browser what to cache (or what not to). The second part is in the `applicationCache`. This object contains methods to trigger updates and to swap the latest cache into the browser. It also has events firing off it that the author can use to notify the user that the application might be upgradable.

What about offline and online events?

Indeed, what about offline events? The HTML5 spec has defined offline events and, in fact, offline events have been in some browsers for quite a number of years now. The spec defines two events that should fire on the document: `online` and `offline`. There's still varying support in browsers today, but that's not the problem. Currently these events only work as you'd expect in mobile devices (and given that there are so many mobile devices, it's fair to say I haven't tested every mobile device). However on the desktop, the situation is very different.

These events only fire when the user—yes, that's right, the *user*—explicitly sets the browser to Work Offline. They don't automatically fire when, for whatever reason, the web connection drops or is reestablished.

To further compound the problem, some browsers (for instance, Chrome and Safari) lack a Work Offline menu item, so these events will never be triggered. Frankly, this is stupid in my book, which is why I wouldn't particularly rely on these events in a production application. One possible alternative is to constantly poll your service to ensure it's up, and I'll show you how you can do this using the manifest in the section below entitled "Using the manifest to detect connectivity."

The cache manifest

The manifest is the thing that tells the browser when and what to get from its offline cache, from the Web, or to fall back onto if assets are missing. Once the manifest is loaded or updated, it triggers an update on the `applicationCache` object. To tell the browser to look for a manifest is simple: You add the `manifest` attribute to the `<html>` element, and point it to the file containing your application's manifest:

```
<!DOCTYPE html>
<html lang="en" manifest="/time.appcache">
<!-- my spiffing time app lives here -->
</html>
```

My example application, in all its glory, will show you the time on your machine and the time on my server. Not quite as complex as a Google Docs application, but enough to demonstrate that, when the connection isn't available, instead of showing the server time—which it can't get—it will show you the working app, but with the server time marked as unavailable. **Figure 7.1** shows the application on first load and when online.

FIGURE 7.1 **Move over, Google Apps: Our application tells us the time!**

My complete application requires

- The application page: `index.html` in this case
- `time.js`: the code to tick the clock forward
- `time.css`: simple styles for my app
- `server-time.js`: in this example, let's say this is generated every minute by my server

Everything, with the exception of the `server-time.js` file, will be stored in the manifest. Finally, in addition, I need a file that will be served up in place of `server-time.js` if we're offline. This will be

- `fallback-server-time.js`: contains a notice about being offline

> **NOTE** With the custom .appcache file extension, you will need to use particular methods to ensure this is served to the browser correctly, as you'll see later in this chapter under "How to serve the manifest."

Here's what the contents of my `time.appcache` look like:

```
CACHE MANIFEST
index.html
time.js
time.css


FALLBACK:
server-time.js fallback-server-time.js


NETWORK:
*


# version 8
```

The format of the file is important. You'll see the first line is `CACHE MANIFEST`. This tells the browser that what follows is the source to a manifest file. Within the manifest, files are listed under categories, also known as namespaces. The default category is `CACHE`, and if it isn't stated, all the filenames encountered are put in that category until the browser hits a new category. So with that in mind, I could have written my file to look like the following—and it would have the exact same effect:

```
CACHE MANIFEST


CACHE:
index.html
time.js
time.css


FALLBACK:
server-time.js fallback-server-time.js


NETWORK:
*


# version 9
```

You can repeat a category, too. To append new files to be included in the cache, include them at the end of the file so the manifest reads: cache, fallback, cache. This is perfectly valid, too.

FALLBACK tells the browser that if anything matches the URL on the left, in my case `server-time.js`, and it's not in the

NOTE The web page that includes the manifest (in the `<html>` tag) is also implicitly included in the cache manifest. For this reason, I recommend explicitly including the file, `index.html` in my case, in the manifest so you don't get confused further along in the development of your project.

manifest and it can't be accessed with the existing connection, then serve up the file specified on the right side, in my case `fallback-server-time.js`. The fallback file `fallback-server-time.js` is included in the files that are cached by the browser, just as files are in the `CACHE` category. We'll look at the fallback category in more detail in the next section.

`FALLBACK` also allows you to use URL paths, so you could use the following:

```
FALLBACK:
server-time.js fallback-server-time.js
/ offline.html
```

> **NOTE** Cachebusting means to forcefully prevent the resource from being cached. In the example of the manifest, this is achieved by changing its contents.

This tells the browser that if `server-time.js` is requested and it's unavailable, then serve up `fallback-server-time.js`. If any other path is requested, such as `/foo.html`, and it's unavailable (either because you're offline or it's not in the cache), the browser will serve `offline.html`. This method can be used to easily define an entire portion of your site to only be available online and redirect the user to offline.html if they try to access a resource while they're not connected. Note that giving this rule that is catching *all* failed requests, it also means that currently, if an image URL results in a 404, it will be served offline.html—so you would need to add multiple sensible rules to your fallback category.

Figure 7.2 shows my time application when the app doesn't have connectivity to the site, and the request for `server-time.js` falls back to `fallback-server-time.js` showing an entirely different message.

FIGURE 7.2 My time application continues to work whilst offline, pulling a different resource for the server-time JavaScript file.

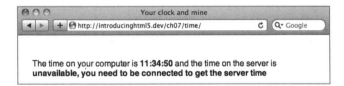

> **NOTE** Browsers like the manifest and don't let go of their cache easily. Make sure you include a comment that has a version number, revision, or timestamp that you can change and force an update to the browser's manifest for your domain.

Finally, I've included a comment in the file, starting with the # symbol (note that comments must be on their own line, too). This tells me the version number. This is important to *cachebust* the manifest. It's not that a comment is required, but *something* in the manifest file must change. Personally I like to use a comment or revision number of MD5 hash of all the files in the application. This change in the manifest file tells the browser to reload the contents of the offline manifest. Also, you can't just change the timestamp on the manifest or any of the assets to force a reload, but changing anything *inside* the manifest *will* force a reload.

In addition to the CACHE and FALLBACK categories, there's the NETWORK category, which already has entries associated with it in our example. This is the *whitelist* category, and what's important about these entries is that they tell the browser that *any* requests to any asset that isn't in our offline cache should go via the Web.

If you're like me, you're probably thinking, "Surely that's the default?" I'm afraid not. If the browser is viewing a page that's running from the AppCache, that is, the page was served up from the manifest, then all resources on that page must match some rule in the manifest; otherwise, they fail to load. This seems odd, but the rule we've already added ensures that we'll never get burnt by this odd behaviour.

We could include more specific URLs, but by putting the * rule in it ensures that *everything* else goes via the Web, and we don't end up with any ugly old broken images.

Network and fallback in detail

Providing fallback content

Both with the FALLBACK and the NETWORK namespaces, there's no pattern matching support—though you might think this if you were looking at an example manifest file with a * character in it; in fact this is a special character that we'll look at in the network whitelist section below.

FALLBACK works by specifying a resource location, or a resource prefix, that is, what the URL *starts with*. Note that there are no regexes going on here; it's just "does it start with...."

When your website is offline, and you're using the AppCache, you could direct all the requests to the payment.html page to an offline version of the page using the following:

```
FALLBACK
payment.html payment-offline.html
```

However, if your site requests /money/payment.html this rule will not match, but we can match on the start of the URL like this:

```
FALLBACK
/money/ payment-offline.html
```

Now any request that starts with /money/ for a URL whilst we're offline *and* whilst the URI is unavailable in the cache will have the payment-offline.html served up instead.

Using the network whitelist

The NETWORK namespace works in a similar way to the FALLBACK namespace, in that you can specify a full URL to whitelist, or you can specify a prefix to match against.

There is also a special rule that if the NETWORK rule contains only a * symbol, then any and all URLs that are requested, that aren't in the application cache, will go via the network. You'd think this would be normal behaviour, but without this flag the browser is actually *unable* to make the web request. This is both true when online *and* offline. Seems a little batty, right?

It's as if once the manifest file is in place, the browser is running all of it's request routing though that file, and if there's not a rule matching the request, the request will fail. This goes for both local assets to the domain *and* remote assets. This is the area that has possibly caught me out the most times—so it's worth remembering!

This * character is an *open whitelist* and it's important because it allows any asset that you've not accounted for in your manifest to be requested. So if you don't have this rule and use something like Google Analytics, the requests made to Google's servers that track the usage on your site will fail, because the manifest is in use, and there's no cached copy of this request, nor fallback or network rule to allow the request to be made.

In general, I'd recommend having a final rule that sets the whitelist as open. This should help during development and avoid too many debugging headaches:

```
NETWORK:
/remote/
*
```

If you've also supported Firefox 3.6, you'll need to include the following two lines which act the same way as the * rule (and I know this looks like the wildcard rule I said didn't exist, it just seems that Firefox made a little mistake along the way—the new versions of Firefox are all fixed and ignoring these two lines now):

```
http://*
https://*
```

These NETWORK rules tell the browser that all requests to anything starting with /remote/ will go via the network, and any other requests will go via the network (i.e. the web)—and now my Google Analytics will be correctly tracked if my visitor is online.

How to serve the manifest

> **NOTE** Changing the mime types on your web server is beyond the scope of this book, but your hosting company can point you in the right direction.

There's one last hurdle to jump before you can take your application completely offline: You need to serve the manifest file properly, meaning it must have the extension `.appcache` and it must have the right mime type.

If you're using a common web server like Apache, you need to add the following to your mime.types file:

```
text/cache-manifest appcache
```

There's multiple ways to serve up the right content type depending on your server of choice; just ensure the web server is sending the text/cache-manifest file header when you request any file with the `.appcache` extension. You can test this by checking the headers of the file requested using a tool like curl:

```
curl -I http://mysite.com/time.appcache
```

That should return (something like) this:

```
HTTP/1.1 200 OK
Date: Mon, 13 Sep 2010 12:59:30 GMT
Server: Apache/2.2.13 (Unix) mod_ssl/2.2.13 OpenSSL/0.9.81
¬DAV/2 PHP/5.3.0
Last-Modified: Tue, 31 Aug 2010 03:11:00 GMT
Accept-Ranges: bytes
Content-Length: 113
Content-Type: text/cache-manifest
```

Now that your server is sending the right headers, and your manifest file is ready to be used, pat yourself on the back. Let's take a look at it in action.

The browser-server process

When working with the offline applications, it's useful to understand the communication process between the browser and the server. If at all possible, I recommend running the following command on your servers to *tail* your access logs whilst refreshing your page using the cache manifest to see exactly what's being pulled. It will show you whether the files from your manifest are actually being requested and served up by your server:

```
tail -f logs/access_log
```

Watch out for dodgy foxes!

Firefox boasts support for offline applications, but it doesn't quite work as smoothly as other browsers, and there are a few important bugs to be aware of. If you're testing with Firefox, make sure you're also checking what's actually being requested from your server by monitoring the server logs. The browser should *always* request the manifest on every single visit (or refresh) of your domain. Older versions of Firefox (3.6 and 4) don't re-request the manifest, meaning that you're stuck with the manifest and resources that the browser downloaded the first time, regardless of any changes you may have made! There is hope! You can tell the browser never to cache the manifest file by adding the following code to your server config or .htaccess (or similar) file:

```
<filesMatch ".appcache$">
  Header set Cache-Control "max-age=0, private, no-store, no-cache,
  ¬ must-revalidate"
</filesMatch>
```

If you're using mod_expires for Apache, you need to include the following in your httpd.conf:

```
<IfModule mod_expires.c>
  ExpiresActive on
  ExpiresByType text/cache-manifest "access plus 0 seconds"
</IfModule>
```

You also send custom headers on requests for .appcache files and send a no-cache header:

```
Header set Pragma "no-cache"
```

I will caveat this whole sidebar with the simple fact that Firefox upgrades are moving faster than, well, a fox that's on fire. It's quite possible that by the time you read this, we'll have Firefox 13 and it won't be an issue. It's also quite possible that when this book is released, Firefox's latest release won't have this issue—but this no-cache rule won't do any harm—so go ahead and plug it in.

When you visit a web page that makes use of the cache manifest, such as my time example, here is what happens:

1. Browser: requests **http://introducinghtml5.com/examples/ch07/time/**

2. Server: returns index.html

3. Browser: parses index.html and requests all the assets in the page, images, CSS, JS, and the manifest file

4. Server: returns all requested assets

5. Browser: processes the manifest and requests all the items in the manifest, regardless of whether it's just requested them. This could effectively be a double request for your application if you're caching all the assets

6. Server: returns the requested manifest assets

7. Browser: application cache has updated, and triggers an event stating so.

Now the browser has fully loaded the cache using the files listed in the manifest. If the manifest hasn't changed and the browser is reloaded, here's what happens:

1. Browser: re-requests **http://introducinghtml5.com/ examples/ch07/time/**

2. Browser: detects that it has local cache for this page and serves it locally

3. Browser: parses `index.html`, and all assets in the local cache are served locally

4. Browser: requests the manifest file from the server

5. Server: returns a 304 code notifying the browser that the manifest hasn't changed.

Once the browser has its cache of assets, it serves them locally first and then requests the manifest. As shown in **Figure 7.3**, Safari is loading all the assets for my time application, but at the same time I'm monitoring the access log for the app, in which we can see *only* `time.appcache` and `server-time.js` is being requested over the connection.

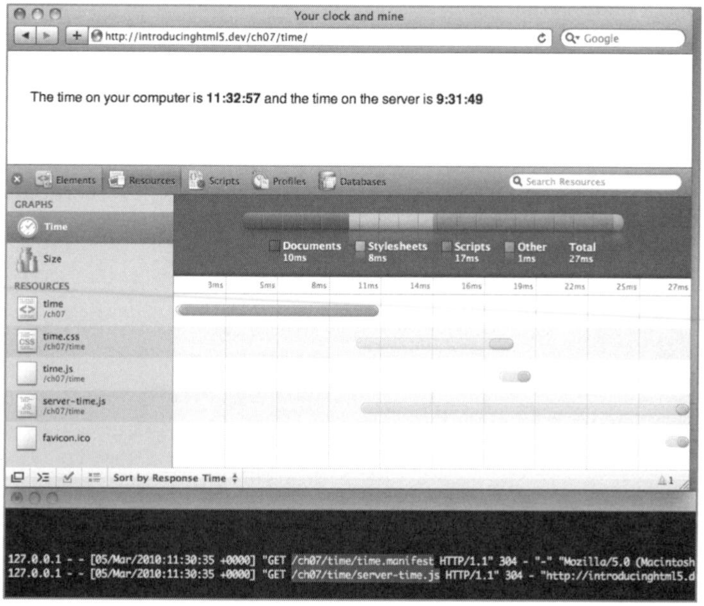

FIGURE 7.3 Safari makes a request for the app loading using the local cache and requesting only the manifest and server-time from the server. This time, you re-request the app—but the manifest has changed. If the manifest has changed, the process from Step 1 through 4 is exactly the same, but next the browser needs to reload the cache.

1. Browser: re-requests **http://introducinghtml5.com/ examples/ch07/time/**

2. Browser: detects that it has local cache for this page and serves it locally

3. Browser: parses `index.html`, and all assets in the local cache are served locally

4. Browser: requests the manifest file from the server

5. Server: returns the updated manifest file

6. Browser: processes the manifest and requests all the items in the manifest

7. Server: returns the requested manifest assets

8. Browser: application cache has been updated, and triggers an event stating so.

However, it's important to know that even though the assets may have changed, any previously loaded assets will not have changed (for example, images don't suddenly change, and old JavaScript functions haven't changed). In fact, at this point in the application's life, none of the new cache is available. Only when the page is reloaded will the new cached assets become available.

We'll look at how we can get our hands on these new assets by looking at the applicationCache object.

applicationCache

The applicationCache is the object that notifies you of changes to the local cache, but also allows you to manually trigger an update to the cache. Only if the manifest has changed will the applicationCache receive an event saying it has updated.

In the process list from the previous section, once the browser has finished loading the cache with the files from the manifest, the update event fires on the applicationCache. You could use this event to tell users that the application they're using has been upgraded and they should reload the browser window to get the latest and greatest version of your app. You can do this using a simple event listener and a notification:

```
applicationCache.onUpdateReady = function () {
  // the cache manifest has changed, let's tell the user to
```

```
  // reload to get whiz bang version 2.0
  if (confirm("Do you want to update to the latest version
  ¬ of this app?")) {
    // force a refresh if the user agrees
    window.location.reload();
  }
};
```

However, what if you wanted to tell the user what had changed? Or even perhaps try to dynamically reload some portion of the functionality. Strictly speaking, it's possible, but it might be tricky depending on your application. Nonetheless, to load the newly downloaded cache into memory, you can use the applicationCache.swapCache() method:

```
applicationCache.onUpdateReady = function () {
  applicationCache.swapCache();

  // the cache manifest has changed, let's tell the user to
  // reload to get whiz bang version 2.0
  notifyUserOfUpgrade();
};
```

Although swapping the cache removes the old cache and loads in the new cache, it doesn't actually swap images or reload any code. This happens only if the asset is manually reloaded or the entire window is reloaded. However, you could force a manual reload on one of these assets by dynamically creating a new DOM node for a script or image you wanted to reload.

For example, let's say that you have a file in your manifest that has the latest version description in version.js. If the browser has an upgrade ready (that you detected through the update ready event), inside the notifyUserOfUpgrade function you'll load the version.js file. Loading this file re-executes the JavaScript that's inside the version.js file and you'll be able to show the user the latest list of changes if he reloads the application.

I think that, generally speaking, the swapCache has very limited practical use. But the update ready event is very useful to tell users that they might want to reload the browser to get the updated application code, a bit like a normal desktop application telling us there's a new upgrade ready to be downloaded. Except in this case, the upgrade has already been downloaded behind the scenes for us.

Debugging tips

No doubt you're already thinking, "This sounds complicated." It is and it isn't. Once you're a dab hand at offline apps, it's easy. But how do you debug when you have your first run-in with it not working?

Browser debug tools vary widely, and as much as we'd love all their tools to work the same, sometimes it's just easier to add the debug information to our development process.

Currently the best tool I've come across is Google Chrome's web inspector, specifically because it reports the progress of the application caching, but also tells me whether it's using a local version or not.

Figure 7.4 is jsconsole.com, which uses the appcache to work offline. This is the output in Chrome's web console when we visit for the first time:

FIGURE 7.4 jsconsole being loaded for the first time in Google Chrome, http://jsconsole.com.

Notice how in **Figure 7.5** each asset is being logged and cached. These can also be seen individually in the resources panel:

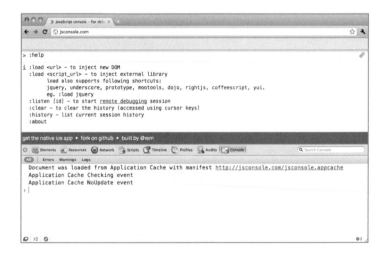

When I refresh jsconsole.com after the manifest is loaded, only the manifest file is requested and the application doesn't need updating, as shown in the log in **Figure 7.6**.

I'm sure the other browsers' tools will eventually give you more information (if they haven't already by the time this book is printed), but you could also bind to the individual applicationCache events, like updateReady, and so on, to get some idea of what your site is doing during start-up.

Using the manifest to detect connectivity

Part of HTML5 includes a property on the navigator object that is *supposed* to tell you if the browser is online or offline, via

`navigator.onLine`

However, as we've already seen when discussing online and offline events, this property changes only when a user explicitly sets the browser to work offline (with the exception of some mobile device browsers). As a developer, what you'd really want is to detect whether or not the browser can connect to your application server. A far more reliable way to do this is by using the cache manifest's FALLBACK category. By including a FALLBACK rule in our manifest, you can pull in a piece of JavaScript and detect whether you're online or offline.

Your manifest:

`CACHE MANIFEST`

```
FALLBACK:
online.js offline.js
```

online.js contains:

`setOnline(true);`

offline.js contains:

`setOnline(false);`

In your application you have a function called testOnline that dynamically creates a script element that *tries to load* the online.js JavaScript file. If it succeeds, the setOnline(true) code is run. If you are offline, behind the scenes the browser falls back on the offline.js JavaScript file, which calls setOnline(false). From there, you might want to trigger the applicationCache.update():

```
function testOnline(fn) {
  var script = document.createElement('script')
  script.src = 'online.js';

  // alias the setOnline function to the new function
  ¬ that was
  // passed in
  window.setOnline = function (online) {
    document.body.removeChild(script);
```

```
    fn(online);
  };

  // attaching script node trigger the code to run
  document.body.appendChild(script);
}

testOnline(function (online) {
  if (online) {
    applicationCache.update();
  } else {
    // show users an unobtrusive message that they're
    ¬ disconnected
  }
});
```

Killing the cache

As I mentioned earlier in this chapter, the browsers get pretty sticky with the cache. It's easy to get stuck in a cycle where you can't clear the cache to test a change you've made. So far, the spec has no method to programmatically clear the cache (for example, you can't do it from the applicationCache object).

With that in mind, during development I strongly urge you to avoid using the cache manifest. Make sure your application development is completely finished, and only then move on to adding the manifest attribute. That said, once you've got the cache in place, how do you go about clearing it? Manually.

Upgrading to a new cache should be as simple as changing the contents of the manifest file. As I said before, you can use a comment that includes a version number or similar.

> **NOTE** When you clear the cache, make sure there aren't any windows still open with your application that uses the manifest.

What if you want to start again, or what if you want to remove the manifest attribute all together? You'll only be able to do this during development because it requires you to clear the browser's cache (and depending on the browser, it's tucked away in different places). This isn't something you can do programmatically: only the user of the browser can actively clear their offline cache.

For Safari, you need to empty (or clear) the cache. By *cache* I mean anything that's been stored to help your browsing experience go faster.

Safari clears the cache for everything except the particular window that you have visible, so when you refresh, it's still got the cache manifest included. This goes for the iPhone in particular.

For Chrome, you can navigate to chrome://appcache-internals/ where you can specifically remove a cache for a URL.

For Firefox, you need to open Preferences, go to the Advanced tab, and select the Network tab. From there you can clear individual domains' cache.

For Opera, open Preferences, navigate to Advanced, and select Storage. From there you can individually remove a URL's storage. Although they call this section *persistent storage* (suggesting that it refers to `localStorage` and `sessionStorage`) there appear to be extra URL entries with data stored, often in the form of the domain with a hash at the end, for instance html5demos. com/$7b8e3c7f. It's unclear exactly what this is (clearing this last one empties neither the AppCache nor the `localStorage`) but to be on the safe side I'd recommend removing both.

Summary

In the past, websites often failed to work when users weren't connected to the Internet. Browsers are now beginning to support offline use, coupled with the ability to detect whether or not a browser is currently online or offline (with a few workarounds). You now know how to make your web apps work, even without direct web access.

CHAPTER 8

Drag and Drop

Remy Sharp

SO WE'VE COME to the black sheep chapter of our book: drag and drop. It's not a black sheep in that cool way, like Darth Vader's version of the Imperial TIE Fighter; no, sadly it's the black sheep you want to leave alone in a field, and let it do its own thing. Some better men have even worse things to say about the spec.

So why is it here? Why is it in the HTML5 spec—and yes, drag and drop actually is part of the real HTML5 spec. Well, it's here because Microsoft Internet Explorer added drag and drop back in 1999 in IE5—yep, that long ago. Since then, Safari had implemented IE's API, so Ian Hickson, the HTML5 editor, reverse engineered the API, did all the hard work to understand exactly what was going on (describing the MSDN documentation as having a "*vague hand-wavy description*"), and documented the API.

NOTE Go to
http://ln.hixie.ch/?start=
1115899732&count=1 to see
details of Hickson's
investigation.

Now we're in the position where Firefox, Safari, Chrome, and IE support this API. It's not a good API—in fact, it's probably the worst API—but it's got some real-world implementations, so it's worth understanding what it's capable of.

Throughout this chapter, you'll be forgiven for exclaiming "WTF?" as we wind our way through the rabbit's warren that is the drag-and-drop API and look at some of the interesting functionality that it can bring to your applications. This API, as its name implies, allows you to drag items and drop them anywhere in the browser. But this functionality is not limited to the browser. You can drag elements *from* the browser *to* external applications—like another browser window, or Photoshop, or a text editor—and the application can prepare the dragged data so that it's compatible with the drop target. This lends itself very well to the idea that HMTL5 is a web applications spec, and is giving us developers more functionality that borrows from desktop computing.

Getting into drag

Let's start with the absolute minimum required to achieve the wonder that is dragging and dropping. By default, all links, text nodes (or selections of text), and image elements are draggable. This means that you don't have to do anything to tell the browser that these things can be dragged around the page.

Our simple demo will have a drop zone and a couple of images that you can drag into the drop zone. And when you drop them, the image source will appear in the drop zone (**Figure 8.1**).

FIGURE 8.1 All images and links are draggable by default. With a little more code, you can make them droppable too.

Since there's nothing to be done to the draggable images, you just need to hook up the drop zone, which requires the following event handlers:

1. Drag over: Tells the browser *this* is an element that accepts drop data.

2. On drop: Once *something* has been dropped on the element, the browser does something with the dropped data.

> **NOTE** As used in this section, "drop zone" simply means a place that a user drops something. I am not referring to the recently added W3C attribute **dropzone** discussed in the sidebar "Native drop zones" later in this chapter.

I'm explaining the absolute minimum required to achieve drag and drop, but this minimum method will only work in Safari. I'll then walk you through the tweaks required to get it to work in Firefox, Chrome, and IE.

The other thing worth mentioning is that the specification up on **http://dev.w3.org/html5/spec/editing.html#dnd** says that there are *three* events you need to handle drag and drop. That isn't the case, at least certainly not in practice. You need three events to get it working in all browsers, except for Firefox and Safari.

Let's put all these caveats aside for a minute and crack on with our demo. The following listing is the über-minimalistic source you need to see the drag-and-drop API in action:

```
<!DOCTYPE html>
<title>Simple drag demo</title>
<style>#drop { height: 100px; border: 5px solid #ccc; }
¬ </style>
<img src="http://img.tweetimag.es/i/rem" alt="@rem" />
<img src="http://img.tweetimag.es/i/brucel"
¬ alt="@brucel" />
<div id="drop"></div>
<script>
  var drop = document.getElementById('drop');
  drop.ondrop = function (event) {
    this.innerHTML += '<p>' + event.dataTransfer.
    ¬ getData('Text') + '</p>';
  };
  drop.ondragover = function () { return false; };
</script>
```

I'm using the minimal HTML required just to keep things short. You can see from the previous code that I'm grabbing a reference to the div#drop element and then setting two inline event handlers: ondrop and ondragover.

When *something* is dropped on the drop element, it triggers the drop event and you're able to read the event.dataTransfer object. The default data type is Text, so you can use the getData method and ask for the Text data type. In the case of an image, the text will be the source of the image (typically IE gives us null for the Text data type, but you'll fix that later). For links, the href is the set data and for plain text that's been selected and dragged, the text itself is the set data.

Here's where it starts to get a little strange. To tell the browser that the drop element can accept items being dropped on it, you need to *cancel* the dragover event. Since I'm using an inline event handler (namely ondragover) I can return false. This prevents the default browser action. What *is* the default action? It's unclear from the spec, but it would be fair to say the default action would be to leave the object in the control of the browser. If I were using addEventListener, I would have to use event.preventDefault().

So that you're completely clear—because, frankly, it's not terribly obvious—here's a quote from the spec:

"If the drop is to be accepted, then this event (dragover) has to be canceled."

So now that you've got your first drag and drop working, what about those tweaks I mentioned? Let's fix Firefox first; this is easy. When you drop the image on the drop zone in Firefox, it actually redirects the browser off to the value of getData('Text') for you if it looks like a link—that is, image sources and link hrefs. So that's easy: In the drop event, you prevent the browser's default action. If you're using inline handlers, you'll return false, or event.preventDefault(), so our drop handler now looks like this:

```
drop.ondrop = function (event) {
  this.innerHTML += '<p>' + event.dataTransfer.getData
  ¬ ('Text') + '</p>';
  return false;
};
```

Now, IE. Getting it working in IE isn't actually as painful as it could be. This is most likely because *they* came up with the API in the first place. IE doesn't listen to the dropover event, it listens for the dropenter event—and it's *this* event you need to cancel for IE to play ball. So let's add another event handler and return false, too. Since you're doing the same thing, I've created a function to return false:

```
function cancelEvent() { return false; }
drop.ondragenter = cancelEvent;
drop.ondragover = cancelEvent;
```

Again, since you're making it work in IE, IE doesn't pass in the event object to our inline handler, so you need to change the drop event handle to grab the global event object if you didn't receive one.

You also need to cancel the event from bubbling up the DOM to prevent new windows opening. Typically return false should handle this (as it does in the other browsers), but IE needs a helping hand with event.cancelBubble=true.

```
drop.ondrop = function (event) {
  event = event || window.event;
  this.innerHTML += '<p>' + event.dataTransfer.getData
  ¬('Text') + '</p>';
  event.cancelBubble = true;
  return false;
};
```

One final issue to fix: When you drop the image in IE or Chrome, you get "null" as the text in our drop zone. To fix this you need to set some data under the Text data type once the element starts to drag, using the dragstart event:

```
var imgs = document.getElementsByTagName('img'),
    i = imgs.length;
while (i--) {
  imgs[i].ondragstart = function (event) {
    event = event || window.event;
    event.dataTransfer.setData('Text', this.getAttribute
    ¬('alt'));
  };
}
```

Now you can see that I've set some data whose type is "Text" based on the alt attribute on the image. Now when the image is dropped, and the Text data type is read, you'll get the Twitter screen names instead of the image source. This drag-and-drop demo works in IE5 onwards, Firefox, Chrome, and Safari. More importantly, it's the setData method that really shows off the possibilities of the drag-and-drop model, but equally exposes some potential issues in the specification.

Interoperability of dragged data

By using the setData and getData methods on the dataTransfer object, we can pass data from elements inside our application to other pages of our app, or across browser windows—as 280 Slides has prototyped, when dragging one slide from one window to another completely separate document (**Figure 8.2**). You can also accept or send data to native desktop applications.

FIGURE 8.2 **An early prototype of how drag and drop could work in 280 Slides.**

Dragging data to other applications

So long as you know what the accepted content types are, you can set the data type to accept that particular content type. For example, on a Macintosh, it's possible to drag text snippets to the desktop. I can construct my own content, set the content type to text/plain, and when I drag the text to the desktop, a text snippet is created with my content (**Figure 8.3**):

```
img.ondragstart = function (event) {
  event = event || window.event;
  // here be one long line
  event.dataTransfer.setData('text/plain',
    'This is the screen name for ' + this.getAttribute
    ¬ ('data-screen_name') +
    ', whose image can be found here: ' + this.src);
};
```

FIGURE 8.3 Dragged content from my web page creates a desktop text snippet.

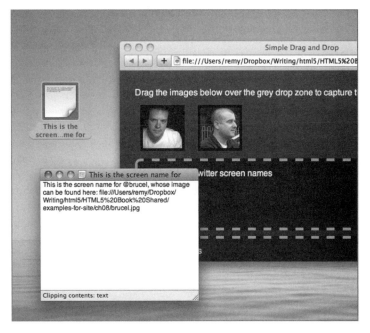

One final note about setData: It only accepts strings. This means you can't store a "complex" JavaScript object in a content type. However, there's an easy enough solution around this: JSON.stringify.

All the latest browsers ship with native JSON encoding (stringify) and decoding (parse), so you can stringify our complex object and set it against a content type. For the older browsers you can include the JSON library from **https://github.com/ douglascrockford/JSON-js** which will plug support for JSON stringify and parse.

Problems with setting drag data

Native desktop applications have had drag and drop for some time now and have had years to get the APIs right. One huge advantage that native applications have is that the setting of data doesn't actually happen, or execute, when the user starts dragging. It happens when the user drops.

There is an important reason for this: When you drop, you need only one content type.

> **NOTE** In total, there're seven drag-and-drop events. You've seen `dragenter`, `dragover`, `drop`, and `dragstart`. The others are `dragend` (the complement to `dragstart`), `dragenter`, and `dragleave`. The enter and leave events fire on the drop zone as the dragged item enters the element.

Having to construct the different content types on the `dragstart` event makes you perform possibly unnecessary code execution. For example, if I were to allow the user to drag a canvas element to Photoshop, I would want to encode it as a Photoshop-compatible file and store it in the correct content type. But what if I'm also supporting *other* formats along with Photoshop? I'd have to do *all* that encoding at the point in which the `dragstart` event fires, but the user will, at best, only drop it on a single application. What if they're just dragging the element around to play? You've still run all that execution, a huge waste of processing for more complicated applications. If your application is simple, you may not see any performance issues; but if it's a full-fledged application, you need to consider your options. Perhaps you don't support all those formats. Perhaps you support only one compatible format. Perhaps you don't even support drag and drop.

There are proposals to fix this (along with proposals to scrap the entire drag-and-drop model and start again), but for the medium term, this is a problem you'll have to work around.

How to drag any element

This is where the HTML5 spec added some new content to the API. Enabling *any* element to be dragged is incredibly easy. Take your div and add the new attribute: `draggable`. For example:

```
<div draggable="true">This element be draggable</div>
```

Of course I said *incredibly* easy. Well, it works in Firefox; any element that has the draggable attribute can now be dragged around the browser. Of course, since it's a new addition in HTML5, it doesn't come as standard in IE, so forget about it working there. Perhaps it will work in IE9 or later. More incredible is getting it to work in Safari 4.

Although it's blindingly simple to enable any element to be draggable using the `draggable` attribute, for reasons that are still beyond this author and many other bloggers, to get any element to drag in Safari 4 you need to give it a specific CSS style. That's right, to enable a *behaviour* you need to define a *presentational* attribute. This has been fixed in Safari 5 so the CSS isn't required, but for older Safari versions you'll need the following CSS to target elements with the `draggable` attribute:

```
[draggable] { -webkit-user-drag: element; }
```

Native Drop zones

No, we're not talking about the place where local parachutists land. There's a new dropzone attribute available in the drag-and-drop specification. This can be applied to the area that you want to *drop* data onto. The attribute accepts the following values: copy (the default), move, and link which control the feedback to the dragged item. In addition to the feedback value, you can also include the accepted *kinds* of data the drop zone supports. For example:

```
<div dropzone="copy s:text/plain f:image/png"> Drop 'em on my head </div>
```

This would *allow my script* to copy any dragged content whose content type was either plain text or a PNG image. The 's:' stands for *string* and 'f:' stands for *file*. Currently nothing else is supported in the spec.

I suspect that the idea is to remove the need for the dragover and dragenter shenanigans. However, as there's absolutely no current browser support for this feature, I can't be entirely sure. It's certainly a move in the right direction toward enhancing and simplifying the drag and drop API, but until we see it land in a browser, I'm afraid this is just a glimpse of what drag and drop should be, rather than being useful today!

This uses the CSS attribute selector (the square brackets) to find all the elements with the draggable property enabled, and then applies the behaviour to enable the user to drag the element.

Aside from the CSS fudge that you have to add to kick Safari 4 into life, dragging any element isn't too hard, and it means you can now create complicated objects in the DOM that the user can move around and drop into other windows or applications.

Adding custom drag icons

You can add your own custom drag icon when dragging an element. On the dragstart event, you can use the setDragImage method to associate your own image with the cursor at a specific offset to the regular cursor image.

There is, of course, a small caveat: It doesn't work in IE, and in Safari, you can't override the cursor if dragging text, images, or links. But we're optimistic—let's create our own custom drag icon:

```
var dragIcon = document.createElement('img');
// set the drag icon to the mini twitter logo
dragIcon.src = 'http://img.tweetimag.es/i/twitter_m';
// later in the code...
element.ondragstart = function (event) {
  event.dataTransfer.setDragImage(dragIcon, -10, -10);
  // and do some other interesting stuff with dataTransfer
};
```

The result is a nice little bespoke drag icon that better represents the data you're moving around (**Figure 8.4**). To keep things consistent with the madness that is the Drag and Drop specification, the coordinate system for the drag image is the inverse of what you'd expect. Since all (or all that I can think of) web technology coordinate systems work with the centre point being the top left, you might think that setting a negative offset would put the drag image -10 up and -10 left. No, in fact you'd be wrong, obviously... it actually puts the image 10 below and 10 to the right. Really the rule of thumb with Drag and Drop is: all bets are off.

FIGURE 8.4 We've created a custom Twitter cursor when dragging Twitter-related data around.

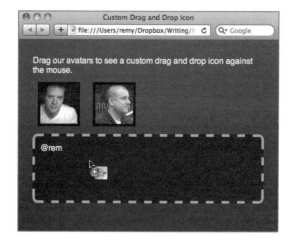

Accessibility

If you've made it this far undeterred by the warnings and dead bodies throughout this specification, then hopefully the application with drag and drop that you're implementing will come under the question of accessibility. Is the drag and drop API accessible, or can I make it accessible?

Well, as you'd expect with this specification, there's a good intention. So yes, the API has been designed with accessibility in mind. It's not terribly clear, but the latest thinking is that the user should be able to control dragging and dropping using the keyboard copy and paste model.

The process is supposed to be: Navigate to the element you want to drag, copy to the clipboard using the keyboard shortcuts, and then navigate to the drop zone, and paste using the keyboard.

As you've probably already guessed, no browser has implemented this (yet).

However, you can prepare your drag-and-drop demos by including ARIA support. You will need to set ARIA attributes on dragstart to indicate that the element is being dragged. We also need to now bind to the dragend event to remove the ARIA attribute. We should also use visual cues to indicate to the user what elements can be dragged and *where* they can be dropped. I'm not going to cover this detail, but Gez Lemon wrote a detailed article on adding ARIA and general accessibility to nonnative drag and drop, but the advice also applies to the native drag and drop provided by this API: **http://dev.opera.com/ articles/view/accessible-drag-and-drop/**

```
var drop = document.getElementById('drop'),
    boxes = document.getElementsByTagName('div'),
    i = boxes.length;

while (i--) {
  if (boxes[i].getAttribute('draggable') != undefined) {
    boxes[i].ondragstart = function (event) {
      event = event || window.event;
      this.setAttribute('aria-grabbed', 'true');
      // set the drop targets up for ARIA support
      drop.tabIndex = 0; // for keyboard support
      drop.setAttribute('aria-dropeffect', 'copy');

      // then do something fancy with dataTranfer.setData
    };

    boxes[i].ondragend = function () {
      this.setAttribute('aria-grabbed', 'false');

      // reset the drop targets
      drop.tabIndex = -1; // for keyboard supportZ
      drop.removeAttribute('aria-dropeffect');
    };

    boxes[i].tabIndex = 0; // for keyboard support
    boxes[i].setAttribute('aria-grabbed', 'false');
  }
}
```

In the previous code, you're searching for the divs that have the draggable attribute. Then you add the ARIA support starting in the dragstart event. Once the element begins to drag, you set the aria-grabbed attribute to true, so that an assistive device can feedback. You're also now making the drop zone an element that can accept keyboard focus using tabIndex = 0 and finally you're saying the drop effect should be 'copy'. You could mirror the allowedEffect and dropEffect in the native drag and drop, but for now you'll remain focused on the ARIA support.

Next, you add the new dragend event handler, and once the element is no longer being dragged, you remove the aria-grabbed attribute and reset the drop zone attributes, that is, no tabIndex and no dropEffect. Lastly, you initialise the draggable element by setting the tabIndex and the aria-grabbed flag.

With this code, users can move around your application and its drag-and-drop components, and their screenreaders (if they support ARIA) will feed back the current state of the operation.

However—and this is a big *however*—since no browser has implemented the keyboard support for native drag and drop, you will most likely have to consider rolling your own drag and drop using JavaScript to handle everything—a rather sad ending to what is a particularly common operation on the Web.

Summary

The drag and drop API isn't in a great state and can be difficult to implement across all the browsers your application may support. In fact, you may have to fall back to an old-school JavaScript-based solution to drag and drop where the support is lacking.

However, native drag and drop, combined with newer APIs like the File API (out of the scope of this book, but it allows the browser to read files directly from within JavaScript, without the need for any submission and interaction with the server) allows users to drag files straight into the browser. This functionality is appearing as beta features in applications such as Gmail, allowing users with browsers that support the bleeding edge drag and drop API, if there is such a thing, to experience the very latest technology. Beyond browser support, accessibility is another big hurdle at the moment.

You'll need to carefully consider whether native drag and drop is the right choice for your application.

CHAPTER 9

Geolocation

Remy Sharp

IN THE UK, when red telephone boxes were still a common sight, inside each box was a printed note indicating the address you were calling from. This was so that if you had to call the police or an ambulance you knew where you were. Of course, this also helped after a hazy Friday night, calling home for a lift because you didn't know where you were. This is the essence of Geolocation—except without the beer.

The geolocation API has absolutely nothing to do with the HTML5 specification, and was created by the W3C rather than the WHATWG. In fact, it was never even part of the original Web Applications specification (though it does now reference the HMTL5 specification), but it's so darn cool that we had to include it in this book. In actuality, it's a key API when it comes to applications and adding some wicked—yes, wicked—social interaction.

The API is incredibly simple to work with, and you can easily enhance your web apps if they make use of any geo data by plugging this API into the app and saving users from having to finger or scroll all over your map to find themselves.

Currently, Internet Explorer 9 and at least the latest and previous versions of all other browsers have support for the geolocation API—not a bad state to be in for a bleeding edge technology. In addition, many smart phones and their mobile browsers support the geolocation API, including iOS, Andriod's WebKit, Firefox Mobile, and Opera Mobile. In addition, if you're using Open Web technologies to build native mobile applications, PhoneGap, the framework for deploying Open Web mobile apps, provides the geolocation API as well.

Sticking a pin in your user

The geolocation API gives us a way to locate the user's exact position. There are already lots of applications that make use of this API, ranging from mapping, as seen on Google Maps in **Figure 9.1**, to location-based social networks such as Gowalla and Google Buzz.

FIGURE 9.1 Google Maps detects geolocation support and adds the "locate me" functionality.

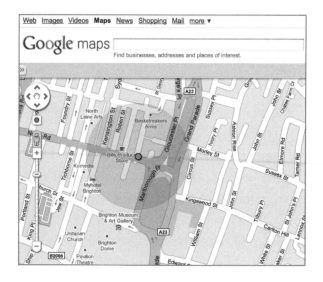

The geolocation API offers two methods for getting the geo information from your user:

1. getCurrentPosition is a one-shot method for grabbing the user's current location.

2. watchPosition keeps an eye on the user's position and keeps polling at regular intervals to see if that location has changed. watchPosition mirrors getCurrentPosition's functionality, but if the user's position changes, it will also tell your code. Note that even though watchPosition is polling your position, it will *only* call your callback if the position has changed. To stop watching, or polling, you pass the return value from watchPosition to clearWatch which we'll see later on.

Both getCurrentPosition and watchPosition work asynchronously to ascertain the user's location. However, if this is the first time your site has asked the user for their location, the browser will show some kind of dialog (as we'll see in a moment) asking for permission to share their location. If the visitor doesn't agree to share their location, the geolocation API will call the error handler if you've provided it with one.

The specification says:

"User agents must not send location information to websites without the express permission of the user."

So it's up to the browser to prompt users to inform them that we're trying to grab their current position. Different browsers handle this in different ways. Firefox, for example, offers a non-modal, non-blocking alert (**Figure 9.2**). This means your application continues to execute. In fact, currently all desktop browsers ask for permission the same way, in that it doesn't prompt the user with a blocking message.

FIGURE 9.2 Firefox being asked to share the user's location.

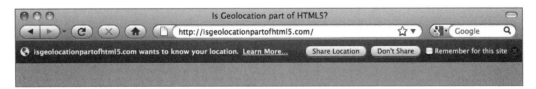

Mobile browsers, including Mobile Safari and Opera Mobile, prompt the user with a modal dialog each time a call is made to the API, stopping all code execution until the user responds (**Figure 9.3**). Mobile browsers like Firefox Mobile and WebKit on Android do not block the page from running, but still clearly prompt the user for a response.

FIGURE 9.3 Mobile Safari with a modal dialog, blocking the app from continuing.

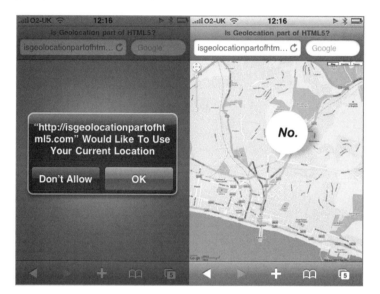

API methods

The geolocation API exists inside the navigator object and contains only three methods:

- getCurrentPosition
- watchPosition
- clearWatch

The watchPosition and clearWatch are paired methods. They work the same way as setInterval, and setTimeout. watchPosition returns a unique identifier, that can be later cancelled by passing the value to clearWatch.

As I mentioned before, getCurrentPosition and watchPosition mirror each other and take the same arguments:

- success handler

- error handler

- geolocation options

A simple use of the geolocation API would be to just pass a success handler to the getCurrentPosition method:

```
navigator.geolocation.getCurrentPosition(function
¬(position) {
  alert('We found you!');
  // now do something with the position data
});
```

Got you: the success handler

If the user permits the browser to share his geolocation and there's no other error, the success handler is called, which is the first argument to getCurrentPosition and watchPosition.

The handler receives a Position object containing two properties: a coords object (containing coordinate information) and a timestamp. The coordinates object is where the interesting stuff is sitting. There are really two grades of data in the position object. The first grade appears in all the browsers with geolocation support:

- readonly attribute double latitude

- readonly attribute double longitude

- readonly attribute double accuracy

Note that accuracy is the measurement of the coordinates' accuracy in meters. You could use this to show a radius of accuracy if you were mapping the user's position.

Although it's difficult to confirm manually, it's likely this data is being provided by the browser vendor's own service. For instance, Google has a big database of location data which—when combined with information about your request, the hardware, your IP, and a bit of black magic—finds your position. This data simply represents a snapshot of the user's position, and doesn't contain any information that could help you work out their speed, or direction of travel. We'll look at the voodoo magic used to ascertain the visitor's location at the end of this chapter.

Using the coordinate data, you could easily map the user's current position on something like a Google map:

```
if (navigator.geolocation) {
  navigator.geolocation.getCurrentPosition(function
  ¬(position) {
    var coords = position.coords;
    showMap(coords.latitude, coords.longitude,
    ¬coords.accuracy);
  });
}
```

In a lot of applications, it's likely that the user will be offered a manual way to set his current position. If the geolocation method is available, the site may offer the advanced functionality, progressively enhancing the page or the whole experience. An example can be seen at **http://owlsnearyou.com**. When visiting the site, if geolocation is available, it reloads the page with your position loaded (**Figure 9.4**), showing you where you can go owl hunting, if that's the activity that gets you going after a day of HTML5 development. If geolocation isn't available, it simply asks you to enter your location.

FIGURE 9.4 **An example of progressive enhancement using geolocation.**

The second grade of data inside the coordinates object is supported, but by default most (currently all) desktop browsers will return null. However, if the device has something like a GPS on board, the values can be determined, at which point the values can be null, 0, or a floating point:

- readonly attribute double altitude
- readonly attribute double altitudeAccuracy
- readonly attribute double heading
- readonly attribute double speed

We'll look at how to use this second grade of data next.

Getting your hands on speed

More and more, we're seeing smartphones, tablets, and notebooks with onboard GPS. On these devices—depending on the specific web browser and OS integration provided—the geolocation API can provide a lot more information than just a one-off set of coordinates (latitude, longitude, accuracy)—instead giving access, through the second-order data, to speed, altitude, and heading information as well.

In most cases, when you make a simple geolocation request, you'll get only the latitude, longitude, and accuracy, and in most cases this is enough for your application.

However, you can get your hands on the speed, altitude, and heading through the geolocation API.

In most cases today, you'll need to tell the API to use highaccuracy to enable the GPS device. Be aware that using the GPS will quickly drain the device's battery, so make sure you're using the technology because you need it, not just because you can.

In order to calculate the current speed, the device needs to average the difference between a series of discrete location measurements (or something to that effect?). For this reason, you'll need to use geolocation.watchPosition and update the current speed as it comes in:

```
var speedEl = document.getElementById('speed');
navigator.geolocation.watchPosition(function (geodata) {
  var speed = geodata.coords.speed;
  if (speed === null || speed === 0) {
    speedEl.innerHTML = "You're standing still!";
  } else {
    // speed is in metres per second
    // multiply by 2.23 to get miles per hour
    speedEl.innerHTML = (speed * 2.23693629) + "Mph";
  }
}, function () {
  speedEl.innerHTML = "Unable to determine speed :-(";
}, { enableHighAccuracy: true });
```

In addition to the speed of the device, you can also get the altitude, altitude accuracy, and heading. If these values aren't available—either because of the device or because the geolocation can't get that particular piece of data—then the returned value will be null.

Geo 404: the error handler

The second argument to the `getCurrentPosition` and `watchPosition` methods is the error handler. This is particularly important if you want to provide some alternative method of location (such as manually) or you want to notify the user of any errors in getting his position. The error handler may trigger if the user denies his position, but it could be that the user has given you permission and you are now watching his position on a mobile device and the phone has gone out of reception. This too would cause the error handler to trigger.

The error handler receives a single argument containing a position error object with two properties:

* `readonly attribute unsigned short code`
* `readonly attribute DOMString message`

The code property will be one of the following:

* `PERMISSION_DENIED` (numeric value 1)
* `POSITION_UNAVAILABLE` (numeric value 2)
* `TIMEOUT` (numeric value 3)

The message property is useful for developing and debugging but wouldn't be appropriate to show the user. It's not because it's some cryptic rubbish from the GPS onboard chips, but because it's bespoke to each browser (as it's not defined in the specification), but also because it's rather *computery* speak—not friendly to your visitor. The message property isn't always available (as it's not currently in Firefox 3.6+).

To give you an idea of how the error handler can be used, here's a simple example:

```
if (navigator.geolocation) {
  navigator.geolocation.getCurrentPosition(function
  ¬(position) {
    var coords = position.coords;
    showMap(coords.latitude, coords.longitude,
    ¬coords.accuracy);
  }, function (error) {
    var errorTypes = {
      1: 'Permission denied',
      2: 'Position is not available',
      3: 'Request timeout'
    };

    alert(errorTypes[error.code] + ": means we can't
    ¬determine your position");
  });
}
```

If your page uses this code and the user, when prompted, doesn't allow the page access to the current location information, they'll receive a stern alert box "Permission denied: means we can't determine your position."

> ## The alternative error: on success
>
> When I once visited a page that was supposed to detect my location, whilst working from home in Brighton on the south coast of England, the map placed me dead in the centre of London. I checked under the hood using browser's web console and could see the accuracy of the geolocation request was set to 140,000 meters—that's about 90 miles of inaccuracy; as a radius that's pretty damn inaccurate! It's understandable how the site wasn't sure exactly where I was. I would strongly recommend that while developing applications that use geolocation you also check the accuracy of the success call. If the accuracy is set to such a large value, it might be worth ignoring the data altogether, treating it the same as an error, and providing your normal fallback mechanisms—such as asking the user to enter his location manually. However, the accuracy is all about context. If your application was helping me to find the closest hospital, I'd expect it to be accurate to about city size. If your application was offering a county view of the current weather system, it would be fine if the accuracy was to 90 miles—as it still puts me in England.

Configuring the geolocation

Finally, the third argument to both `getCurrentPosition` and `watchPosition` contains the geolocation options. All the geolocation options are *optional*, as you've seen, and are constructed as follows:

- `enableHighAccuracy` (Boolean, default false)
- `timeout` (in milliseconds, default infinity [represented by 0])
- `maximumAge` (in milliseconds, default 0)

For example, to request high accuracy and a two-second timeout, and to never use old geo data, call `getCurrentPosition` using the following options (where `success` and `error` are pre-defined functions):

```
navigator.geolocation.getCurrentPosition(success, error, {
  enableHighAccuracy: true,
  timeout: 2000,
  maximumAge: 0
});
```

We already encountered `enableHighAccuracy`—it tells the device to try to get a more accurate reading on the latitude and longitude—`timeout` tells the geolocation lookup how long it should wait before giving up and triggering the error handler. However, it won't start counting down if it's waiting for the user to approve the request. If it does timeout, the error code is set to 3 (TIME-OUT). Setting a zero timeout (the current default) tells the browser to never time out and keep trying.

Finally, maximumAge tells the browser whether or not to use recently cached position data. If there is a request that is within the maximumAge (in milliseconds), it is returned instead of requesting a new position. maximumAge can also be Infinity, which tells the browser to *always* use a cached position. Setting the maximumAge to zero (the default value) means the browser must look up a new position on each request.

How it works under the hood: It's magic

The geolocation API uses a few different techniques in acquiring the user's position. It is black magic to most people, including myself, but it's worth having an idea of what's going on under the hood as it will affect the accuracy of the position data.

GPS is one of the obvious methods for getting position data. More computing devices, ranging from mobile phones to laptops, are being fitted out with GPS. Assuming there's a clear enough line to the GPS ground station (which picks up readings from satellites to triangulate the user's position—yep, more black magic), then you'll have a very accurate reading. GPS can also give you altitude, speed, and heading, which we saw in the second grade of properties in the coordinates object when the high accuracy option was enabled.

Another method is using network information, which would be typical if used via a desktop browser such as Firefox. The network information could use Wi-Fi triangulation and IP addresses to make a best guess at the user's location. The developer makes a call to the browser's geolocation API, which in turn makes a call to a third-party service such as Skyhook or Google. Although this may be less accurate than GPS, it could make for a very good backup as GPS doesn't work very well indoors or in high-rise urban locations.

Overall, it's not terribly important to know what makes geolocation tick, but if you need to get the high accuracy, be wary of using the more power-hungry devices such as GPS and of killing your user's battery.

All in all, it's some very cool black magic.

Summary

If there's any aspect of geolocation in your application, then you'd be a fool not to include this amazingly simple API. The work is virtually zero to implement. Really the work would be in creating the user interface. What's particularly important to me as a developer is that regardless as to *how* the browser is determining my user's location, it will work the same—whether they're using a desktop machine, laptop, or mobile phone—the code remains exactly the same, and easy.

Since IE9 and all other browsers come with geolocation, support is in a good state. What's more is that we can use polyfill techniques to fall back on to JavaScript-based geolocation using traditional IP lookup services (which you'll see in the polyfill chapter towards the end of this book).

Just remember that geolocation should be used to progressively enhance the page, rather than forcing your user to rely on the data that comes back from the geo-lookup—as it may not be accurate enough for your application.

CHAPTER 10

Messaging and Workers

Remy Sharp

WEB MESSAGING AND WEB WORKERS are different APIs but all have the same communication API, which is why I will discuss them together. Only the Messaging API is part of the official HTML5 spec, but both of these APIs are valuable additions to any web application.

Messaging allows applications to send messages from one domain to another, something that Ajax security policies have long prevented for good reason, but is now starting to open up with the right security measurements in place.

> **NOTE** The new XMLHttpRequest Level 2 object (http://www.w3.org/TR/XMLHttpRequest2/), out of scope for this book but already in WebKit and Firefox, supports cross-domain requests (with the right level of server security). It also includes progress events for monitoring uploads.

Browsers are effectively *single-threaded* applications, in that when JavaScript is running or perhaps being parsed, the page isn't rendering. Equally, when JavaScript is performing a long and complicated function, the whole browser can be seen to lock up. What a Web Worker does is introduce a simplified idea of *threads* for browsers. A worker allows me to ring-fence a particular block of code and it will run without affecting the browser at all in a new, concurrent thread of operation, allowing the main browser thread to continue uninterrupted.

Chit chat with the Messaging API

I wanted to show you the Messaging API first because the Web Worker, WebSocket, and Server-Sent Event APIs (the latter two discussed in the next chapter) all use this common method of communication. So think of this as your gentle primer on communication.

The Messaging API has very good support across all browsers—yes, including Internet Explorer (IE)—and offers a simple API for posting plain text messages from one origin (or domain, to you and me) to another. For example, if you want to send some information to a window you have in an iframe, you can do it using the Messaging API. This will still work if the window is on a completely different domain than the site hosting the iframe.

Sending messages across domains

If Bruce has a document that wants to communicate with my document—say either in an iframe or perhaps in a pop-up window—it needs a reference to the `window` object (of my document) and he can then call the `postMessage` method to pass some message to it. The JavaScript in Bruce's document will look like this:

```
var t = document.getElementsByTagName('iframe')[0];
t.contentWindow.postMessage('favourite instrument?',
¬ 'http://brucelawson.co.uk');
```

The target origin being passed to `postMessage` in the second argument is required, and it must match the origin of your `contentWindow` object (the target window, my document in this example). If the origins don't match, a security error will be thrown, stopping the script from continuing. If the origin isn't passed in, the JavaScript will throw a syntax error—not helpful, but something to watch out for if you forget. One last tip: Remember to wait for the target to finish loading. The target is still a document that needs to be parsed and loaded. If the browser hasn't loaded the document and you try to send it a message, the JavaScript will fail entirely with a similar syntax error.

My document is being referenced via an iframe on Bruce's page, and it contains the following JavaScript:

NOTE This code list uses `addEventListener` rather than `onmessage` because previous versions of Firefox didn't appear to respond to `onmessage` on the `window` object. This is best practice anyway, but it would mean we also need to hook IE using `attachEvent`, which I've not included in my example.

```
window.addEventListener('message', function (event) {
  if (event.data == 'favourite instrument?') {
    if (event.origin == 'http://remysharp.com') {
      event.source.postMessage('brand new clarinet',
      ¬ event.origin);
    } else if (event.origin == 'http://brucelawson.co.uk') {
      event.source.postMessage('rusty old trombone',
      ¬ event.origin);
    }
  }
}, false);
```

My script sets an event listener for messages being passed to the `window`. Inside the event object is a data property containing the message that was sent. Along with the data property, there are a number of other useful properties sitting inside the event: origin and source.

The `event.origin` gives me the domain that the message came from. I can use this, as I have in the previous code listing, to determine whether I want to process the message. This is policy control at a very rudimentary level.

The `event.source` points back to the window object making the original call to my document, that is, Bruce's document. This is useful to be able to communicate back and forth. Of course, your `onmessage` event handler could do a lot more, like make an Ajax request to the server on the same domain.

What about sending more than strings?

In the examples I've shown you so far, I've passed only strings in messages back and forth. What if you want to send more than just a string? What if you have an object with properties and values?

Well, the good news is the specification describes what's supposed to happen when a browser has to safely send data from one source to another. It describes how to clone the data and how it should be treated.

However, most browsers don't support this process. In fact, most browsers simply coerce the object into a string. That sucks for you and me. It means that instead of the nicely constructed object, you'll get [object Object] in the event.data property. In fact, we saw this before in Chapter 6, "Data Storage," where we try to store objects in localStorage. So in the same way we got around the issue with localStorage, you can use JSON.stringify to convert your JavaScript object into a string, pass it to postMessage, and then, on the receiving side, convert it back to a native JavaScript object using JSON.parse.

Using JSON.stringify and JSON.parse will be useful methods for transferring more complicated objects from window to target, as we'll see in the next section on Web Workers (and the next chapter on WebSockets and Server-Sent Events).

Threading using Web Workers

Web Workers are part of a separate specification to the HTML5 spec, but they are a key feature in building web applications.

A worker is a way of running a discrete block of JavaScript in a background process to the main browser. This is effectively a *thread*. What this means is that the worker runs in the background without interfering with the main browser thread.

The browser is already responsible for requesting and parsing files, rendering the view, and executing JavaScript, running the UI/chrome, and anything that consumes the browser's processing time causes all other jobs to wait. This is where Web Workers come to the rescue.

Why use a worker?

If you've ever written any dodgy JavaScript that goes haywire, causing your browser to start fuming like it's about to explode, then you've experienced the single-threadedness of browsers. Eventually, if the browser's smart, it'll give you the option to terminate the dodgy code, something like **Figure 10.1**.

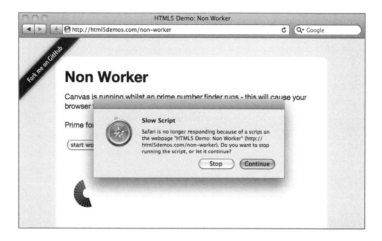

FIGURE 10.1 Some browsers will interrupt JavaScript that's gone wild, and give you the option to nuke it into space.

More worrying, though, are the much more subtle issues. Say you've written the latest and greatest web application that does the most amazing photo manipulation. You're using all the *l33t* skills you learnt from this book—canvas, storage, offline applications—but when it comes to adding a photo filter, it takes 30 seconds. It's not the 30 seconds that's the problem; it's the fact that your user can't do *anything* in the browser for those 30 seconds. What if your user changed her mind and wanted to cancel the filter? Obviously this is a situation you want to avoid.

This scenario is perfect for a Web Worker because all the filter processing can happen in the background, and the main browsing window—and the rest of your web application—is left alone to continue to be responsive to your visitor's requests.

Creating and working with workers

You can test for Web Worker support by checking whether or not the object is undefined:

```
if (typeof Worker != "undefined") {
  // do the jazzy stuff
}
```

Now that we know we've got support (Safari, Safari Mobile, Chrome, Opera, Firefox, and IE10 all support Web Workers) we can go about creating a new worker:

```
var worker = new Worker('my_worker.js');
```

A new worker object is fired up, reads in the my_worker.js JavaScript file, and is now happily running and ready to be used.

At this point, you'd be forgiven for thinking that you can call methods inside the worker from your document, and that data can be returned from the worker to your document. Poppycock! No, in fact, to work with a worker, everything must be communicated through posting messages between the worker and your document. It's like some scene from *Romeo and Juliet*, exchanging letters of love between the browser and the worker.

The *only* way you get can information to the worker is via postMessage:

```
worker.postMessage('hello worker!');
```

Note that the postMessage in the Web Workers, unlike postMessage in the Messaging API, only requires a single argument. The only way you can receive information from the worker is via the onmessage event handler:

```
worker.onmessage = function (event) {
  alert('The worker just sent me this: ' + event.data);
};
```

You should now be recognising the postMessage/onmessage combination from the Messaging API from earlier in this chapter. You remember how we can only send and receive strings in the Messaging API? You won't be surprised to know, then, that the Web Workers have the same constraint.

Equally, the code *inside* the worker must also communicate using the postMessage/onmessage combo. However, a Web Worker doesn't have the same access as your normal document: It's very much sandboxed and has access to only a select few APIs and functions, as I'll show you in the next section.

The only other method available to you via the worker object is terminate, which does exactly what it says on the tin. The worker ceases to run and the worker object becomes limp and useless. In particular, you can't resume the worker; you'd have to create a brand new one.

What you can do inside a worker

Within a Web Worker you don't have access to such pleasures as the DOM. In fact, if you need to do anything with the DOM, you're going to have to *prepare* the work in the worker, and then pass it to the parent document to do the actual DOM manipulation.

NOTE Currently there are no Web Worker implementations that support accessing IndexedDB, though there are fixes in the works. In the first edition of this book, it was Web SQL Databases that weren't supported; since that's changed, and the IndexedDB spec is still fairly new, I'd expect support to come fairly quickly once IndexedDB implementations have settled down.

However, there are a number of things you can do in a worker (according to the specification):

- postMessage and listen for inbound messages via onmessage

- close, to end the current worker

- Set event listeners

- XMLHttpRequest, for Ajax requests

- Timers, such as setTimeout, setInterval, and their clearing counterparts

- All the core JavaScript functions: eval, isNaN, escape, and so on.

- Location object, the href of the worker script

- WebSockets (which we'll discuss in the next chapter)

- EventSource (also in the next chapter)

- Web SQL Databases (only implemented in Safari and Chrome)

- IndexedDB

- Web Workers

- importScripts

The following code is all I need in my_worker.js to communicate with the document from the earlier code listing:

```
this.onmessage = function (event) {
  if (event.data == "hello worker!") {
    postMessage("hello there, right back at you");
  } else {
    postMessage("Can't you see I'm busy, leave me alone");
  }
};
```

It's useful to know that, in a normal document, this keyword would refer to the global scope, the window object. Here in the worker, the global scope is the worker instance. It also means that the this keyword inside of setTimeout and setInterval is the worker instance (where this would otherwise be the window object).

In these examples so far, our worker hasn't done anything particularly special. How about a worker that searches for prime numbers? This requires a super tight loop in JavaScript constantly spinning around looking for values that match a prime. All this and at the same time allowing your visitor to draw on a canvas while your app searches for prime numbers? Perhaps a strange use case, but we have workers to come to your rescue.

The main document will handle starting the worker and drawing on the canvas. The only code that's offloaded to the worker is the prime number searching.

```
var worker = new Worker('prime.js'),
    prime = document.getElementById('prime');
worker.onmessage = function(event) {
  prime.innerHTML = event.data;
};
```

The page continues to handle mousedown, mousemove, and mouseup events to draw on a canvas on the page. Inside the prime.js script we have:

```
onmessage = function (event) {
  // doesn't matter what the message is, just start the job
  run();
};

function run() {
  var n = 1;
  search: while (true) {
    n += 1;
    for (var i = 2; i <= Math.sqrt(n); i += 1)
      if (n % i == 0)
        continue search;
    // found a prime!
    postMessage(n);
  }
}
```

When the prime.js worker receives any message, it starts the prime number search. When you run this prime number drawing extravaganza of an application, everything runs smoothly, and you're able to create your perfect work of art whilst also searching for primes as seen in **Figure 10.2**.

FIGURE 10.2 Everything you could ever need: prime number and drawing executed without interruption thanks to Web Workers.

Matryoshka dolls: workers inside workers

If you had a watchful eye, you would have spotted that you can also create new workers from *within* a worker. Currently, only Firefox and Opera support this, but it's part of the spec, so you should expect that other browsers will be updated to include this feature.

What this means is that you could spawn one worker, which then goes and splits its job into lots of delegated little jobs and passes them to sub-workers. Let's go back to the example of applying a complex filter to a photo in your super-sexy online image web app. To speed up the processing of the image—assuming it made sense in the filter—you could split the image up into regions and pass each region of image data to a sub-worker.

As each worker returns, you reduce the pending count and, once all the workers have finished, the main worker returns the final processed image data to the parent document. It looks something like this (I've left out some functions from the listing as this is just to demonstrate the idea):

```
var pendingWorkers = 0,
    results = {},
    workingWidth = 100;

onmessage = function (event) {
  var imageData = JSON.parse(event.data),
      worker = null;

  pendingWorkers = getNumberOfWorkers(imageData.width
  ¬ / workingWidth);
  // reset any old results
  results = {};

  for (var i = 0; i < pendingWorkers; i++) {
    worker = new Worker('photofilter.js');
    worker.postMessage(JSON.stringify({
      imageData: imageData,
      x: i * workingWidth,
      width: workingWidth
    }));
    worker.onmessage = storeResult;
  }
};

function storeResult(event) {
  var result = JSON.parse(event.data);

  buildUpImageData(result);

  pendingWorkers--;
  if (pendingWorkers <= 0) {
    postMessage(JSON.stringify(results));
  }
}
```

When the message is received from the sub-worker, the main worker above decreases the number of outstanding sub-workers. Once all the sub-workers have returned their slice of the image data, the final result is returned to the parent document.

The photofilter.js sub-worker would contain the following code to process just a small region of the image data:

```
onmessage = function (event) {
  var data = JSON.parse(event.data);
```

```
// perform some amazing feat of image processing
var imageData = amazingImageProcess(data.imageData,
¬data.x, data.width);
postMessage(JSON.stringify({
  imageData: imageData,
  x: data.x
}));

// self close
close();
};
```

Notice also how photofilter.js, once it's done performing its task, calls the close() method. This allows the worker to terminate itself, since it's no longer needed.

Importing scripts and libraries to your worker

The concept of Web Workers is very much about modularising a block of code or functionality and running it in a stand-alone environment (that is, the worker itself). But Web Workers can also load external JavaScript files and libraries via the importScripts method.

This is one of the few worker-specific methods. It accepts a list of URLs and loads them into the worker synchronously. You can load one script at a time, or you can load multiple scripts from within the worker:

```
importScripts('xhr.js');
importScripts('prime.js', 'number_crunch.js',
¬'captain_crunch.js');
```

Each script is processed one at a time. The script must be on the same origin as the worker—the same domain, cname, and so on. The worker then synchronously loads the JavaScript into itself, returning to continue only once the script has finished processing.

Sharing a load with SharedWorkers

Another type of Web Worker is the SharedWorker, currently supported only in Chrome, Safari, and Opera. A shared worker is pretty much like an average Web Worker except that multiple documents can access the same instance of the worker. This means that if you have several pop-ups or several iframes, all those documents can access this single shared worker and this single shared worker will serve all those documents.

This would be useful, for example, for applications like Gmail or Facebook, where client-side data needs to be maintained, such as messages for the user, and you have several different windows open.

The worker can access and manage the website's client-side Web SQL Databases and IndexedDB (both discussed in Chapter 6). It can also maintain the connection with the server, handling all the data that's coming in and out—perhaps even via a WebSocket to the server, as we'll see in the next chapter—so that data is handled in real time. The shared worker can then maintain all the changes to the client-side messages database and push all those updates via `postMessage` to each of the pop-ups, iframes, and so on.

This means that there's no chance of data getting out of sync— or chance of race conditions if each of the pop-ups, iframes, and so on was individually connecting to the server and trying to each manage the client side—since the shared worker is the single point of contact for all of that type of work.

The `SharedWorker` works slightly differently when it comes to communication. For starters there's the concept of ports—this is an array-like object that contains a reference to each of the communication channels the shared worker has. Also, if you bind to the message event using `addEventListener`, you have to manually start the worker, which I'll show you in the following code sample.

In addition, within the worker the connect event fires when the `SharedWorker` is created, which can be used to keep track of how many connections the worker has to other documents.

The documents creating the `SharedWorker` contain the following code:

```
var worker = new SharedWorker('messages.js');
worker.port.addEventListener('message', function(event) {
  var messages = JSON.parse(event.data);
  showNewMessages(messages);
}, false);
worker.port.start();
```

In the preceding code block, you can see we're accessing the worker via the port property. This is how you interact and, in fact, distinguish between shared and nonshared workers. As the example binds to the message event using addEventListener, the worker must be connected manually using the .start() method. The code wouldn't need this if it used onmessage. Next is the messages.js worker:

```
importScripts('xhr.js');
importScripts('database.js');

var connections = [];

onconnect = function(event) {
  connections.push(event.ports[0]);
}

var xhr = new XHR('/get-new-messages');
xhr.oncomplete = function (messages) {
  database.updateMessages(messages);

  for (var i = 0; i < connections.length; i++) {
    connections[i].postMessage(JSON.stringify(messages));
  }

  xhr.send(); // causes us to loop forever
};
xhr.send();
```

When a client document connects to the worker, the connect event is fired, which allows me to capture the connection port. This is collected through the event.ports[0] reference, even though there will never be more than one item inside the ports property. However, the worker reference is inside this, so we can use this to post messages and receive messages.

As you see in the previous example, when the Ajax oncomplete function runs, I loop through all the connected ports and send them each a message of the new email messages that have come in. This way the connected clients act as dumb terminals, oblivious to any of the real work going on to store the messages in the client-side database.

Debugging a worker

We've gotten to the point in web development where the tools for debugging are so much better than ten years ago. All the latest browsers come with their own JavaScript debugger (though Firefox still requires Firebug as a plugin); it's a haven of debugging when compared to the bad old days of using alert boxes left, right, and centre.

While with a Web Worker, now you're working in a sandboxed environment, so there is no access to the console debuggers. There's no native way to do `console.log("who's the daddy?")` in a worker. To compound this hurdle, there's not even an alert box we can use.

However! There is hope yet. The WebKit folks have kindly thought about this problem, and in the *scripts* panel the developer tools offer a debug checkbox next to Web Workers (in both Chrome and Safari). This changes how Web Workers actually run (behind the scenes they're running in a `setTimeout`), but it does mean you can include `console.log` in your code to help you debug as seen in **Figure 10.3**.

FIGURE 10.3 Check the Debug check box to allow the developer to run `console.log` inside a Web Worker.

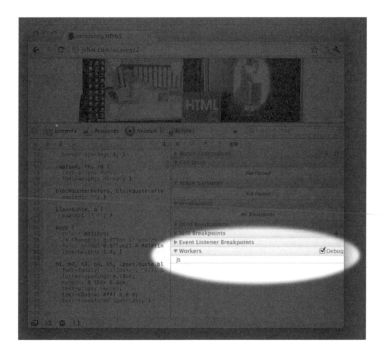

It's great that Chrome and Safari have debugging tools, but what if you want to debug in Firefox, too? You'll need to create your own system for posting debug messages. However, as with all communications from your worker—be it a debug message or results from a worker's delegated tasks—you'll need to have some agreed language between your workers and your main document to differentiate between each of those different message types, and this will depend entirely on your application. For instance, you could prefix debug messages with the keyword "log:"

```
importScripts('xhr.js');

var xhr = new XHR('/someurl');
xhr.oncomplete = function (data) {
  log('data contains ' + data.length + ' items');
};
xhr.send();

function log(msg) {
  postMessage('log ' + msg);
}
```

Note that xhr.js is my made-up XMLHttpRequest script that returns me some JSON data—you'll have to make your own!

In the main page in the onmessage event, I'll be looking for prefixes in messages and actioning them:

NOTE It's possible for a worker to get aborted or terminated through a method unknown to your code. If your worker is being killed off by the browser for some reason, then the `worker.onerror` event is going to fire. If you're closing the worker manually, you're having to do this from within the worker via `.close()` so you have the opportunity to notify the connected documents that your worker is closing.

```
var worker = new Worker('xhr_thang.js');
worker.onmessage = function (event) {
  var data = event.data.split(' '),
      action = data.shift(), // grab the first word
      msg = data.join(' '); // put the message back
      ¬ together

  if (action == 'log') {
    console.log(msg);
  } else {
    // some other action
  }
};
```

In this example, my agreed grammar is that all messages are prefixed with an action. This could be log, set, run, or some other action. What's important is that I now have a way to inspect data that's inside the worker by sending data to my log function when I'm not testing in Safari or Chrome.

It's also useful to be able to poke around inside a worker, something I've found to be exceptionally useful when experimenting in JavaScript. In a nonworker environment, I can pop open my console of choice (Firebug or Dragonfly, for example) and from within there, I can log out and inspect all the properties on the window object, the document, and then their properties, just to see what's supported and what I can play with. Since a worker is a closed environment, I need to do this manually. So one of the online examples for this book includes a console that allows you to inspect a Web Worker and test code inside the worker and see what it produces. You can see the worker console at **http://introducinghtml5.com/examples/ch10/echo.html** (**Figure 10.4**).

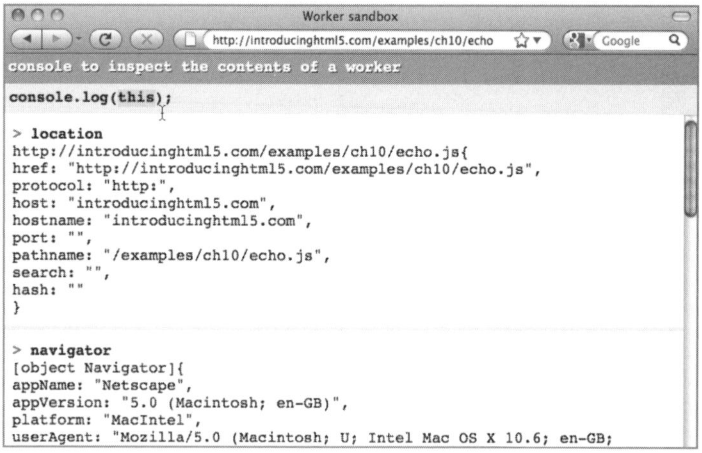

FIGURE 10.4 A demo console to inspect inside a Web Worker.

```
Worker sandbox
http://introducinghtml5.com/examples/ch10/echo          Google

console to inspect the contents of a worker

console.log(this);

> location
http://introducinghtml5.com/examples/ch10/echo.js{
href: "http://introducinghtml5.com/examples/ch10/echo.js",
protocol: "http:",
host: "introducinghtml5.com",
hostname: "introducinghtml5.com",
port: "",
pathname: "/examples/ch10/echo.js",
search: "",
hash: ""
}

> navigator
[object Navigator]{
appName: "Netscape",
appVersion: "5.0 (Macintosh; en-GB)",
platform: "MacIntel",
userAgent: "Mozilla/5.0 (Macintosh; U; Intel Mac OS X 10.6; en-GB;
```

Summary

There are a number of APIs that use similar messaging techniques—we'll cover more in the next chapter. Once you've got your head around all the different ways you can communicate within your web app, you have all the tools at your disposal to create multi-threaded, multi-window, cross-domain thingamajigs.

Web Workers absolutely provide what has been eagerly awaited: the ability to run background JavaScript jobs that don't lock your user out of a browsing experience. Now that you've seen that it's easy-peasy, I'm confident your websites will be safe from the beach ball of death!

CHAPTER 11

Real Time

Remy Sharp

THE REAL-TIME WEB is one of those golden eggs of the Internet. Very cool when you come across it, but perhaps quite daunting when it comes to building it. This chapter will show you the choices of technology and how spectacularly simple the client-side code is.

There are two options to add a real-time aspect to your web application: Websockets and Server-Sent Events. WebSockets let you create a connected stream to your server (for server boffins out there: a TCP connection), and allow two-way, real-time communication between the server and the client. The typical *hello world* app is a chat client, but the possibilities of use are endless. Sockets go a long way toward replacing Comet-based code. Comet uses a variety of—often quite hackish—techniques to achieve real-time, streaming data from a server. WebSockets simplify this process on the client side, as we'll see later in this chapter.

Server-Sent Events, also known as EventSource, push messages sent in real time from the server to the browser client. These are perfect for applications that need information from a server without necessarily having to wait for any user interaction or input, like streaming prices or live chart updates, or live information that you're monitoring.

WebSockets: working with streaming data

The WebSockets specification is one of the shiniest new APIs outside the realm of HTML5, but it's actually really important for some of the real-time-based web applications that have emerged recently.

WebSockets give you a *bidirectional* connection between your server and the browser. This connection is also real time and is permanently open until explicitly closed. This means that when the server wants to send your client something, that message is immediately pushed to your browser.

This is what Comet succeeded in doing. Comet created a real-time connection to your server, but it would do it using a variety of different hacks. Ultimately, if none of these hacks worked, it would eventually fall back down to Ajax polling, which would constantly hit your server and that doesn't scale up very well.

> **NOTE** If the browser doesn't natively support WebSockets, you can fake it using Flash. Visit **https://github. com/gimite/web-socket-js** to see Hiroshi Ichikawa's Flash-based polyfill for WebSockets.

If you have a socket open, your server can push data to all those connected sockets, and the server doesn't have to constantly respond to inbound Ajax requests. This is the move from polling to pushing, from reactive to proactive. This is what Comet was achieving through hacks, and this is what WebSockets achieve natively in the browser.

Sockets solve latency of real-time applications

Low latency is a massive benefit of WebSockets. Since your socket is always open and listening, as soon as data is pushed from the server, it just has to make its way to your browser, making the latency exceptionally low in comparison to something like an XMLHttpRequest-based Ajax request.

To take something like Google Wave—the now defunct real-time web-based email and collaboration tool—as an example, if you have lots of people all in the same document, and you're all typing, you want to send all those keystrokes to all the connected people as soon as the keystrokes happen. However, if you're using vanilla Ajax to do that, you would have to create a new XHR object every time a key is hit, and every one of those requests will contain all the headers that are sent with a normal XHR request—like the user agent string, the referrer URL, the accepted content type, and so on. That's a lot of data for what was essentially a single keypress.

With sockets, on the other hand, because the connection is always open, you need only send the information about the keystroke, which would then be disseminated to all the connected clients via the server, and *only* that single piece of information would be sent.

The data sent has gone from Ajax—which will be perhaps 200–300 bytes of data—to a socket connection, which will be just a few—around 10–20 bytes of data—making our application much more responsive, with faster transfer around the connected sessions.

The simple WebSocket API

The WebSocket API is also exceptionally easy to work with. Currently, browsers only support sending strings (with the exception of Firefox and Web Workers), which we've seen in Chapter 10 with the Messaging API and Web Workers using postMessage and onmessage. Sockets work in almost exactly the same way.

> **NOTE** Regarding the ws:// server protocol, writing about how to set up the server side is beyond the scope of this book, but there are already several libraries out in the wild that can add the WebSocket protocol to your existing setup. Using servers like Node.js, I was able to get a WebSocket server up and running in around 20 minutes. Visit **http://remysharp.com/ slicehost-nodejs-websockets/** to see how I documented the process.

This means that you can't (currently) send binary data—but I'd argue that in the web world we're used to working with JSON and it's not a particularly big deal to encode to JSON as the messages come in from a socket, since we're already doing it for JSON Ajax requests.

The API is limited to the essential methods for creating the connection, sending data down the socket, receiving, and closing the socket. There's also an error handler and a state flag, which tells our app if the socket is currently connecting, open, closing, or closed. Once you've closed a socket, it can't be reopened, so you'll need to create a new socket.

Creating a new WebSocket is easy and very much like creating a new Web Worker. The protocol of the URL must be `ws://` but the rest of the URL can be structured just as you would a normal URL, to be:

```
var socket = new WebSocket('ws://myserver.com/tweets:
¬8080/');
```

For this example, I'm going to be listening only to the messages that come from the tweets URL. Each is a new tweet from Twitter that my server has been set up to listen for (**Figure 11.1**).

FIGURE 11.1 A streaming connection showing tweets that my server was listening for.

The messages from the server are being delivered as JSON messages, forwarded on from Twitter's streaming API. So when they come in, I'll convert the JSON to data and render the tweet on the screen:

TIP The URL that you use for the WebSocket doesn't have to be the same origin as your document. This means you can connect to servers from third-party services, which expands the possibilities of what can be done.

```
socket.onmessage = function(event) {
  var tweetNode = renderTweet(JSON.parse(event.data));
  document.getElementById('tweets').appendChild(tweetNode);
};
```

Now in as many as four lines of JavaScript (excluding the renderTweet function, which just massages the incoming parsed JSON data into a workable HTML fragment to append to the page), I've got streaming real-time tweets on my page.

Doing more than listening with a socket

As I said before, there are more methods available on a socket than just listening. Since a chat application is the *hello world* of Comet, I felt it only fair to show you a simple example of what chat would look like using WebSockets:

```
var socket = new WebSocket("ws://my-chat-server.com:8080/"),
    me = getUsername();

socket.onmessage = function(event) {
  var data = JSON.parse(event.data);
  if (data.action == 'joined') {
    initiliseChat();
  } else {
    showNewMessage(data.who, data.text);
  }
};

socket.onclose = function () {
  socket.send(JSON.stringify({
    action: 'logoff',
    username: me
  }));
  showDisconnectMsg();
};

socket.onopen = function() {
  socket.send(JSON.stringify({
    action: 'join',
    username: me
  }));
};
```

This simple pseudo code shows you how the same techniques we used in the Message API can help with getting around the limitations of plain text. The WebSocket API really is as simple as that. All the negotiation is done out of sight by the browser for you; all the buffering is done for you (though you can check the current bufferedAmount on the socket). In fact, the communication process is even easier than setting up an XHR object!

Server-Sent Events

These are situations where you want to have simple push-based messages that come from the server. Server-Sent Events are well suited to applications like real-time price updates, or latest headlines, or some real-time, one-way information that needs to get to the browser. If you instead need real-time, two-way communication, you want WebSockets as we saw earlier in this chapter.

Server-Sent Events come through the EventSource object. They're quite similar to WebSockets in their use. You create a new EventSource, passing it a URL to connect to. The browser immediately begins to establish a connection.

The EventSource object has a few simple events:

- Open: when the connection has been established
- Message: when a new message comes in—the event's data property contains the raw message
- Error: if something goes wrong

What makes EventSource unique is the way it handles dropped connections and message tracking.

If the EventSource connection is dropped for any reason, the API automatically tries to connect. If you use message IDs, when the EventSource reestablishes its connection it will tell the server which message ID it last saw. This allows the server (if your application requires it) to easily send the client the backlog of messages it missed.

Say for instance you had created a real-time charting application that tracked every time Bruce mentions his favourite pink cuddly toy on Twitter. This charting app will plot Bruce's sentiment against the current time—so you know if he's happy with the colour, texture, and general feel of the thing or not.

Since the browser just needs to passively receive data from the server, Server-Sent Events are a good match.

Now let's assume that while you're carefully monitoring Bruce's adorations on your app, you lose the connection. When you return online, EventSource will tell the server that the last message ID was 69; the server is now up to message ID 78. So the application on the server realises that you've missed a bunch of messages, and the server will send back all the messages from 70 onwards. Your client code doesn't change in any way, since each of those missing eight messages will just trigger the message event, and everything will be plotted accordingly.

Here's an example of said application:

```
var es = new EventSource('/bruces-pink-toy');

es.onopen = function () {
  initialiseChart();
};

es.onmessage = function (event) {
  var data = JSON.parse(event.data);
  chart.plot(data.time, data.sentiment);
};
```

Server-Side Events—the server side technology

On the server side, you could use a PHP-based setup (LAMP for instance), but since Apache (the *A* in LAMP) doesn't support persistent connections very well, it will keep dropping the connection, and the EventSource will keep on reconnecting automatically. This will effectively result in something more akin to an Ajax polling application.

This isn't the best way of doing things, but I appreciate that PHP probably has the lowest barrier of entry for most of us, so knowing that it can still work is useful. To take real advantage of the EventSource, you need a persistent connection to the server, and your typical LAMP setup isn't going to cut it.

You can, and probably should, opt for an event-based server. Going into great detail about this is way beyond the scope of this book, but I'd recommend looking at Node.js (a JavaScript-based server platform) or something like Twisted for Python.

The server needs to keep the connection open to the client, and it must send the client a header with the mime type text/event-stream.

The server needs to send new messages as such:

```
id: 1\n
data: { "semiment": "like", "time": "2011-06-23 16:43:23"
¬ }\n\n
```

Two new lines indicate the end of the message. If we were sending just plain sentences (rather than JSON in Bruce's case), the API supports sending multiple lines as such:

```
data: Here's my first really, really, really long line,
¬ but -\n
data: I've not just finished there, I've got more to
¬ say.\n\n

data: Since I follow two blank lines, I'm an entirely new
¬ message\n\n
```

In the example above, only *two* messages would be sent. Also notice that I'm not using any IDs either—they're not mandatory, but if you want to support the *picking up where you dropped off* feature, you'll want to include the IDs.

A simple EventSource server

What follows is some very simple Node.js code to accept connections to an EventSource-based server and send messages. Again, it's beyond the scope of this book to explain the server logic, but it should give you a starting point. I've also simplified the solution so the server just notifies connected users about the user agent string of *other* visitors that are currently connected to the same service. We'll keep Bruce's special toy charting experiment for another day!

```
/** When they create a new Event Source */
response.writeHead(200, {'Content-Type':
¬ 'text/event-stream', 'Cache-Control': 'no-cache'});
// get the last event id and coerce to a number
var lastId = req.headers['last-event-id']*1;
if (lastId) {
  for (var i = lastId; i < eventId; i++) {
    response.write('data: ' + JSON.stringify
    ¬ (history[eventId]) + '\nid: ' + eventId + '\n\n');
```

```
    }
}

// finally cache the response connection
connections.push(response);

/** When a regular web request is received */
connections.forEach(function (response) {
    history[++eventId] = { agent:
    ¬ request.headers['user-agent'], time: +new Date };
    response.write('data: ' + JSON.stringify
    ¬ (history[eventId]) + '\nid: ' + eventId + '\n\n');
});
```

My client-side code looks like this:

```
var es = new EventSource('/eventsource');
es.onmessage = function (event) {
    var data = JSON.parse(event.data);
    log.innerHTML += '<li><strong>' + data.agent +
    ¬ '</strong><br> connected at <em>' +
    ¬ (new Date(data.time)) + '</em></li>';
};
```

A very simple application, but behind the scenes all the hard work happens thanks to real-time, push-based events from the server.

Implementation support

Support isn't too bad for EventSource. Chrome, Safari, Firefox, and Opera handle it just fine, while—at the time of writing, at least—whether or not IE10 will support EventSource sadly remains a mystery (but I still have every faith). However, because Event-Source reverts to polling, it's very simple to replicate this API to create a polyfill using JavaScript and Ajax (you can see a few examples online here: **https://github.com/Modernizr/Modernizr/wiki/HTML5-Cross-browser-Polyfills** under "EventSource").

One thing I've noticed is that if you create a new EventSource during or immediately after the page has loaded, some browsers will keep their "loading throbber" running, making it look like the page has more to load even when that's no longer the case. I'm unclear if this is a bug in the implementations or if it's a specially crafted feature to keep us developers on our toes, but I've found that simply waiting for the document to finish loading and then wrapping your EventSource initialisation code in a setTimeout(init, 10) helps to avoid that unsightly and nasty throbber.

Summary

This chapter has equipped you with the very best in buzzword compliancy: real time. At the same time, adding a real-time dimension to your website could give you the competitive edge, and now that you've seen how easy the JavaScript is, I expect it's hard to resist. Obviously there is some server-side hickery pokery to be done, but once that's in place, you'll quickly be able to attract all those short attention span users. Now go build something a-maze-zing.

CHAPTER 12

Polyfilling: Patching Old Browsers to Support HTML5 Today

Bruce Lawson and
Remy Sharp

SO, THANK YOU for reading this far. By now we've probably whetted your appetite with new structural elements, piqued your interest with the new APIs, and you're champing at the bit to start using all these new cool things. But Internet Explorer 6, 7, and 8 stand in your way. Not for long, gentle reader.

Introducing polyfills

When you decorate your house, you find cracks or holes in walls and wooden surfaces that need to be filled so that the surface is level. To achieve this, you use a white filler paste that gives you a smooth, level surface upon which you can paint, hang wallpaper, or otherwise decorate.

This chapter introduces *polyfilling,* which is a way to fill the holes in browser support using JavaScript (or any appropriate technology such as Flash *if* it makes sense) to level the playing field.

We've seen that the HTML5 shiv allows new HTML5 elements to be styled in oldie. But what about all the exciting APIs we've introduced?

The method is

> **NOTE** Shivs vs Shims: Did Bruce & Remy mean "shiv"? Yes folks. The HTML5 shiv was coined by John Resig who later admitted (or realised) that he really meant shim, but the name stuck, so now it's the HTML5 shiv. It's a bit stabby, but it works.

- Code your page according to the standard APIs and test in browsers that support all the features you need to use.

- Using JavaScript, feature-detect each of the features that your site requires to work.

- If a feature is unavailable in the browser, lazy-load a polyfill script that fakes support.

- Pat yourself on the back and have a cup of tea and a custard cream.

There is a downside: really creaky browsers might end up loading a lot of scripts, so performance could be terrible. This is a matter of testing thoroughly.

You might also be somewhat surprised at this hacky approach. After all, isn't the point of HTML5 to let us make modern web apps without hacks and fallbacks? Well, yes, it is. The crucial difference with the polyfilling method is that new browsers use only the modern standards, without any hacks. The hacks are only there to patch up old browsers; this approach has been termed "regressive enhancement," because we're hacking for a dwindling number of old browsers, rather than hacking forever after.

> **NOTE** Just remember that a polyfill isn't progressive enhancement—nor does it particularly support graceful degradation. A polyfill typically *requires* JavaScript in the first place.

The polyfilling method also means clean code; we code to the spec in our markup and scripts in the first instance, and only (optionally) load additional hacks using our off-the-shelf polyfilling scripts. It's what marketing types call a "win-win situation," because they're not always wrong about everything.

What makes a polyfill different from the techniques we have already, like a shim, is this: if you removed the polyfill script, your code would continue to work, without any changes required *in spite of the polyfill being removed.*

Feature detection

Detecting support for a particular technology is the first step in deciding whether or not your application needs a polyfill. Note that I say *detecting support*, rather than just browser sniffing, declaring that this particular browser is lacking a particular feature and therefore we'll fix it using our hack.

With feature detection you've future proofed your polyfill. That way if the user upgrades their browser to one that supports the required technology, your polyfill sees the native feature is there and doesn't run. Equally, the user could still be using the same old browser, like IE7, but could have installed some super power extension that gives them all the tasty HTML5 goodness. Any user agent sniffing would have failed in this instance, whereas feature detection leaves you feeling smugger than Bruce when he's wearing his "I'm smug" t-shirt.

With detecting support in mind, not *everything* can be detected, which we'll come on to.

There are different ways to detect support in browsers, and often it comes down to the specific technology you're trying to support, but the key thing to remember is that if you're writing a polyfill, make absolutely sure your feature detection works correctly in all the browsers you plan to support.

In the majority of cases, though, feature detection is just a matter of testing whether a function or property exists in the current browser.

Detecting properties

For example, along with the `document.body` shortcut property, in HTML5 we now have `document.head`. Not so exciting, but still useful when you want to inject some script element, for instance. As this is simply a property, it's easy to test for its existence and to set it if it's not available:

```
if (document.getElementsByTagName('head')[0] !==
¬ document.head) {
  document.head = document.getElementsByTagName('head')[0];
}
```

When simplified, it looks like this:

```
document.head || (document.head =
¬ document.getElementsByTagName('head')[0]);
```

In our code, we're testing for `document.head`, and if it has a *falsey* value (in fact, undefined), we explicitly set `document.head` to the head element. However, rarely in the wastelands of cross-browser support is anything that simple. The potential problem with this code is that if you were to generate an iframe dynamically in JavaScript, its document wouldn't have the head property unless you ran this code against it. Not a big problem—we just rerun the code—but it's worth bearing in mind (hat tip to Mathias Bynens for the code, and Lea Verou for flagging iframes).

Another common detection method is to test for the existence of a particular property in an HTML element. For example, to test if the browser has native support for the `details` element, we create the element and then test if the open property (which we know is part of the standard details implementation) exists, so we create this element on the fly, and test if said property is present:

```
if (!'open' in document.createElement('details')) {
  // does not have native support, let's polyfill it...
}
```

What we're asking here is: does the open property exist on the details element. It doesn't have to be in the DOM to give us an accurate reading of true or false.

Detecting new functions

If you don't know already, in JavaScript, everything is an object (and there are lots of great books dedicated to this particular aspect of JavaScript). Since we're in the browser, the global root variable is the `window` object, and functions and methods are properties on this `window` object. Because of this, we can test for new functions, methods, and constructors in the same way as we did when we were looking for property values.

When I want to test if `sessionStorage` is available natively in the browser, I can do:

```
typeof window.sessionStorage !== 'undefined'
```

However, older versions of Firefox (3.x in particular) will throw a security exception if cookies are disabled for this particular line of code (as we touch on in Chapter 6). As I want this polyfill to support old versions of Firefox, rather than throwing exceptions all over the place, I'll wrap the test in a try/catch:

```
var sessionStorageAvailable = (function() {
  try {
    return typeof window.sessionStorage !== 'undefined';
  } catch (e) {
    return false;
  }
})();
```

> **NOTE** It's also worth mentioning now that Mark Pilgrim, author of "that other HTML5 book," *HTML5: Up and Running*, put together an absolutely amazing and possibly near definitive list of methods to detect features in browsers. Go to **http://diveintohtml5.org/everything.html** to have a look.

As we've already seen, each property and method you're aiming to polyfill will have its own intricacies when testing in the browsers you plan to support. But this is part of web development which we're all well and truly used to.

Detecting everything when JavaScript isn't your forte

If JavaScript isn't your bag, there's still hope for you yet. The Modernizr project (**http://modernizr.com**), maintained by Faruk Ateş, Paul Irish, and Alex Sexton, is a small JavaScript library that gives you a complete programmatic view of what your browser does and doesn't support.

Don't be confused by the name though; the library won't *modernise* your browser, but it will give you the starting point to easily detect support for over 40 different new aspects of HTML5 and CSS3. If you wanted to improve your JavaScript, or even just for the curious, it's worth popping the hood on Modernizr as it's a great way to learn how some features can be detected. You might find that some places are ugly to look at as browsers sometimes lie about their support or don't completely follow the specifications.

Performance of feature testing and polyfills

A question that's usually asked when JavaScript is proposed to solve a deficiency in the browser is: "What's the performance?"

Of course, any additional JavaScript that runs in the browser (even if it's just a one-liner that tests for the presence of a particular feature) will have a performance impact. However, when it comes to real-world use, a very large proportion of feature detection tests are going to be micro-snippets of code that won't have any effect on your application at all. Runtime will be in the milliseconds, which we'd say is negligible in most situations.

What you should also remember is that JavaScript engines are really fast. As the newer and faster browsers are less likely to need polyfills, extensive patches, or helper scripts—and instead require only that you run a few tests—there will be little or no cost for users with modern browsers.

Even for older browsers, which have slower JavaScript engines, there will still be no significant cost in the feature detection, but there may be some wait time to load the polyfill. This may be unavoidable, as we're trying to drag these old browsers into today's world, albeit kicking and screaming.

What's particularly important is that you don't polyfill everything including the kitchen sink (sorry, I couldn't resist the poor man's DIY joke). When you're including JavaScript to do what the browser can't do natively, it will always cost a little bit of performance. If you include a lot of redundant functionality that you won't make use of, then it's obviously a waste. Try to include only what you absolutely need. If you're building the next Super Bruce & Super Remy adventure game using canvas, and find that polyfilling slows IE6 down to a grinding halt *and* your main audience is IE6 users: don't use it! As the developer you need to make the judgment call as to whether the selected technology is the right tool for the job.

The undetectables

As we've already alluded to, there are definitely nuances in writing a polyfill for one technology to the next. However, there are also the black holes, those undetectable technologies.

A simple example of an "undetectable" is a technology that gives a false positive when tested.

Let's take, for example, the `contenteditable` attribute from Chapter 2. If you test for the attribute using the methods we've seen so far, it will tell you that `contenteditable` *is* supported, but really the problem is that on a device like Safari Mobile (pre-iOS 5) the keyboard doesn't actually focus to the editable area, so in reality it's not supported, regardless of the feature detection test.

It's hard to say exactly what is and isn't available to feature test. So long as you're testing your polyfill against all the browsers your site plans to support, you'll find whether or not the feature can be truly and reliably detected.

If you'd like a head start on those undetectables and determining the environments in which they're undetectable, the Modernizr project (**https://github.com/Modernizr/Modernizr/wiki/Undetectables**) has a page dedicated to those technologies.

If a feature can't be detected, what's the solution? Well, it's nasty, but one answer could be to browser sniff. It's an unreliable technique because the browser doesn't always tell the truth about its version or even its name—even today Microsoft Internet Explorer claims to be a Mozilla browser! What you should also be wary of with user agent sniffing is that there are future browser versions that your code might pick up incorrectly. It's a very wobbly ground on which to rely.

Where to find polyfills

As with most JavaScript snippet libraries, polyfills are scattered around the Web, but Paul Irish, like a superhero flying out of the deepest, darkest corners of the Web, started a wiki page collecting all the ones he could find (**https://github.com/Modernizr/Modernizr/wiki/HTML5-Cross-Browser-Polyfills**). Since this page is a wiki, it has grown over time with many contributions from the web development community, including our fine selves, with polyfills that provide all sorts of solutions ranging from canvas, SVG, Web Forms, WebSockets, EventSource, details element, data-* attributes, and many, many more.

In addition, this resource doesn't *just* include polyfills, but shims and other useful libraries as well.

CSS Polyfills

The concept of polyfilling applies to CSS3, also: CSS3Pie (**http://css3pie.com**) and IE-CSS3 (**http://fetchak.com/ie-css3/**) make IE6–8 capable of rendering a few of the most useful CSS3 decoration features. Meanwhile, selectivizr (**http://selectivizr.com**) is a JavaScript utility that emulates CSS3 pseudo-classes and attribute selectors in IE6–8. eCSStender (**http://ecsstender.org**) is another polyfill. Of course, CSS is never required for a site to function in the same way an API is—if it is, you're doing it very wrong. And please note: CSS3 has nothing to do with HTML5. Think of this as bonus information, because we love you.

A working example with Modernizr

So now you're armed to the teeth with feature detection techniques, and you've written your amazing polyfill script that will smooth out the cracks in browsers when people visit your site, but how do you make it all work?

We'll show you how to use Modernizr combined with a super duper useful tool called yepnope (by Alex Sexton and Ralph Holzmann at **http://yepnopejs.com**) to firstly detect whether the browser supports the technology you need, and, if it doesn't, load a polyfill and then get on with loading the rest of your application.

Since the nice folks behind Modernizr care so much about you, yepnope already comes bundled *inside* Modernizr with the `Modernizr.load` method, so you don't even have to worry about it.

Let's say your application is going to use `sessionStorage`. You've found the `sessionStorage` polyfill Remy wrote, but it also requires JSON support, so we'll need to test for both `sessionStorage` *and* JSON support before our application can start properly.

```
Modernizr.load({
  // first tests
  test: function () {
    return !!window.JSON;
  },
  nope: 'json2.js'
}, {
  // second tests
  test: Modernizr.sessionStorage,
  nope: 'sessionStorage.js'
},
// now once we're all good to go, include app.js
'app.js'
});
```

Make sure you're using a version of Modernizr that you built yourself. This is easy if you just go to the Modernizr website: select the pink Production button and build yourself. From here you can select the features you want to test for. The advantage is that your visitor downloads less code when visiting your website.

You include the Modernizr JavaScript file, and then the code above, which simply tells Modernizr to run two tests before including the app.js file (which would include all your application code). Although we're calling Modernizr, all the testing and conditional loading is happening in the magic yepnope library. You don't have to worry about that; just focus on specifying the feature tests required before your code gets run.

The first test is checking that JSON is available natively. This isn't part of HTML5, but hey, we included geolocation in this book, and *that's* not part of HTML5 either! The point is that you polyfill any technology if you want to level the playing field. If the test fails— say the browser is IE7, which doesn't have JSON natively available—our code will go ahead and load the json2.js file.

Next, we test for sessionStorage support. Since we chose to build this version of Modernizr to test for sessionStorage, this value will be available as either true or false depending on support. If false, the sessionStorage.js polyfill is loaded (note that from our example above, it will read the sessionStorage.js file from the relative path on your domain).

Finally, once all tests are complete and all required polyfills are loaded, the app.js file is loaded and your application can start up properly, safe in the knowledge that even if it's running in a dirty old browser like IE6, it can still use the latest, snazziest technology like `sessionStorage` and JSON.

Summary

We've seen that it's possible, and relatively simple, to make HTML5 apps work in old browsers by performing feature detection (as by design, most—but sadly not all—HTML5 features can be programmatically detected) and patching in support with helper script. However, it's important to be aware that polyfills probably won't perform as well as their native counterparts, and that older browsers like IE6 will be further slowed down by their non-performing JavaScript engines. It may well be better in these cases to avoid polyfilling and provide a completely different fallback solution.

AND FINALLY...

Hopefully, you've been enlightened by our brief foray into the new structures and APIs that you can use.

There are loads more cool but not-yet-implemented things in the spec that we haven't shown you. For example, you'll be able to register the browser as a content handler (`registerContent-Handler`) so that clicking a document, photo, or video on your desktop opens the browser and goes to a web application that can edit that document, complete with application toolbars (using `<menu>` and `<command>`), all built with HTML5. Awaiting implentation.

Forget the marketing BS of "Web 2.0." We're at the beginning of Web *Development* 2.0: powerful languages like HTML5, SVG, and CSS3 will revolutionise the way we build the Web. Browsers support more and more aspects of these languages, and you can be certain that further support is being added daily.

But it's vital that we remember that we are dealing with *web* development. The Web is based on URLs and hyperlinks, and it's a method to deliver content. If your amazing demo is basically contentless `div`s being flown around the screen by JavaScript; or if your content is text-as-pixels scripted with canvas; if you *require* a mouse or a touchscreen; or if you have no links, no content, and no URLs to bookmark or link to; or if you generate all your markup from unreadable obfuscated JavaScript, ask yourself: am I developing for the Web, or am I reinventing DHTML or Flash intros that just happen to run in the browser instead of a plugin?

Of course, have a play with the new features. Experiment with the new markup structures, manipulate video on the fly, and build fun and attractive games and apps that use canvas. By reading this book, you're demonstrating that you're an early adopter, you're ahead-of-the-curve, so please set a good example for your colleagues: respect those visitors who have older browsers or assistive technologies.

Thanks for buying this book and sticking with us. Pop by **introducinghtml5.com**; all the code (and more) is available.

Bon voyage: Enjoy building incredible things. kthxbai.

—Bruce Lawson and Remy Sharp
Birmingham, and Brighton, September 2011

INDEX